Passionately Inclusive: Towards Participation and Friendship in Sport

AF003809

Detlef Dumon, Annette R. Hofmann, Rosa Diketmüller, Katrin Koenen,
Richard Bailey und Constanze Zinkler (Hrsg.)

Passionately Inclusive: Towards Participation and Friendship in Sport

Festschrift für Gudrun Doll-Tepper

Waxmann 2017
Münster • New York

Bibliografische Informationen der Deutschen Nationalbibliothek
Die Deutsche Nationalbibliothek verzeichnet diese Publikation in der Deutschen
Nationalbibliografie; detaillierte bibliografische Daten sind im Internet über
http://dnb.dnb.de abrufbar.

Print-ISBN 978-3-8309-3729-6
E-Book-ISBN 978-3-8309-8729-1

Waxmann Verlag GmbH, 2017
Steinfurter Str. 555, 48159 Münster
www.waxmann.com
info@waxmann.com

Umschlaggestaltung und Satz: Anke Thomas
Gedruckt auf alterungsbeständigem Papier, säurefrei gemäß ISO 9706

Printed in Germany
Alle Rechte vorbehalten. Nachdruck, auch auszugsweise, verboten.
Kein Teil dieses Werkes darf ohne schriftliche Genehmigung des Verlages
in irgendeiner Form reproduziert oder unter Verwendung elektronischer
Systeme verarbeitet, vervielfältigt oder verbreitet werden.

Die Fotos stammen aus privaten Archiven und wurden uns von den Autoren und
Autorinnen sowie von Fotografen und Fotografinnen zur Verfügung gestellt.

Inhalt

Editorial Note 9

1. Life and Legacy 11

Zum 70. Geburtstag von Gudrun Doll-Tepper
Thomas Bach 13

Maßstäbe setzen und Barrieren abbauen
Friedhelm Julius Beucher 17

Diplomatin des Sports
Klaus Böger 21

Promoting Participation in Sport
Sir Philip Craven 25

Saluting Professor Gudrun Doll-Tepper
Mary Davis 29

Exemplary Leadership and Advocacy: The Early Years
Karen P. DePauw 31

Visionär und nachhaltig
Herbert Dierker 37

Adapted Physical Activity ohne Grenzen
Maria Dinold 39

Vielseitig und menschlich engagiert für Sportdeutschland
Alfons Hörmann 45

Gemeinsam nach vorne schauen
Jan Holze 49

What Else Could Possibly Be Said...
ICSSPE Executive Office Team 53

Celebrating a True Path-Finder
Darlene A. Kluka 57

2017 – Zeit zum Feiern
Tobias Knoch, Isabel Flory und Matthias Thaler 61

A Personal Thank You
Uri Schaefer 65

Mauern überwinden und Knoten lösen
Guido Schilling 67

Eine Paralympische Siegeshymne
Wolfgang Schrödter 69

An Encounter with Professor Doll-Tepper and the Development of Adapted Sports in Japan
Tomoyasu Yasui 73

2. Changes and Challenges 77

Der Beitrag des (organisierten) Sports für die Entwicklung junger Menschen
Wolf-Dietrich Brettschneider und Erin Gerlach 79

The Effects of Technology Supported Brain Breaks on Physical Activity in School Children
Fatma Sacli Uzunoz; Ming-Kai Chin; Magdalena Mo Ching Mok; Christopher R. Edginton; and Hrvoje Podnar 87

Organismus und Mechanismus
Gunter Gebauer 105

**Zwei Seiten einer Medaille: Olympische Idee und Identität –
Eine Gedankenskizze und ein Fragenkatalog**
Andreas Höfer 115

Jeder Sport hat (s)einen Preis...
Detlef Kuhlmann 125

Für den Erhalt des *Youth Leadership Programmes*
Wilfried Lemke 133

Empowerment and Inclusion through Sport – A Universal Language
Marianne Meier 141

Olympic Education: History, Theory and Practice
Roland Naul and Deanna Binder 159

Handball – From a Women's Game to a Men's Sport
Gertrud Pfister 175

Institutes of Higher Education and the Olympic Games
Uri Schaefer 195

**Frauen im Sport: Totales Eigenleben
Ein Gespräch mit Shokouh Navabinejad**
Guido Schilling 205

**Inklusion im schulischen und außerschulischen Sport –
im Fokus der Heterogenitätsdimension Behinderung**
Heike Tiemann und Sabine Radtke 209

***Frauen an die Spitze* – Förderung von Frauen im
gemeinnützig organisierten Sport in Deutschland**
Petra Tzschoppe 223

Editorial Note

Given the history of sport and physical education, a human life seems rather short; and the various fields in which huge developments have occured since the second half of the last century may make a life seem even shorter. However, in the diverse areas of sport and physical education as well as in their respective academic and policy activities, we observe improvements in various forms, initiated, supported and promoted by *beacons* who give light where direction is needed.

The following contributions uniquely reflect what the authors associated when approached with the request to contribute to a *Festschrift* for Gudrun Doll-Tepper on the occasion of her birthday in 2017. The authors are witnesses, friends and colleagues of such a guide; enthusiastic, persistent, a team player able to play in various positions.

At the same time, the authors themselves are influential actors who have left their footprint on the landmap of sport, sport science and physical education. This said, the publication will provide a record for a period that has produced rapid changes in the world of sport. Despite many negatives, we are witnesses of developments which have opened the doors a bit further for parts of society, for persons with different abilities, social, economic and cultural backgrounds and for girls and women. Many of us are aware that Gudrun Doll-Tepper has been a driving force for these – on global, national and local level.

The concept for this publication was developed by the International Council of Sport Science and Physical Education (ICSSPE) and the German Olympic Sports Confederation (DOSB) and was led by Annette R. Hofmann, Rosa Diketmüller and Detlef Dumon. In the first part, authors, who have accompanied Gudrun in various parts of her life as a professional, volunteer or in academic life, share a variety of personal moments; in the second part, authors offer papers which are related to one of the many work areas Gudrun Doll-Tepper is engaged in.

We express our sincerest thanks to all, for the time they have taken to turn the idea of a *Festschrift* into something real, for their thoughts and for their respect, their empathy for their areas of work and for a unique friend, colleague, chief, chair, president, and employer.

We appreciate that Gudrun Doll-Tepper's network of colleagues and friends goes of course far beyond this publication. It becomes visible when you accompany her during national and international sporting events and conferences and it has been documented in earlier publications.[1]

We are optimistic that the publication which has been financially supported by ICSSPE and the DOSB, will be a source of information for future generations of scientists, teachers, coaches, paid and unpaid professionals in sport, may it be Adapted, Olympic or Paralympic Sport, as it provides very personal views and insights in the great phenomena sport, physical education and physical activity. Finally, it is our intention – and we assume that this request will be second by Gudrun Doll-Tepper – that we all, authors, readers and editors, jointly work towards a human society that provides opportunities for everybody to contribute to the development of a healthy and just world.

The Editorial Team

---

[1] Tiemann, H., Schulz, S. & Schmidt-Gotz, E. (2007). *International Inklusiv Interdisziplinär. Perspektiven einer zeitgemäßen Sportwissenschaft.* Schorndorf: Hofmann; Borms, J. (2008). *Directory of Sport Science. 5th Edition. Featuring A Journey Through Times – The Changing Face of ICSSPE.* Berlin/Champaign.: ICSSPE/Human Kinetics.

1.
Life and Legacy

Zum 70. Geburtstag von Gudrun Doll-Tepper

Thomas Bach
Präsident Internationales Olympisches Komitee und Olympiasieger im Fechten

Im September 2015 wurde die *Agenda 2030 für nachhaltige Entwicklung* von allen Mitgliedsstaaten der Vereinten Nationen verabschiedet. Nie zuvor hat sich die internationale Staatengemeinschaft auf so weitreichende und umfassende Ziele einigen können. Es war auch ein historischer Moment für die Olympische Bewegung, denn der Beitrag des Sports zum Erreichen dieser weltweiten Nachhaltigkeits- und Entwicklungsziele wurde dabei ausdrücklich hervorgehoben. So ist zum ersten Mal die tragende Rolle des Sports als *wichtiger Ermöglicher* für nachhaltige Entwicklung und Frieden von der Staatengemeinschaft anerkannt worden.

Die Frage, welche Potenziale im Sport stecken und wie er zu nachhaltiger Entwicklung unserer Gesellschaft beitragen kann, hat auch die Arbeit von Prof. Dr. Gudrun Doll-Tepper geprägt. In ihrer langen wissenschaftlichen Karriere und in ihrem ehrenamtlichen Engagement für den Sport hat sie sich erfolgreich dafür stark gemacht, dass die Gesellschaft die Potenziale des Sports erkennt und für sich nutzt. Sport ist für Professor Gudrun Doll-Tepper seit jeher eine Herzensangelegenheit. Kern ihrer Arbeit ist es, *den Menschen für den Sport Mut zu machen*, wie das Munzinger Sportarchiv über Gudrun Doll-Tepper schreibt. Sie selbst sagte einmal über ihre Arbeit: *Letztlich geht es um Potenziale, die der Mensch entwickeln kann*.

Seit vielen Jahrzehnten bringt sich Gudrun Doll-Tepper als Wissenschaftlerin und als ehrenamtliche Führungskraft in den Sport ein. Ihr geht es dabei um Wissensaustausch und internationale Vernetzung. Inklusiver Sport, das gemeinsame Sporttreiben von Behinderten und Nicht-Behinderten, Sport in Schule und Verein, Sport für Frauen und vor allem die Bildungspotenziale des Sports gehören zu den Schwerpunktthemen ihrer Arbeit. Gudrun Doll-Tepper verkörpert die Olympischen Werte von Freundschaft, Exzellenz und Respekt und hat sie in ihrer Arbeit stets vorangestellt. Sie hat sich in ihrer Karriere große Verdienste um die Olympische Bewegung erworben.

Deshalb ist sie auch in die höchsten Gremien des Sports berufen worden. Als Präsidentin des Weltrates für Sportwissenschaft und Leibes-/Körpererziehung

(ICSSPE) setzte sich Gudrun Doll-Tepper mit unermüdlichem Engagement für die Sportwissenschaft ein und wurde 2016 zur ersten ICSSPE Ehrenpräsidentin ernannt. Sie entwickelte ICSSPE mit ihrer zupackenden Art weiter und stellte die Organisation modern auf. Dazu zählte auch die Einführung einer Amtszeitbegrenzung für das Ehrenamt, das sie konsequent für ihre Nachfolger freimachte, als sie selbst die Grenze erreicht hatte.

Seit 2008 gehört Gudrun Doll-Tepper der Kommission *Frauen im Sport* des Internationalen Olympischen Komitees (IOC) an und seit 2015 zudem der Kommission *Olympische Erziehung*. Als Vorsitzende der Deutschen Olympischen Akademie ist Gudrun Doll-Tepper prädestiniert für diese Aufgabe. Die DOA, 2007 gegründet, spielt bei der Olympischen Erziehung und der Wertevermittlung in Deutschland eine tragende Rolle.

Engagiert hat sich Gudrun Doll-Tepper aber auch im Internationalen Paralympischen Komitee (IPC), im Landessportbund Berlin, im Deutschen Sportlehrerverband sowie einer Reihe anderer Organisationen. Für dieses Engagement erhielt sie eine Vielzahl von internationalen und nationalen Auszeichnungen.

Über 350 wissenschaftliche Beiträge zum Sport hat Gudrun Doll-Tepper in ihrem Berufsleben als Autorin oder Co-Autorin verfasst. Diese sind für den Sport unersetzlich. Zwei möchte ich an dieser Stelle gesondert erwähnen: Es sind ihre Artikel zum Olympischen Kongress im Jahr 2009 in Kopenhagen: *Is competetive Sport still appealing?* und zum Thema *Promoting Sport in Countries affected by disaster: The role of the International Olympic Committee*. Beide Themen beschäftigen das IOC auch in diesen Tagen und wir sind froh, dabei auf den Rat von Gudrun Doll-Tepper zählen zu können.

Liebe Gudrun Doll-Tepper,
über viele Jahre habe ich eng mit Ihnen zusammenarbeiten dürfen, von 1998 bis 2006 im Nationalen Olympischen Komitee für Deutschland, dem Sie als persönliches Mitglied angehörten, und von Mai 2006 an im DOSB-Präsidium, in dem Sie seit der DOSB-Gründung Vizepräsidentin für Bildung und Olympische Erziehung sind. In den vielen Jahren unserer Zusammenarbeit habe ich Sie stets als anpackende, nach vorne schauende und ebenso konzeptionell wie programmatisch denkende Persönlichkeit erlebt, die Menschen Mut macht.

Das habe ich im Sport gelernt, heißt eine Kampagne, die in Deutschland von einem Landessportbund gestartet worden ist. Dass der organisierte Sport in Deutschland heute der größte nichtstaatliche Bildungsträger ist, hat auch mit Ihrer Arbeit und Ihrem Einsatz für den Sport zu tun. Auch für die öffentliche Anerkennung des Sports von Menschen mit Behinderung haben Sie entscheidende Impulse geliefert.

So ist Ihr Engagement, die Werte des Sports in die Gesellschaft zu tragen, Inspiration für uns alle. Durch solch vorbildlichen Einsatz von Ihnen und vielen anderen ist der Sport erst zum *wichtigen Ermöglicher* für nachhaltige Entwicklung und Frieden in der Welt geworden.

Zu Ihrem 70. Geburtstag gratuliere ich Ihnen herzlich und möchte Ihnen für Ihre Verdienste rund um den Sport außerordentlich danken. Ich freue mich auf die weitere Zusammenarbeit sowie die persönlichen Begegnungen.

Maßstäbe setzen und Barrieren abbauen

Friedhelm Julius Beucher
Präsident Deutscher Behindertensportverband e.V.

Sehr gerne beteilige ich mich an der *Überraschungsidee*, Prof. Dr. Dr. h. c. Gudrun Doll-Tepper anlässlich ihres 70. Geburtstages mittels einer Festschrift für ihre Verdienste und Leistungen zu würdigen. Dieses tue ich sowohl als Präsident des Deutschen Behindertensportverbandes wie auch als langjähriger und freundschaftlich verbundener Wegbegleiter der Jubilarin.

In den vergangenen Jahrzehnten hat der Sport von Menschen mit Behinderung einen enormen Bedeutungszuwachs erfahren. Die Gründe hierfür sind vielfältig. Der Beginn dieser enormen Wandlung kann sicherlich bei den Paralympischen Sommerspielen 1988 in Seoul/Südkorea und der Gründung des Internationalen Paralympischen Komitees (IPC) 1989 verortet werden (vgl. Doll-Tepper, 2007). Seit jener Zeit steigt die Zahl der teilnehmenden Nationen sowie der Athletinnen und Athleten kontinuierlich an, um zuletzt bei den Paralympischen Spielen 2016 in Rio de Janeiro in Brasilien mit 4.328 Athletinnen und Athleten aus 159 Ländern seinen derzeitigen Höhepunkt zu finden. Daneben gibt es mit den World Games von Special Olympics sowie den Deaflympics jedoch noch weitere große Sportveranstaltungen, die dazu beitragen den Sport von Menschen mit Handicap voranzubringen. Wenngleich es im Vergleich zu Athletinnen und Athleten ohne Behinderung noch Luft nach oben gibt, spielt der Sport von Menschen mit Behinderung gegenwärtig sowohl in den Medien als auch in der Wirtschaft eine immer größere Rolle. Ebenso im Bereich der Wissenschaft führte der Sport von Menschen mit Behinderung insgesamt, also sowohl im Breiten-, Präventions- und Rehabilitationssport als auch im Leistungssport, lange Zeit ein Schattendasein. Hier ist insbesondere einzelnen engagierten Personen zu danken, die dieses Thema unermüdlich bearbeiten und so Wissenslücken schließen. Ohne Zweifel ist Gudrun Doll-Tepper diesem Personenkreis nicht nur zuzuordnen, sondern sie hat hier auch weltweit Maßstäbe gesetzt. Mit ihrem langjährigen Engagement und vielfältigen Aktivitäten ist sie eine unermüdliche Kämpferin für den Sport von Menschen mit Behinderung. Wie keine andere in der Szene außerhalb des Deutschen Behindertensportverbandes setzt sie sich insbesondere auch für die Gleichrangigkeit von Menschen mit körperlichen und geistigen Behinderungen ein. Dadurch leistet sie einerseits einen unverzichtbaren Beitrag für Menschen mit Behinderung selbst, andererseits aber auch für die gesamte Gesellschaft, in der es gilt, Barrieren in den Köpfen abzubauen und einen Bewusstseinswandel herbeizuführen.

Durch die beschriebenen Entwicklungen ist der Sport von Menschen mit Behinderung zwischenzeitlich auch in der Politik angekommen und wird bei relevanten Vorhaben größtenteils mitgedacht. Einen maßgeblichen Beitrag hierzu hat auch die UN-Behindertenrechtskonvention (UN-BRK) geleistet, die durch die Ratifizierung des Deutschen Bundestages im März 2009 auch in Deutschland Gesetzeskraft erreicht hat. Basierend auf dem Grundsatz der Inklusion verpflichtet die UN-BRK alle staatlichen Stellen die gleichberechtigte und diskriminierungsfreie Teilhabe von Menschen mit Behinderung in allen gesellschaftlichen Bereichen zu fördern. In Artikel 30 Absatz 5 der UN-BRK ist der Sport als relevanter Bereich ausdrücklich aufgeführt. Die Arbeit des Deutschen Behindertensportverbandes ist bereits seit langem darauf ausgerichtet, dass alle Menschen gleichermaßen nach ihren individuellen Wünschen und Voraussetzungen selbstbestimmt und gleichberechtigt an Bewegungs-, Spiel- und Sportangeboten teilhaben können und entspricht somit auch den Vorgaben der UN-BRK. Neben der enormen positiven Bedeutung der Konvention bedeutet diese für den Sport zugleich eine große Herausforderung und geht mit vielfältigen Fragestellungen einher, wenn es um die gleichberechtigte und selbstbestimmte Teilhabe von Menschen mit Behinderung im Sport geht. Beispielhaft seien an dieser Stelle nur die Frage der Teilnahme von Athletinnen und Athleten mit Behinderung an Olympischen Spielen und Weltmeisterschaften, die Strukturen des organisierten Sports national und international sowie die Bedeutung von inklusivem Schulsport genannt. Ein Blick auf die lange Liste ihrer Publikationen zeigt, dass sich Gudrun Doll-Tepper bereits seit Langem mit vielen dieser Fragestellungen intensiv auseinandergesetzt hat und sie sich bereits in der Zeit vor Inkrafttreten der UN-BRK und bevor der Begriff der Inklusion handlungsleitend wurde, eine umfangreiche Sachkenntnis und einen wertvollen Erfahrungsschatz erarbeitet hat. Damit ist sie aktuell ohne Zweifel eine führende Expertin in ihrem Fachgebiet und sowohl national als auch international anerkannt und geschätzt. Völlig zu Recht ist daher aus meiner Sicht auch ihre erneute Berufung im Mai dieses Jahres in die Kommission *Olympische Erziehung* sowie die Kommission *Frauen im Sport* des Internationalen Olympischen Komitees (IOC) erfolgt. Ich bin mir sicher, dass sie mit ihrer Beteiligung ihre Expertise, ihre Erfahrungen und das weitreichende Wissen über die Paralympische Bewegung und den Sport von Menschen mit Behinderung in die Arbeit der Kommissionen einbringt und die Diskussionen damit bereichert.

Der internationale Spitzensport und die dahinter stehenden Sportorganisationen stecken bereits seit längerem in einer Glaubwürdigkeitskrise und die Gründe dafür sind ebenso vielfältig wie die Auswirkungen. Die Ablehnung von Sportgroßveranstaltungen im eigenen Land und das abnehmende Interesse an Weltereignissen wie den Olympischen Spielen sind nur zwei Beispiele dafür. Mit der gewachsenen Bedeutung des Spitzensports von Menschen mit Behinderung muss leider festgestellt werden, dass Themen wie Doping und Manipulation auch im Paralympischen Sport Einzug gehalten haben und eine ständige Herausforderung für alle Beteiligten sind. Besonders deutlich wurde dies im Juli 2016, als der erste Teil des sogenannten McLaren-Berichts vorgestellt wurde. Der kanadische Jurist Richard McLaren hat darin eindrucksvoll ein staatlich gelenktes Dopingsystem in Russland aufgedeckt, welches den gesamten russischen Sport – also auch den Paralympischen Sport – eingeschlossen hat. Wenige Wochen vor Beginn der Olympischen und Paralympischen Spiele in Rio de Janeiro haben IOC und IPC sich zu einem ganz unterschiedlichen Vorgehen entschlossen. Während das IPC konsequenterweise das Russische Nationale Paralympische Komitee suspendiert hat und der Russischen Paralympischen Mannschaft damit eine Teilnahme in Rio verwehrt blieb, hat das IOC die Verantwortung an die Internationalen Fachverbände übertragen, was zu einer uneinheitlichen und nicht nachvollziehbaren Bewertung und schließlich zu einer Teilnahme der Russischen Mannschaft bei den Olympischen Spielen in Rio führte. Auch dieses aktuelle Beispiel zeigt deutlich, dass der gesamte Sport vor der großen Herausforderung steht seine Integrität zu schützen und wieder zu stärken. Wesentliche Grundlage hierfür ist die Diskussion und die Rückbesinnung auf die Werte, die den Sport ausmachen. Olympische und Paralympische Werte müssen dabei gleichberechtigt betrachtet und bezogen auf aktuelle Herausforderungen fortentwickelt werden. Vertreterinnen und Vertreter der Wissenschaft, wie Gudrun Doll-Tepper, müssen in diesem Dialog gehört werden und eine wichtige Rolle einnehmen.

Entsprechend der Vision des IPC *to enable Para athletes to achieve sporting excellence and inspire and excite the world* bereichert und inspiriert Gudrun

Doll-Tepper mit ihrer Arbeit und ihrem Engagement die Welt des Sports. Durch regelmäßige Besuche bei Sportwettkämpfen und anderen Veranstaltungen des Behindertensports sowie ihre Mitarbeit im Kuratorium des Deutschen Behindertensportverbandes und vielen anderen nationalen und internationalen Organisationen zeigt sie ihre große Wertschätzung und leistet einen unverzichtbaren Beitrag für den Sport von Menschen mit Behinderung.

Meine vielen Begegnungen mit Gudrun Doll-Tepper haben Anfang der 1990er Jahre begonnen, wo sie mich in der ihr eigenen Art – freundlich, aber unablässig und bestimmt – als (damals noch) jungem Abgeordneten über die Arbeit des *Weltrates für Sportwissenschaft und Leibes-/Körpererziehung* informierte und konsequenterweise auch meine Mithilfe bei der Finanzierung einforderte. Dem folgten unzählige Gremiensitzungen, Konferenzen und damals schon als Höhepunkte der stete Besuch der Paralympics seit Atlanta 1996. Genauso erinnere ich mich, dass wir stets ebenso viel gelacht wie diskutiert haben und ich dankbar bin für die langjährige vertrauensvolle und zuverlässige Zusammenarbeit. Im Laufe der Zeit ist aus einer sachlichen Begegnung eine Freundschaft entstanden und ich gratuliere Gudrun Doll-Tepper zu ihrem Geburtstag von ganzem Herzen und wünsche ihr, dass sie, in welcher Funktion auch immer, dem Sport noch lange erhalten bleibt. Gudrun, du wirst gebraucht!

Literatur

Doll-Tepper, G. (2007). International Developments in Sport for Persons with a Disability. *Sobama Journal, 12,* 7–12.

International Paralympic Committee: https://www.paralympic.org/the-ipc/about-us; June 2017.

Diplomatin des Sports

Klaus Böger
Präsident Landessportbund Berlin

Meine erste Begegnung mit Gudrun Doll-Tepper stand im Zusammenhang mit ihrer Tätigkeit als Vorsitzende des Weltrats für Sportwissenschaft und Leibes-/ Körpererziehung. Als damaliger Sport- und Bildungssenator war meine Verwaltung Anlaufstelle in einer Reihe von Angelegenheiten, die sich um diese für das Renommee der Sportmetropole in jener Zeit so wichtige Institution rankten. Ich lernte Gudrun Doll-Tepper schnell schätzen als selbstbewusste Verhandlerin und verlässliche Partnerin. Ihr Wort galt.

Selbstverständlich haben auch wir Wort gehalten, insbesondere was Sitz und Finanzierung des Weltrats in Berlin anging. Dem Rechnungshof hat das damals überhaupt nicht gefallen. Wir mussten unangenehme Fragen über uns ergehen lassen. Aber am Ende stachen unsere Argumente. Mit einer übertriebenen Buchhaltermentalität kann man selbst besten Ideen und Projekten vorzeitig den Garaus machen.

Als ich 2009 dann das Präsidentenamt im Landessportbund Berlin übernommen habe, gehörte Gudrun Doll-Tepper diesem Gremium bereits über ein Jahrzehnt an. Höchst engagiert war sie zunächst Präsidialmitglied für Frauensport gewesen, hatte aber alsbald zu ihrer eigentlichen Leidenschaft, dem Ressort *Wissenschaft, Bildung und Internationales*, gefunden. Dort ist sie bis zu ihrem Ausscheiden im Jahr 2015 unsere zuständige Vizepräsidentin gewesen, hat für die Stadt und ihren Sport Netzwerke geknüpft.

Für eine Stadt, die dutzendweise Städtepartnerschaften pflegt und sich laufend um die Akquise neuer und attraktiver Sportgroßevents bemüht, sind Persönlichkeiten mit exzellenten internationalen Verbindungen buchstäblich Goldes wert. Das wusste Gudrun Doll-Tepper natürlich auch und trug dementsprechend selbstbewusst vor. Meist war ihr Auftritt bereits die sprichwörtliche *halbe Miete*, wenn etwas auf Anhieb gelungen ist.

Besonders verdient gemacht hat sich die weltweit wertgeschätzte und hoch geachtete Hochschullehrerin um die Einwerbung sowie die erfolgreiche Durchführung des SportAccord 2005. Von der Generalversammlung aller rund 100 internationalen Sportverbände und Dachorganisationen der olympischen Sommer- und Wintersportverbände ins Leben gerufen, ist der Kongress die wichtigste Zusammenkunft von Funktionsträgern des Sports überhaupt. 1.400 Führungspersönlichkeiten aus der Welt des Sports, Sponsoren, Sportrechte-Vermarkter und -Anwälte, Architekten, Mediziner, Politiker und Medienvertreter kamen damals in unserer Stadt zusammen, um über Schlüsselfragen des Weltsports zu beraten. Parallel tagte auch die IOC-Executive in Berlin, wodurch der SportAccord zusätzliche Aufwertung erfuhr.

Seit dem Olympischen Kongress 1981 in Baden-Baden hat es in Deutschland keinen derartig hochkarätigen sportiven Gipfel gegeben. Um die Konferenz SportAccord, die mit einer IOC-Exekutivsitzung verbunden ist, beneidet man Berlin nun landesweit. Den finanziell klammen Hauptstädtern ist ein sportpolitischer Coup gelungen. Noch nie war ein Treffen von IOC-Funktionären in Berlin von derartiger Leichtigkeit ..., schrieb eine Berliner Zeitung im Anschluss.

Eingeweihte wussten natürlich, dass auf der Bühne und hinter den Kulissen vor allem Gudrun Doll-Tepper die Fäden zog. Bereits beim *SportAccord* 2003 in Madrid, den ich als Senator besuchte, hatte ich festgestellt, wie viele wichtige Vertreter des Weltsports sie persönlich kennt und wie anerkannt sie in diesen Kreisen ist. Nicht zuletzt deshalb gelang es uns gemeinsam mit dem damals als Bundesinnenminister zuständigen Otto Schily, den *SportAccord* zu dessen dritter Auflage für Berlin einzuwerben.

Gudrun Doll-Tepper war oft gleichzeitig auf den verschiedensten Ebenen tätig: als Wissenschaftlerin, als Hochschullehrerin, als Beraterin für Politik, Wissenschaft und Gesellschaft, als Führungspersönlichkeit in Sportorganisationen, als internationale Botschafterin des deutschen Sports, als Sachwalterin der Belange der Frauen im Sport. In Frankfurt, Brüssel, Lausanne oder Peking war sie genauso zu Hause wie in Berlin. Es machte ihr Spaß. Dabei verstand sie Interessenskonflikte geschickt zu vermeiden, erklärte sich nötigenfalls auch einmal für *befangen* und nahm an einer Abstimmung erst gar nicht teil, wenn sie divergierende Loyalitätspflichten für unvereinbar hielt.

Gudrun Doll-Tepper ist eine couragierte, eine geradlinige Persönlichkeit. Die Neugier junger Jahre hat sie sich bis heute bewahrt. Mit ihren Studierenden pflegt sie einen Umgang auf Augenhöhe. Wer je Gelegenheit hatte Gudrun Doll-Tepper an der Universität zu beobachten, war verblüfft, wie fast *familiär* sie mit den jungen Leuten umging. Der Autorität als Lehrkraft tat das keinen Abbruch. Viele der *Ehemaligen* hielten den Kontakt auch über die Universitätszeit hinaus.

Das offene Ohr für die Menschen an der Basis ihrer zahlreichen Wirkungskreise hat sie nie verloren. Überall wird sie aufgenommen wie eine gute Bekannte. Dabei ist sie durchaus fordernd, aber Fordern und Fördern stehen bei ihr in einem ausgewogenen Verhältnis. Sich selbst verlangt sie stets am allermeisten ab, ist dabei sogar noch ausgesprochen produktiv, wie die Veröffentlichungsliste in ihrer wissenschaftlichen Vita ausweist. An ihren Manuskripten arbeitet sie selbst im Zug, im Flieger, im Hotel. Intensive Reisetätigkeit ist für den Aufbau internationaler Kontakte schier unverzichtbar.

Der Landessportbund hat die rührige Sportwissenschaftlerin inzwischen zu seinem Ehrenmitglied gemacht. Von ihren Netzwerken zehrt der Berliner Sport bis heute. Berlin hat allen Grund Gudrun Doll-Tepper dankbar zu sein. Zum großen Geburtstag die besten Wünsche!

Promoting Participation in Sport

Sir Philip Craven
President International Paralympic Committee 2001–2017

It is a great pleasure to congratulate Professor Gudrun Doll-Tepper, a woman who has done so much to advance the Paralympic Movement globally, on the occasion of her 70th birthday.

Throughout her international professional career, Professor Doll-Tepper has been a giant in the advocacy of sport participation. Her philosophy has been simple: by encouraging people to participate in sport, the world will be a better place for all, and who can disagree?

From an early stage in her career she realised that the human body has unlimited potential and that by bringing sport and society together you can achieve a common goal. Since then she has gone on to become a pioneer and global leader for social inclusion through sport with a worldwide reputation for championing equal rights, whatever a person's abilities, gender, religion or family background.

Thanks to her outstanding work, she has helped to amplify the IPC's aspiration to make for a more inclusive society for people with an impairment through Para sport.

It is fair to say that thanks to her boundless enthusiasm, infinite energy and immense passion for both people and sport, millions of people with an impairment now enjoy better, more enriched lives as a result of her work.

What impresses me the most is that she is one of the world's loudest voices on the need for inclusive education and the necessity to transform a global system that, in many places, sadly encourages exclusion.

As the UN Convention on the Rights of Persons with Disabilities states everyone has the right to practice sport, and children with an impairment must have an opportunity to participate in regular schools and in regular physical education, exclusion in the education system sends out the wrong message to other areas of society.

Like Professor Doll-Tepper, I truly believe that sport is life's great educator, sport can have a seismic impact on society and it is essential that the practice of sport for all is engrained in every school curriculum around the world.

I know from my own experiences as a wheelchair basketball player that many precious life skills are acquired by the regular practice of sport, such as hard work, fair play, honesty and integrity. For me sport is the antithesis of war; it improves self-discipline, respect and tolerance and leads to a greater understanding of why in life you must play by the rules. Where else can you pit two fierce rivals head-to-head in peaceful conflict other than in sport?

Through human interaction in sport you sub-consciously realise that you can be good at something, raising your self-esteem. You practice self-determination, and quickly understand that it is easier to achieve a common objective through teamwork rather than by working as a group of individuals.

Apart from the obvious health benefits, sport helps the individual to help themselves, and enables them to achieve personal freedom. It awakens their hearts, minds and souls so that they can discover with a passion their own talent.

When people realise their dreams and use the energy within their own bodies and minds to develop themselves and their nations for the good of all, then this planet will become a better and more peaceful place. Sport really can achieve the common good.

Back in 1993 at the first VISTA conference[1] in Jasper, Canada, Gudrun Doll-Tepper brought together an ad hoc committee that would later go on to become the IPC Scientific Committee, a group she chaired for many years. Her objective was to formulate a sport science strategy for athletes with an impairment and today she is seen as a leading global expert in this area authoring and co-authoring hundreds of publications in sport science, sport pedagogy, and adapted physical activity and sport for persons with an impairment.

---

1 VISTA is the name for a series of conferences under the leadership of the International Paralympic Committee.

Gudrun Doll-Tepper and Sir Philip Craven

In her former role as the President of the International Council of Sport Science and Physical Education (ICSSPE), she helped bring together the four leading organisations in sport, sports medicine and sports science to create a new scientific conference. With the co-operation of the IOC, IPC, ICSSPE and the International Federation of Sports Medicine (FIMS), the International Convention on Science, Education and Medicine in Sport (ICSEMIS) was born, bringing together multiple experts from around the world just prior to the Olympic and Paralympic Summer Games.

As a result of her outstanding work in sports science, physical education and sport for people with an impairment, she has rightly received multiple prestigious awards. In 1999 she received the Distinguished Service Cross of the Federal Republic of Germany for her contribution to disability sport, physical education and sport science. At the Salt Lake City 2002 Paralympic Winter Games I had the pleasure to present her with the Paralympic Order, the highest accolade anyone within the Paralympic Movement can achieve, which was followed by the IPC Paralympic Scientific Award in 2009.

When you look at what she has achieved, it is hard to believe she has fitted all of this into just 70 years! Professor Doll-Tepper, from everyone within the Paralympic Movement and all those around the world who have directly and indirectly benefitted from your work, we wish you a very happy 70th birthday.

Gudrun, enjoy the celebrations!

Saluting Professor Gudrun Doll-Tepper

Mary Davis
Chief Executive Officer Special Olympics International

It is our great privilege to write a few sentences about Professor Gudrun Doll-Tepper, a very good friend of Special Olympics in Germany but also of Special Olympics globally.

Professor Doll-Tepper, a renowned and great University Professor, conducted Adapted Physical Activity courses at the *Freie Universität* in Berlin, including some Special Olympics topics in her lectures and classes for students. She was a great promoter of Special Olympics Germany and Special Olympics Europe-Eurasia. During her work for the International Federation of Adapted Physical Activity (IFAPA) and the International Council of Sport Science and Physical Education (ICSSPE) she always supported the Special Olympics Movement and supported Special Olympics workshops and mini-symposia. Her presentations at several IFAPA conferences always included an angle on Special Olympics.

Thanks to Professor Doll-Tepper many students started volunteer programmes and later on became a Special Olympics coach. This was very helpful to develop the Special Olympics Germany Programme, which is one of the largest in the world.

Professor Doll-Tepper attended many Special Olympics Germany National Games as well as World Games as an Honored Guest. The Special Olympics Family is extremely fortunate to have such a charismatic and great friend and supporter.

We all in the Special Olympics movement wish Professor Doll-Tepper many further years in good health and a lot of energy to continue supporting people with all kinds of disability in sports and active life.

Sincere best wishes for a very happy birthday celebration!

Exemplary Leadership and Advocacy: The Early Years

Karen P. DePauw
Virginia Tech and Speaker ICSSPE Associations' Board 1999–2004

Professor Dr Gudrun Doll-Tepper is an advocate and enthusiastic leader of sport science and adapted physical activity and has been throughout her professional life. Her accomplishments and awards are many and well deserved. It has been my sincere pleasure to know her for more than 30 years and an honor to work with her in the early years and further development of the International Federation of Adapted Physical Activity (IFAPA), the International Paralympic Committee (IPC) and the International Council of Sport Science and Physical Education (ICSSPE). Under her leadership, sport science and adapted physical activity have received world-wide recognition.

The narrative which follows provides a brief review of those years and selected memories of our work together. I share some observations and reflections of Gudrun's efforts and contributions. Although the stories are not necessarily detailed here for the reader, they will likely trigger memories that were shared in our individual and shared journeys as young and emerging professionals/ scholars to advocates and leaders. Gudrun's leadership within the sport science world continues to this day while my journey has taken me into the world of global higher education, in particular graduate education.

As I reflect upon the many and varied contributions of Gudrun Doll-Tepper, I know that her strong academic preparation and extensive teaching experiences and athletic endeavors initially in Berlin and throughout Germany provided the solid foundation upon which she could draw upon as she actively engaged in the further development of sport science. She has shared that she was influenced by many leaders including the likes of Ernst (Jonny) J. Kiphard (1923–2010), an early leader in psycho-motor learning. Kiphard was her friend and I had the opportunity to learn from him and the connections to leaders (e. g., Jean Ayres, Marianne Frostig) in the United States whose work influenced my thinking and early beginnings in adapted physical activity. Many special professional and personal moments were shared with Jonny and Gudrun which I greatly appreciate.

Gudrun's spheres of influence were many. Originally founded in the 1973, Gudrun played a significant leadership role in building IFAPA into a vibrant international association. It was through the IFAPA international symposium (International Symposium on Adapted Physical Activity – ISAPA) that I first met Gudrun when she attended the 1981 ISAPA held in New Orleans, Louisiana (USA). I sensed the positive energy and her enthusiasm for physical activity and sport for individuals with disabilities. Shortly thereafter I would also learn that she had a strong commitment to advancing girls and women in sport. We shared similar values and spent many hours that have now extended into years promoting inclusion in physical activity and sport.

Once engaged with IFAPA, her passion was clear and her leadership fostered the opportunity to invigorate IFAPA. She expanded the global scope of IFAPA and through the hosting of the 1989 Symposium in Berlin set high standards and provided a model for the symposia which would follow in the years to come. Gudrun served on the IFAPA board in several capacities, initiated modernisation and updates to the organisation and structure of the association and ultimately served as IFAPA president. We served together on the IFAPA board for at least 12+ years. She developed the Elly D. Friedmann Award for Outstanding Adapted Physical Activity Contributions which honors those who have made significant professional contributions and she too was recognised as a recipient.

Beginning during the IFAPA years, Gudrun worked closely with the leadership of the newly developing International Paralympic Committee (IPC). In particular, she helped establish the IPC Sports Science Committee and worked tirelessly to advance the Paralympic movement. She advocated for the right of athletes with disabilities to be recognised as athletes. In collaboration with then IPC President Robert Steadward, she helped organise meetings, workshops and symposia to promote a meaningful research agenda and training for athletes and coaches alike. Among these I recall meeting Phil Craven who was a coach at that time and who would ultimately be known as Sir Philip Craven, President of the IPC (2001–2017) and IOC member.

It is clear to me that Gudrun played a significant role in fostering connections that would later have a significant impact upon future decisions including the incorporation of the Paralympics alongside the Olympic movement. I recall several meetings at the IOC Lausanne headquarters and in Atlanta at the 1996 Olympic Games with IOC President Juan Samaranch with the goal of bringing the Paralympics within the umbrella of the Olympic movement. I distinctly remember staying on the same floor as IOC President Samaranch (and the security checks when returning to my room) and waiting for Gudrun to share the results of her meeting with him. Although it took some time, the combined efforts of many including Gudrun resulted in an agreement that the Olympics and Paralympics would be held in the same year in the same location which is the common practice today.

I also remember our first foray into ICSSPE at one of their annual gatherings in Cologne, Germany in the early 1990s. As representatives for IFAPA, we were present to observe the international association firsthand and to help promote the inclusion of adapted physical activity and disability sport. I recall her skills in navigating the interactions with the long serving ICSSPE members and the ways in which she gained their respect. This was the beginning of her involvement with ICSSPE which would ultimately lead to her election as President of ICSSPE and years of outstanding service and significant progress on the sport science arena. With her commitment and service as President, ICSSPE became stronger and would realise a strong leader of sport science in the world.

During this time, she strengthened relationships with other international associations (e. g., AIESEP, IAPESGW) and global agencies (e. g., UNESCO, WHO). These relationships and collaboration would lead to many regional and international congresses and seminars. Gudrun has literally spent hundreds of hours networking, planning, organising, and implementing highly successful and influential gatherings. She initiated the World Summits on Physical Education which helped promote the quality of physical education worldwide and inclusion of individuals with disabilities. She also played a significant role in the transformation of the scientific congresses held prior to the Olympic Games into the multi-disciplinary professional conference known as the International Convention on Science, Education and Medicine in Sport (ICSEMIS) which brought together the IOC, IPC, ICSSPE and FIMS (International Federation of Sports Medicine). Although the first official ICSEMIS (2008) was held in Guangzhou, China, the efforts to incorporate adapted physical activity and disability sport began earlier in congresses held in Thessaloniki (2004) and Brisbane (2000), thanks again to Gudrun's efforts.

Gudrun Doll-Tepper and Karen DePauw

For years, we often attended the same conferences, served on panels and gave keynotes, authored papers together and meetings to advance adapted physical activity and disability sport. This continued from the 1980s until the Scientific Congress held in China before the 2008 Beijing Olympic when my academic administrative position (my »day« job) required me to reduce my involvement with the discipline of APA and sport science. Her leadership and responsibilities continued and her efforts have touched and influenced many.

We were active collaborators and I was pleased to work with her to advance adapted physical activity and disability sport on an international scale. In the early years, we visited colleagues in sport centers and universities and attended many conferences mostly around Europe. We spent many days and nights in Berlin. We have shared a hotel room in the winter without heat or electricity (Vienna), shared space in residence halls (Israel, Turkey) and accommodations across the spectrum of multi-starred hotels around the world. We attended many conference meals and banquets, dined in fine restaurants, shared many conversations with colleagues in coffee houses and bars, and very often grabbed meals *on the go*. As the statement implies, there was so much to do with seemingly so little time. These years with IFAPA, IPC, and ICSSPE took us to many countries around the world. These included in no particular order Australia, Norway, Switzerland, Brazil, Turkey, Spain, Israel, Germany, Belgium, Sweden, Finland, Italy, Greece, Canada, the United States, Japan, Korea, China, Denmark and probably more.

It is delightful to be able to see the results today after the years of advocacy and dedicated service. Adapted physical activity and sport science are better because of the efforts of exemplary leaders like Professor Dr Gudrun Doll-Tepper.

Thank you Gudrun for your dedication, leadership and wonderful memories!

Visionär und nachhaltig

Herbert Dierker
Abteilungsleiter Sport, Senatsverwaltung für Inneres und Sport, Berlin

Sehr geehrte Frau Professorin Doll-Tepper, liebe Gudrun,
die Anrede beschreibt unsere Beziehung gut: Einerseits haben wir uns in zahlreichen offiziellen Arbeitskontakten getroffen und andererseits auch persönlich sehr gut kennengelernt – aber der Reihe nach.

Im März 1982 kam ich als junger Assistent aus dem idyllischen Studentenstädtchen Münster an das Institut für Sportwissenschaft der Freien Universität Berlin in der damals noch geteilten Großstadt. Der Einstieg in die Arbeit am Institut fiel mir sehr leicht, weil ich mit Prof. Dr. Gertrud Pfister eine tolle Chefin hatte und vor allem, weil ich von solch netten Kolleginnen und Kollegen wie Dr. Christoph Dahms und dir empfangen wurde. Zahlreiche und intensive Gespräche fanden über die Entwicklung des Instituts statt, so hat uns die immer wiederkehrende Frage eines Neubaus des Sportinstituts tief bewegt – leider erfolglos, wie wir heute wissen. Auch unsere besonderen Vorlieben für bestimmte Sportarten, wie z. B. das Skifahren, haben uns verbunden.

Anscheinend habe ich nicht nur bei dir, sondern auch bei den anderen *Mittelbauern* einen vertrauenswürdigen Eindruck hinterlassen, so dass ich unsere Interessen im Direktorium des Sportinstituts vertreten durfte. Auch dadurch gab es immer wieder Gelegenheit über das zum Teil spannungsgeladene Verhältnis der unterschiedlichen Gruppen hinaus in einen intensiven Gedankenaustausch zu treten.

Besonders interessant fand ich damals schon deine Beschäftigung mit dem Thema *Sport für Menschen mit Handicap*. Dieses Thema hast du mir durch das von dir 1989 als IFAPA Vorsitzende zu verantwortende internationale Symposium *Adapted Physical Activity* nahegebracht. Neben allen Inhalten dieser Konferenz erinnere ich bis heute das tolle Logo – und vor allem deine Einladung an uns alle in ein nettes Lokal unweit des ICC. Nebenbei sei erwähnt, dass meine damalige Freundin und heutige Ehefrau eine kompetente Fahrerin eines *nigelnagelneuen* silberfarbenen Mercedes Cabrio für den Kongress war. Wichtig war auch, dass ich in diesem Zusammenhang unseren gemeinsamen Wegbegleiter und Freund der Paralympischen Bewegung Harald von Selzam kennenlernte.

Eine der in meiner Erinnerung besten Ideen hattest du dann bei der Berliner Bewerbung für die Olympischen Spiele 2000, bei der Christoph, Harald und ich nun mitwirkten, auf den Weg gebracht. Berlin positionierte sich dank deiner Initiative eindeutig und bewarb sich von Beginn an sowohl für die Olympischen als auch für die Paralympischen Spiele – damals eine völlig neue Idee. Im Verlaufe des Bewerbungsprozesses zogen die anderen Bewerberstädte nach. Heute ist die gemeinsame Veranstaltung dieser beiden faszinierenden Ereignisse bereits eine Selbstverständlichkeit. Ich glaube, du hast den entscheidenden Stein ins Wasser geworfen.

Einige Jahre später warst du für mich eine ganz wichtige Ansprechpartnerin im Vorstand der Führungs- und Verwaltungsakademie des Deutschen Sportbundes mit Sitz am Priesterweg in Berlin. Du hast mich in meiner Arbeit als Direktor begleitet und mir geholfen den schwierigen Weg der strategischen Neuausrichtung dieser Einrichtung erfolgreich zu gestalten. Mit dem Wechsel der Führungs-Akademie, wie sie seit dieser Neuausrichtung heißt, im Jahr 2003 nach Köln haben wir uns ein wenig aus den Augen verloren.

Kein Problem, denn ich kam 2008 als Abteilungsleiter Sport in die Innenverwaltung nach Berlin zurück. Natürlich gab es wieder einen konkreten Arbeitszusammenhang: Du warst damals Präsidentin des *International Council of Sport Science and Physical Education*. Ein Kennzeichen deiner Arbeitshaltung kann an dieser Funktion sehr deutlich herausgestellt werden: Du hast dich für die Organisation eingesetzt, obwohl du im selben Jahr die Verantwortung in andere Hände gelegt hast. In der Folge wird ICSSPE nun als wichtige international agierende Institution dauerhaft vom Land Berlin gefördert – das nenne ich nachhaltig.

Liebe Gudrun, sehr geehrte Frau Professorin, beide Seiten dieser Ansprache finde ich wichtig: Schön, dass wir uns kennengelernt haben, und dass wir ein paar Schritte in deinem facettenreichen Leben zusammen gegangen sind!

Adapted Physical Activity ohne Grenzen

Maria Dinold
Vizepräsidentin ICSSPE und Universität Wien

Auf der Suche nach den Wurzeln des Einflusses Gudruns auf die Entwicklung von Adapted Physical Activity (APA) und meiner Freundschaft mit ihr fiel mir ein Brief von Gudrun vom 5. April 1988 in die Hände. Dieser war an meinen früheren Chef, Professor Raimund Sobotka, gerichtet und wurde von ihm an Dr. Beatrix Eder-Gregor weitergeleitet, die meine Vorgängerin als Universitätsassistentin für Bewegung und Sport (mit Spezialisierung Behindertensport) war.[1]

Dieses Schreiben über die Gründung der EARAPA (*European Association for Research into Adapted Physical Activity*, später *EUFAPA*) führte zur Etablierung einer Kontaktperson für APA in Österreich. Diese Funktion übernahm ich dann auch mit dem Beginn meiner Tätigkeit am Institut für Sportwissenschaft 1994, die übrigens auch mit dem Bedarf für diesen Bereich begründet wurde. Es war ein großes Anliegen von Gudrun das Forschungs- und Praxisgebiet APA im deutschsprachigen Raum zu verbreiten. 1989 gelang es ihr in Berlin das bestbesuchte Symposium (7th ISAPA 1989) zu organisieren und sie bestärkte das kleine Team von Interessierten in Österreich darin eine nationale Organisation – die *Austrian Federation of Adapted Physical Activity (AFAPA)* – 1995 zu gründen. Ihre weiter bestehende Unterstützung motivierte uns 2001 das *13. Internationale Symposium Adapted Physical Activity* in Wien zu veranstalten, das einen großen Beitrag zur inter- und cross-disziplinären Zusammenarbeit für die Arbeit mit Menschen mit Behinderung leistete.

Die immer wieder motivierende und verbindende Art von Gudrun – sei es als Präsidentin von EARAPA, IFAPA oder später ICSSPE – erreichte viele Menschen. Sie wirkte als Mentorin vor allem für Wissenschaftlerinnen auf der ganzen Welt und vergaß dabei nie ihre deutschen Wurzeln, ihre deutlich differenzierte Ausdrucksweise und ihren freundlichen und oft unterhaltsamen Umgangston. Neben ihren Führungspositionen erübrigte sie immer noch Zeit zum Publizieren und Unterrichten, was für viele, wie auch für mich, eine fast unerreichbare Vorbildwirkung hatte und hat.

---

1 Der Brief ist als Faksimile am Ende dieses Beitrags abgedruckt.

Gudrun besuchte meines Wissens alle ISAPAs, zuletzt das Symposium im Juni 2017 in Daegu, Korea. Kein Weg war bzw. ist ihr zu weit, keine Veranstaltung zu lokal, um mit Gleichgesinnten Kompetenz und Wissen in packenden Präsentationen auszutauschen.

Ich freue mich, einige Wege mit Gudrun gegangen und Veranstaltungen mir ihr erlebt zu haben und wünsche ihr natürlich weitere Erfolge und Anerkennungen, wie sie sie sich schon zahlreich verdient hat.

Gudrun Doll-Tepper, Claire Boursier, Maria Dinold und Karen DePauw

EUROPEAN ASSOCIATION FOR RESEARCH INTO ADAPTED PHYSICAL ACTIVITY (EARAPA)
===
Dr. Gudrun Doll-Tepper , Präsidentin
c/o Institut für Sportwissenschaft
Freie Universität Berlin
Rheinbabenallee 14
D- 1000 BERLIN 33

An das
Institut für Sportwissenschaft
der Universität Wien
z. Hd. Herrn Prof. Dr. Sobotka
Auf der Schmelz 6
A - 1150 WIEN

Berlin, d. 5. April 1988

Betr.: European Association for Research into Adapted Physical Activity -
Kontaktpersonen aus europäischen Ländern/ hier: Österreich

Sehr geehrter Herr Professor Sobotka ,

wie Sie bereits wissen, wurde im September 1987 in Brüssel die " European
Association for Research into Adapted Physical Activity (EARAPA) "
gegründet. Diese Vereinigung ist der europäische Zweig der " International
Federation of Adapted Physical Activity (IFAPA)". Ziel der IFAPA/EARAPA ist
es, ein Forum für Fachleute zu schaffen, die sich mit " Adapted Physical
Activity", einem Bereich , der "Bewegung, Spiel und Sport für Menschen mit
Erkrankungen, Behinderungen und Alterssyndromen " umfaßt, in Forschung und
Praxis (Therapie, Unterricht, Erziehung, Freizeit, Wettkampf etc.)
beschäftigen.
Die IFAPA führt im Zwei-Jahres-Turnus internationale Kongresse durch. 1987 fand
das 6. Internationale Symposium " Adapted Physical Activity " in Brisbane/
Australien statt. 1989 wird der nächste Weltkongreß dieser Art in Berlin
stattfinden.(Ankündigung siehe Anlage)
Auch auf europäischer Ebene hat bereits ein erster Kongreß stattgefunden,
bei dem sich 1986 in Brüssel Experten aus verschiedenen Fachgebieten

- 2 -

(Medizin, Psychologie, Pädagogik, Sportwissenschaft etc.) trafen und auf dem die ersten Schritte zur Gründung der EARAPA unternommen wurden. Übereinstimmend wurde dort festgestellt, daß ein intensiver Informationsaustausch und eine bessere Kommunikation innerhalb der europäischen Länder im Bereich " Prävention/ Rehabilitation/Behindertensport - Adapted Physical Activity " dringend erforderlich ist.
Um ein solches Kommunikationsnetz zu entwickeln, wurde beschlossen, sogenannte " Key Persons " in den verschiedenen europäischen Ländern zu identifizieren. Die Aufgaben dieser " Key Persons " sind folgendermaßen definiert :
" Key persons should serve as individuals and not as representatives of institutions ; they should attempt to identify and build a network of EARAPA contacts/members within their respective countries; they should attempt to identify what is happening in their respective countries within the field of adapted physical activity and they should act as link persons between their own national membership and the rest of EARAPA ' s membership through interaction with their fellow key persons . "

Für die meisten europäischen Länder konnten bereits Kontaktpersonen gefunden werden. Ein erstes Treffen dieser Gruppe fand im Dezember 1987 in Lissabon während des AIESEP-Weltkongresses statt. Leider war Österreich bei diesem Treffen nicht vertreten. Eine kontinuierlich mit uns zusammenarbeitende Kontaktperson haben wir bisher in Österreich noch nicht finden können, wenngleich erste Gespräche und Kontakte mit Herrn Professor Dr. Größing (Salzburg) positiv verlaufen sind , und er freundlicherweise die Bereitschaft zur Mithilfe signalisiert hat.
Ich trete nun an Sie , sehr geehrter Herr Professor Sobotka, mit der Bitte heran, uns bei der Suche nach einer Kontaktperson in Österreich - in Absprache mit Herrn Professor Größing - zu helfen, die über entsprechende Kenntnisse in dem genannten Fachgebiet verfügt und bereit ist, auf internationaler Ebene mit uns zusammenzuarbeiten.

Für 1988 liegen folgende Pläne für weitere Treffen vor :
- Während des AIESEP-Weltkongresses in Madrid vom 26.-31. Juli 1988 besteht die Möglichkeit, in der Sektion " Adapted Physical Education and Sport " zu referieren. Darüber hinaus ist ein Treffen zwecks Informations- und Erfahrungsaustausch innerhalb der EARAPA vorgesehen.

- Im Herbst 1988 soll in Newcastle/England ein EARAPA- Seminar zum Thema
" Research Priorities " stattfinden, auf dem der aktuelle Forschungsstand
und zukünftige Forschungsprioritäten von den " Key Persons " der verschiedenen
europäischen Länder vorgestellt und erörtert werden sollen. Eine finanzielle
Unterstützung dieser Tagung ist bei der Europäischen Gemeinschaft beantragt
worden.

Zu Ihrer Information füge ich den EARAPA Newsletter bei. Sollten Sie weitere
Auskünfte benötigen , wenden Sie sich bitte an mich.
Abschließend möchte ich dem Wunsch Ausdruck geben, daß es bald gelingen möge,
Österreich aktiv an der Zusammenarbeit innerhalb der "European Association
for Research into Adapted Physical Activity " zu beteiligen.

Mit freundlichem Gruß

Gudrun Doll-Tepper

Dr. Gudrun Doll-Tepper
- Präsidentin -

Anlagen

Kopie dieses Schreibens an Herrn Prof. Dr. Größing

Vielseitig und menschlich engagiert für Sportdeutschland

Alfons Hörmann
Präsident Deutscher Olympischer Sportbund

Gudrun Doll-Tepper wurde mit der Gründung des Deutschen Olympischen Sportbundes im Jahr 2006 zur *Vizepräsidentin für Bildung und Olympische Erziehung* gewählt. Sie hat in den nunmehr 11 Jahren seit Bestehen des DOSB die Bildungsarbeit in ihrem ganz eigenen Stil geprägt.

Was macht Gudruns eigenen Stil aus? Zunächst einmal ihre Begeisterung, mit der sie sich dem Themenfeld Bildung im DOSB und dem Themenfeld der Olympischen Erziehung in der Deutschen Olympischen Akademie (DOA) widmet. Der DOSB hat das große Glück, dass er Gudrun für dieses Amt gewonnen hat: eine passionierte Sportlerin, eine ausgefuchste national und international erfahrene Vertreterin von Sportorganisationen und dazu noch eine Professorin für Sportpädagogik. Dieses Profil ist für das DOSB-Vizepräsidentenamt *Bildung und Olympische Erziehung* geradezu ideal. Darüber hinaus prägen Gudruns freundliche, integrierende und zugewandte, aber auch durchaus beharrliche und durchsetzungskräftige Persönlichkeit ihre Arbeit.

Im Folgenden möchte ich auf Gudruns Arbeitsschwerpunkte im DOSB eingehen. Dazu muss ich mich auf die herausragenden Meilensteine ihrer bisherigen Amtszeit konzentrieren, denn die Gesamtauflistung ihres Wirkens würde den Rahmen sprengen.

Sportverein und Schule

Gudrun hat gleich zu Beginn ihrer Amtszeit die Verbindung von Sportverein und Schule im DOSB verankert, ergänzend zu den Aktivitäten der Deutschen Sportjugend (dsj). Sie war und ist der Überzeugung, dass dieses wichtige Thema, nämlich den staatlichen Lernort Schule und den gemeinnützigen Sportverein zu einer fruchtbaren Kooperation zu bringen, nur in gemeinsamer Anstrengung gelingen kann. Dabei zeigte sich sehr schnell ihre besondere Gabe, Menschen zusammenzubringen und so auch eine fruchtbare Kooperation zwischen DOSB, dsj und der

Kultusministerkonferenz (KMK) zu gestalten. In regelmäßigen Gesprächen mit der Kommission Sport der KMK stellt sie seither sicher, dass alle – mitunter auch schwierige – Themen zwischen dem gemeinnützigen Sport und den Vertreterinnen und Vertretern des Schulsports immer wieder auf die Agenda genommen werden. Dass sich beide Seiten regelmäßig ihrer jeweiligen Stärken und Unterstützung versichern und an ihren Schwächen arbeiten, lässt sie durch die Erarbeitung und Verabschiedung gemeinsamer Handlungsempfehlungen fixieren. Mit Expertenhearings, Arbeitstreffen und Fachkonferenzen, die sie gemeinsam mit der dsj veranstaltet, sichert sie den Austausch zwischen Wissenschaft und Praxis.

Gesellschaftliche Partner

Die gesellschaftliche Vernetzung, die Gudrun sehr am Herzen liegt, strebt sie auch mit Partnern aus Politik und Zivilgesellschaft an. Gudruns Mission ist es, Menschen zusammenzubringen, Synergien zu schaffen, um dann gemeinsame Ziele zu verfolgen, die im Alleingang nicht oder nur schwer umsetzbar gewesen wären. Ein besonderes Highlight für eine gelungene Kooperation war die gemeinsame Konferenz *Bildung ist viel mehr als Schule*, die der DOSB in Kooperation mit der Evangelischen Kirche Deutschlands (EKD) und der Deutschen Bischofskonferenz (DBK) im April 2012 in Berlin durchgeführt hat. Gudrun war die erste, die es wagte, die Bildungspotenziale des Sports und der Kirchen in der Gesellschaft darzustellen und so mehr Anerkennung für diese Potenziale zu erreichen. Das Ergebnis war eine Veranstaltung mit großer Strahlkraft, in der die drei großen zivilgesellschaftlichen Partner EKD, DBK und DOSB erstmals gemeinsam mit Vertreterinnen und Vertretern aus Gesellschaft und Politik über das Themenfeld Bildung diskutierten. Einig war man sich, dass es vor allem außerschulischer Lernorte bedarf, an denen gesellschaftliches Engagement erfahren und gelernt wird, ohne das das Gemeinwesen nicht funktionieren kann. Dieses Ziel ist auch heute, fünf Jahre später, noch aktuell. Nach wie vor muss darum gekämpft werden, dass diese Bildungsleistungen in Politik und Gesellschaft die notwendige Anerkennung finden.

Inklusion im Sport

Die Ausrichtung von Gudrun Doll-Teppers Lehrstuhl *Integrationspädagogik, Bewegung und Sport* an der FU Berlin zeigt dies eindrucksvoll: Der Sport der Menschen mit Behinderung ist Gudruns Herzenssache schon seit Jahrzehnten. Sie hat sich dafür stark gemacht, dass sich der DOSB mehr für das Themenfeld Inklusion einsetzt. Die Diskussion um das gemeinsame und gleichberechtigte Sporttreiben von Menschen mit und ohne Behinderung im organisierten Sport in Deutschland wurde durch sie entscheidend angeregt. Und wer Gudrun kennt, der weiß, dass sie auch umsetzt, was sie für wichtig und richtig hält: Nämlich die Entwicklung einer Inklusionsstrategie für den DOSB und seine Mitgliedsorganisationen, die sich zum Ziel setzt, die Türen für ein *Mehr* an gemeinsamen Sporttreiben zu öffnen. Um dies zu verwirklichen, hat sie das Projekt *Sport-Inklusionsmanagerinnen und -Inklusionsmanager* initiiert, in dem Menschen mit Behinderung als hauptberufliche Expertinnen und Experten in eigener Sache ihre Erfahrungen und Wissen in die Entwicklung von Sportverbänden und -vereinen einbringen.

DOSB-Lizenzausbildung

Die Rahmenrichtlinien für die DOSB-Lizenzausbildung, quasi das Kern-Curriculum aller Ausbildungen für Übungsleiter und -leiterinnen, Trainer und Trainerinnen, Sportmanager und -managerinnen sowie Jugendleiter und -leiterinnen in den Sportvereinen, ist ein weiterer Eckpfeiler des Amtes der Vizepräsidentin *Bildung und Olympische Erziehung*. Diesen Rahmen inhaltlich und strukturell weiterzuentwickeln, so dass die Ausbildungen im Sport den Anforderungen moderner Bildungsarbeit gerecht werden, ist eine Kernaufgabe von Gudrun. Dass es erstmals gelingen konnte, für die Weiterentwicklung und Qualitätssicherung der DOSB-Lizenzausbildung eine maßgebliche Unterstützung des Bundesministeriums für Bildung und Forschung (BMBF) zu erhalten, war ein großer und richtungsweisender Erfolg. Mit dem durch das BMBF finanzierte *SALTO-Projekt* haben wir wichtige und wirksame Impulse für das Lernen und Lehren mit digitalen Medien in den Sportverbänden gesetzt. Auch hierbei hat Gudrun gezeigt, dass Kooperationen und Zusammenarbeit eine zentrale Grundüberzeugung ihrer Arbeit sind. Aktuell setzt sie ihren Arbeitsschwerpunkt auf die *Schlüsselfunktion Trainerin und Trainer*, ein Schwerpunkt, der im DOSB in seiner Gesamtheit getragen und vorangebracht wird.

Deutsche Olympische Akademie (DOA)

Die beispielhafte Würdigung ihres inhaltlichen Wirkens im DOSB will ich mit dem zweiten Teil ihres Titels als Vizepräsidentin *Olympische Erziehung* abschließen. Gudrun hat als erste Vizepräsidentin des Deutschen Olympischen Sportbundes die für ein NOK von Deutschland obligatorische und wichtige Aufgabe übernommen, die Olympischen Werte in Deutschland zu pflegen und weiter zu verbreiten. Hierzu hat der DOSB im Zuge der Fusion von DSB und NOK im Jahr 2006 unter ihrer Führung die Deutsche Olympische Akademie (DOA) gegründet und zu einer wichtigen Instanz für die Werte in Sportdeutschland entwickelt.

Diese Liste von vielen normalen, aber eben auch einer Reihe von ganz besonderen Aufgaben könnte ich nun noch beliebig fortsetzen, aber diese Beispiele skizzieren den Einsatz unserer Gudrun als unglaublich vielseitig einsetzbare Kollegin wohl recht gut. Explizit hervorheben möchte ich an dieser Stelle noch ihre besonderen menschlichen Fähigkeiten. Sie lebt die Werte des Sports wie Fair Play, Teamgeist, maximale Einsatzbereitschaft und Chancengleichheit mustergültig vor.

Hermann Gmeiner, der Gründer der SOS-Kinderdörfer hat so schön formuliert: »Alles Große in unserer Welt geschieht nur, weil jemand mehr tut, als er muss.« – Gudrun tut seit Langem mehr, als sie tun muss, und hat sich deshalb sowohl innerhalb der Strukturen von Sportdeutschland als auch weit darüber hinaus eine verdient hohe Akzeptanz und Wertschätzung erarbeitet. Wir hoffen, dass wir darauf noch in vielschichtiger Form weiter bauen können...

Gemeinsam nach vorne schauen

Jan Holze
Vorsitzender Deutsche Sportjugend

Die Jubilarin steht und engagiert sich für so vieles im Sport und in seinen Handlungsfeldern; allein die Herausgabe einer Festschrift zu ihrem runden Geburtstag deutet das an. Bei Würdigungen von Alleskönnerinnen und Vielbegabten wie Gudrun Doll-Tepper, der Sportwissenschaftlerin, Inklusionspädagogin, Multifunktionsehrenamtlichen, gerät man schnell in die Gefahr aufzuzählen – und dabei Wesentliches zu vergessen: Nicht nur einzelne Funktionen und Fähigkeiten und Auszeichnungen auszulassen, sondern eben nicht genug den Menschen dahinter zu sehen. Und der einzelne Mensch, der ist Gudrun Doll-Tepper doch so wichtig! Also soll es im Folgenden auch um *sie* gehen, und alle ihre früheren und heutigen Aufgaben und Belobigungen können wir getrost ihrer offen zugänglichen und wirklich sehr beeindruckenden Biografie überlassen.

Ich habe Gudrun Doll-Tepper als eine Persönlichkeit mit herausragender Kompetenz, stets wertschätzendem Verhalten und ständigem Augenmaß kennengelernt, die sich nie von Emotionen leiten lässt, sondern sich immer der Sache dienend und gleichwohl emotional auftretend für die Belange von Menschen und ihrem Sport einsetzt. Ein Mensch, der mich beeindruckt und genauso viele von meinen Mitstreiterinnen und Mitstreitern der Deutschen Sportjugend (dsj), mit denen ich über den Menschen Gudrun Doll-Tepper gesprochen habe. Wir haben in vielen Begegnungen und bei gemeinsamen Projekten erlebt, mit welchem persönlichen Mut und Herz sie ihre Themen anpackt.

Gudrun Doll-Tepper steht für Bildung und Olympische Erziehung; so lautet die Zusatzbezeichnung neben dem Titel der Vizepräsidentin im Deutschen Olympischen Sportbund (DOSB). Sie steht als Pädagogin für den Schulsport, natürlich. Sie unterstreicht gerne, und dem kann ich nur zustimmen, dass der organisierte Sport einer der größten Bildungsanbieter in Deutschland ist. In besonderer Weise steht Gudrun Doll-Tepper für den Sport von Menschen mit einem körperlichen oder geistigen Handicap und den Prozess ihrer Inklusion in den Sport und in die Gesellschaft. Den Sport sieht sie als Intermedium, als Zwischenspiel auf dem Weg zum großen Ziel. Auf dieser Klaviatur ist sie *die* Expertin, und die Deutsche

Sportjugend nimmt in diesem Feld immer wieder gerne ihren Rat in Anspruch. Ideen für sportliche Inklusionsplattformen gehen ihr nicht aus, und immer legt sie den Finger in die Wunde. Nicht nur hier haben Gudrun Doll-Tepper und die Deutsche Sportjugend die gleiche Position: Inklusion muss in unserer Gesellschaft hochgehalten werden, die zukünftigen Generationen erwarten das von uns. Und neben all den Organisationen, die dafür eintreten, braucht es eben auch die Menschen, die diese gesellschaftliche Verantwortung authentisch vorleben, ja, sie personifizieren können, und die es obendrein vermögen, Entscheidungsträger und andere Menschen für die eigene Sache einzunehmen – wie Gudrun Doll-Tepper; auch sie ist eine, die andere mitnimmt. Der wichtigen Aufgabe der Inklusion bereitet sie mit ihrer Kompetenz, ihrem Engagement und als Respektsperson das Feld. Es könnte keine Bessere für diese Rolle geben.

Denn Gudrun Doll-Tepper scheut vor keiner Verantwortung zurück, sie weicht nicht aus, stellt sich den Themen. Solche Menschen ziehen Arbeit magnetisch an. So hat natürlich sie die Führung des Deutschen Sport- und Olympiamuseums in Köln übernommen, sowohl in dessen Verein als auch in der Stiftung. DOSB-Ethikpreis? DOSB-Wissenschaftspreis? Auch hier hält sie die Zügel in der Hand. Im IOC arbeitet sie in den Kommissionen *Frauen und Sport* sowie *Olympische Erziehung* mit. Als Vorsitzende der Deutschen Olympischen Akademie ist ihr die Stimme der Deutschen Sportjugend in Person ihres Vorsitzenden im Vorstand dieser der Olympischen Idee verpflichteten Einrichtung sehr wichtig – und die Deutsche Sportjugend, das kann ich sagen, arbeitet sehr gerne mit und unterstützt die Maßnahmen und Projekte zur Olympischen Erziehung und zur weiteren Verbreitung der Olympischen Werte nach Kräften. Ja, das war soeben eine Aufzählung von Funktionen Gudrun Doll-Teppers, aber hier nur als Mittel zum Zweck, um zu zeigen: Das Ehrenamt ist ihr zum Naturell geworden.

In ihrem bürgerschaftlichen Engagement strotzt Gudrun Doll-Tepper vor Kraft, und ich habe den Eindruck gewonnen, sie ist in den mehr als 15 Jahren, die ich sie jetzt kenne, kein Stückchen gealtert, weder in physischer Hinsicht noch in ihrem Denken. Dafür mag ihre Fähigkeit zum Ausgleich mitverantwortlich sein. Auch wenn Meinungen nie immer gleich ausfallen können, hat sie die Deutsche Sportjugend stets wertschätzend behandelt, unsere Strukturen akzeptiert und den Weg der Partnerschaft gesucht. Wie bei hochintelligenten Menschen wohl nicht unüblich, ist ihr stets die Meinung der anderen wichtig.

Passionately Inclusive: Towards Participation and Friendship in Sport – der Titel dieser Festschrift trifft es. Gudrun Doll-Tepper ist eine Universitätsprofessorin. Und doch nein, sie ist keine Theoretikerin, sondern, so habe ich sie kennengelernt, ihr Handeln ist gekennzeichnet von einem pragmatischen Ansatz, hinter dem immer der Dienst am Menschen steckt. Dieses Ziel verliert Gudrun Doll-Tepper nie aus den Augen, sie ist daher für alle nahbar, und sie ist der Deutschen Sportjugend gerade in der Bildungsoffensive und dem durch die Inklusionsdebatte angestoßenen Paradigmenwechsel des gesellschaftlichen Zusammenlebens eine herausragende Ratgeberin und Unterstützerin.

In einer Zeit, in der Inhaberinnen und Inhaber von Ehrenämtern unter verstärkter öffentlicher Beobachtung stehen, um es vorsichtig auszudrücken, verfügen wir mit Gudrun Doll-Tepper über eine leuchtende Musterfrau, die es einfach als Mensch, der sich dermaßen für andere Menschen engagiert, verdient hat, selber in höchstem Maße anerkannt zu werden und dafür Dank zu empfangen.

Die Zusammenarbeit mit Gudrun Doll-Tepper ist immer erfreulich unkompliziert, viele sagen auch: herzerfrischend.

Dafür herzlichen Dank! Die Deutsche Sportjugend freut sich auf die weitere Zeit mit dir!

What Else Could Possibly Be Said...

ICSSPE Executive Office Team

Despite a progressing globalisation that we observe in our lives, we notice borders that are not easy to cross. To overcome habits in order to foster change it requires inner conviction, energy and a vision. But it is worth trying: No matter how comfortable it may be to continue walking on well-trodden paths, life can offer unique and exciting experiences when leaving these, ideally with a mentor who helps you to become a team-oriented and visionary change-maker yourself.

A few years ago, one of us, as inspector of turns for a swimming competition, observed that when a one-arm amputee swimmer was doing the butterfly stroke, he touched the wall with his remaining arm perfectly correctly according to the rules for Paralympic swimmers – in a competition under the rules of the German Swimming Federation. The senior inspector asked him to disqualify the swimmer – but the inspector balanced the facts: a teen athlete, swimming, practicing every day year-in-year-out, with his able-bodied friends, should not be allowed to be part of a relay team because of a missing arm? On the other hand, there were the competition rules. He was weighing the options, thinking of his boss at work, her conviction to work towards equality and her courage – and he decided against all odds not to disqualify him. A leading newspaper picked up the issue of competition rules for athletes with and without impairment and shortly afterwards, the German Swimming Federation changed its rules. Swimmers with an impairment can now participate in competition under the guiding rules for Paralympic swimmers.

Gudrun Doll-Tepper lives the values of sport. She plays with and for the team, whether as a team-mate, chair or employer. Her professional leadership is characterised by a balanced and visionary approach and nonetheless by fairness, transparency and respect for the interests and needs of partner organisations, colleagues and staff. She leads by example and from the front, or by stepping back and trusting and supporting the colleagues.

Along with all her strategic planning and conduction of business meetings with other leaders and colleagues, she has an eye on her team, her staff, and welcomes everybody with the same friendly smile and an invitation to cooperate.

One of us remembers her first business trip to Edmonton, Canada, soon after she had started working in the ICSSPE Executive Office. She arrived late due to difficulties with the airline. Although the meeting period with a demanding agenda had already started, Gudrun Doll-Tepper, about to chair the meeting, took the time to personally welcome her with the affection we have all experienced, to update and to reassure her that everything would turn out well. This warm welcome helped to release the tension and the work could start.

Also volunteers, among them students and retired people, enjoy the same respect: At the end of the World Championships in Athletics or at similar events where Gudrun Doll-Tepper has met with high-level governmental and sport leaders, she never forgets to thank them for their contribution which only makes the event possible.

Sport, it is said, is a practice ground for life skills, and players of team sports could carry over some of the skills and attitudes needed to succeed in other areas of their life. Whether or not this is true for everyone, it certainly is the case for Gudrun Doll-Tepper. She trusts and thus, provides a unique basis for personal development:

More than twenty years ago, one of us, a second semester student of Physical Education and French, was planning to participate in an exchange programme to France when asked by Gudrun Doll-Tepper whether she would be interested in working as her student assistant and supporting the organisation of an international congress. The young student dropped the plan to go abroad and consequently also her studies of the French language to work for Gudrun and participate in the organisation of what is now known as the famous AIESEP conference in Berlin in 1994. This opportunity, based on the vision and confidence of a leader, formed the basis for a professional career in event and publication planning.

More books with stories such as these could be filled with contributions from people from around the world where Gudrun Doll-Tepper is almost at home as in her home town Berlin which since 1989 again provides opportunities for young people from all over the world to be creative, to learn and to appreciate diversity.

We are grateful to Uri Schaefer, our current President, and to the ICSSPE Executive Board, to support the production of this publication and thus provide another testimony of how sport development and a professional career can benefit so many.

ICSSPE President Uri Schaefer, Gudrun Doll-Tepper, the Executive Office Team and colleagues at MINEPS VI, July 2017

Celebrating a True Path-Finder

Darlene A. Kluka
IAPESGW President 2005–2009 and ICSSPE Vice President

This is the first time that I have been asked to participate in the creation of a *Festschrift*. I was not at all sure about how to approach this specific honour, especially for a woman with the professional reputation of Prof. Dr Gudrun Doll-Tepper. I asked several people to show me examples of a *Festschrift* without luck. I did what any decent researcher would do: I searched! After many hours of searching through *Festschrift* articles on the internet, I found that there appears to be a three-step approach in a *Festschrift* creation. It strangely reminded me of when I first learned to spike in volleyball, using a three-step approach. First, I was to discuss and praise the honoree with superlatives, as *Festschriften* are only created for the very best in the field. Second, because the honoree's work contributes substantively to the field, the work is still unfinished, leaving questions to be answered and positions to be filled for the next generation. And third, to scholarly explore topics that are still unsettled and to include the honoree's work in developing the tapestry of interwoven issues and controversies. Since I believe I can best contribute to the first, this is my contribution to the life and times of Prof. Dr Gudrun Doll-Tepper.

Born in 1947 in Berlin (then West Berlin), Germany, Gudrun Doll-Tepper was a post-World War II arrival. Her place and time of birth were part of an equation that shaped her choices as a young adult seeking her life's purpose. Growing up in the epicenter of the Cold War, in a country surrounded by the remnants of Allied Forces Occupation, it would have been easy for her to remain nationally focused and inward-looking if, for nothing else, survival. This new and increasingly complex Germany seemed to spark her passion for seeing the world differently than people did before and during the war. She increasingly developed ways forward that would provide her dispositions and skills leading toward a common vision of inclusion, advocacy and international development through sport and physical education.

Gudrun Doll-Tepper studied physical education and sport at the *Freie Universität* in Berlin and became increasingly interested in people with disabilities. She worked with several groups dealing with cerebral palsy, learning and intellectual disabilities. Since that time, she has been a part of a dramatic philosophical change in access and opportunities. She came to believe in access, opportunity and choice for those with disabilities. More importantly, she became an advocate for social inclusion. As a remarkably bright student of sport science, she realised that in order to make positive change, there must be a connection between science and practice. She also realised that there must be connections between science, practice, and policy initiatives in order to overhaul systems within society. In short, Gudrun Doll-Tepper discovered, at a relatively young age, that access, opportunity, and choice are cornerstones for any marginalised population in any society. She invests in professional discourse as well as projects, programmes and initiatives that connect physical education and sport science and those with disabilities, girls and women, fostering values, and the Paralympic Movement to those making policy.

She has a remarkable *sixth sense* of determining who powerful stakeholders are and who frequently hold the keys to change. She decided that in order to facilitate change she needed to be in legitimate leadership positions. She served as President of the European Federation for Adapted Physical Activity (EUFAPA) from 1987 until 1993, which directly led to her presidency of the International Federation for Adapted Physical Activity (IFAPA). She also served as Chair of the International Paralympic Committee's Sport Science Committee for a decade. Perhaps her most significant contribution to the integration of sport science and physical education with powerful global stakeholders was her presidency from 1997 until 2008 of the International Council of Sport Science and Physical Education (ICSSPE). Even after the end of her presidency, she continues to find ways to facilitate discussion of inclusion and education through sport and physical activity and use them to open doors that have been previously locked.

Gudrun Doll-Tepper loves meetings. She is at her best when she can be involved in discussions that connect, engage and determine ways forward with people from a variety of sectors in society. She has come to realise that when meaningful discussions are held around issues that have potential to influence societies for better quality of life, she wants to be a part of the discussion and possible solutions.

She is also a synthesiser. She loves to learn about new topics or fields, surveys them broadly, and puts them together in a way that makes sense, not only to herself, but to others. Books, articles, and monographs that she has authored or co-authored, show these syntheses: *Introduction to Adapted Physical Education* and lead editor of *Sport, Education and Social Policy* to list only two. Through her scholarship, she touches on inclusion in a broader sense for all people who lack equal access, opportunity to participate, and personal choices because of religious and cultural backgrounds, sexual orientation, race and ethnicity, and gender.

Gudrun Doll-Tepper, whether knowingly or unknowingly, found herself with service and leadership opportunities in already established professional organisations. Through her involvement with ICSSPE, she became the first woman president of the organisation in its long and prestigious history. Again, she chose a role of inclusion rather than a role of independence to display and use her inclusive leadership style to grow the organisation's membership from less than 100 to over 320 in a decade. She moved the Secretariat from Finland to Germany, hired a fulltime Executive Director, and led the charge for formulated funding from the Berlin and German governments as well as non-governmental sectors. I was fortunate enough to be a part of the Executive Board from 1997 through her presidency and personally participated in what I consider to be the best learning experience I ever had. What a thrill it was to be able to observe someone utilising theory into practice! What an honour to be part of the decision-making team to make ICSSPE a more inclusive and global sport science and physical education organisation! What a joy it was for me, under Gudrun's leadership, to be selected as the first woman on the prestigious ICSSPE Editorial Board! What an opportunity for me to be involved in the initial decision making for the Communities in Crisis Seminar that came from discussions at a conference on Tsunamis and natural disasters!

In my opinion, Gudrun was impressively adept at utilising the *Hedgehog Concept* in the organisation and administration of ICSSPE. First, the leadership began to understand what its members were truly passionate about. She brought together the Executive Board and consultants with whom she had worked through the International Olympic Committee. You can imagine how revolutionary this was – not only were we planning the future of what would become the most-consulted and respected global organisation of its kind, but we used computers and interactive communication face-to-face to make the future! Next, leadership identified what we do better than anyone else – science, service and advocacy for sport science and physical education globally. The affiliations with the International Olympic Committee (IOC), the International Federation of Sports Medicine (FIMS), the United Nations Education, Scientific, and Cultural Organisation (UNESCO), and the World Health Organization (WHO) were formulated and continued to grow. And last, leadership determined where we were good at generating revenue. Gudrun, through her now-extensive network in Germany and Europe, found startup funds for the Secretariat and continued to work on finding additional funding through programmes, projects and initiatives that placed ICSSPE in roles of consultancy and service provision to other international organisations. In a sense, ICSSPE began its reputation as a conduit, and then broker, for its membership.

In short, Gudrun has impacted my professional and personal life in so many ways – more than she will ever realise. We first met in 1996 through my membership in the International Association of Physical Education and Sport for Girls and Women (IAPESGW). I was nominated by Pat Bowen West and Margaret Talbot to serve on the Executive Board of ICSSPE. I did not attend the Dallas meeting because I was working at the International Volleyball Federation (FIVB) Congress and at the Olympic Games in Atlanta at the same time the then Pre-Olympic Scientific Congress was being held. To my shock, I was elected. I was later told that it was highly irregular for someone to be elected at the General Assembly by delegates without being in attendance. This had to be *kismet*!

Gudrun's ability to embrace me with open arms for who I am; to provide me with her presence and attention when engaged in discussion; to instill confidence in me and my abilities; to *womentor* me without announcing that she was *womentoring*; to display a strong, yet sensitive and inclusive, leadership style; to function with honesty, integrity and fairness in decision making; to show me how to politically change the face of sport and physical education without being *political*; to encourage the development of passionate enthusiasm and inspiration in those she touched; and to do it with grace and dignity are the reasons for this *Festschrift* honoring Gudrun. It is with profound gratitude and love to you for allowing me to be in your professional life for over twenty years…

2017 – Zeit zum Feiern

Tobias Knoch, Isabel Flory und Matthias Thaler
Deutsche Olympische Akademie

Gudrun Doll-Tepper kommt 2017 aus dem Feiern kaum noch heraus: Nach dem 10. Geburtstag *ihrer* Deutschen Olympischen Akademie Willi Daume e.V. (DOA) im Mai steht mit ihrem 70. Geburtstag gleich das nächste Jubiläum vor der Tür. Diese Zahl ist aber kein Grund, kürzer zu treten – im Gegenteil: Erst im März übernahm Gudrun Doll-Tepper zusätzlich zu ihren umfassenden sonstigen ehrenamtlichen Verpflichtungen noch den Vorsitz des Deutschen Sport & Olympia Museums in Köln. Diese Bereitschaft zur Übernahme von Verantwortung charakterisiert ihr Leben und Wirken.

Die Liste der Tätigkeitsfelder von Gudrun Doll-Tepper ist lang: Nach ihren Anfängen als Lehrerin an Sonderschule und Gymnasien war beziehungsweise ist sie als Professorin in Leuven (Belgien) und Peking (China), an der Humboldt-Universität und der Freien Universität in Berlin tätig. Die Steigerung des Frauenanteils im organisierten Sport und die Förderung des Paralympischen Sports sind dabei nur zwei ihrer Forschungsfelder. Als langjähriges Mitglied in Kommissionen des Internationalen Olympischen Komitees (z. B. in der Kommission für Olympische Erziehung), als Präsidentin des Weltrats für Sportwissenschaft und Leibes-/Körpererziehung oder als Vizepräsidentin des Deutschen Olympischen Sportbundes (DOSB) – um nur einige ihrer Tätigkeiten zu nennen – ist sie international bestens vernetzt. Die gebürtige und überzeugte Berlinerin ist in der Welt zuhause.

Diese Erfahrungen und Kontakte brachte Gudrun Doll-Tepper über die vergangenen zehn Jahre sehr gewinnbringend in ihre Arbeit bei der DOA ein. Als Zusammenschluss aus dem Deutschen Olympischen Institut (DOI) und dessen Erweiterung um den Aufgabenbereich des Kuratoriums Olympische Akademie und Olympische Erziehung des Nationalen Olympischen Komitees (NOK) für Deutschland wurde diese 2007 gegründet. Nach der Fusion von Deutschem Sportbund und NOK zum DOSB im Jahr zuvor entstand so auch eine Nationale Olympische Akademie für Deutschland, die sich im Auftrag des DOSB primär Aktivitäten im Bereich der Olympischen Erziehung sowie der Förderung der Olympischen Bewegung in Deutschland widmen sollte.

Gudrun Doll-Tepper im Kreis ihrer Vorstandskollegen beim Festakt zu *10 Jahre Deutsche Olympische Akademie* im Kaisersaal des Frankfurter Römer.

Die Wahl Gudrun Doll-Teppers zur Vorsitzenden erwies sich dabei von Anfang an als Glücksfall für die Akademie. Als ausgewiesene Expertin auf dem Feld der Olympischen Erziehung konnte sie bei der Themensetzung wichtige Impulse geben und die Projekte und Aktivitäten der DOA mit ihrem Fachwissen bereichern. Ihre hervorragende nationale wie internationale Vernetzung öffnete der Akademie viele Türen und half, Themen in unterschiedlichen Feldern auf der (sport-)politischen Agenda zu platzieren. Unter ihrem Vorsitz etablierte sich die DOA in der deutschen Sportlandschaft und konnte ihr Profil in den vergangenen Jahren kontinuierlich weiterentwickeln und schärfen.

Unter der Führung von Gudrun Doll-Tepper vereinte die Deutsche Olympische Akademie nicht nur verschiedene Aufgaben ihrer Vorgängerinstitutionen, sondern ging auch eigene, neue Wege. Bestehende Aktivitäten wurden modernisiert und ausgebaut, neue Kooperationen gestartet und zusätzliche Projekte ins Leben gerufen. So gehören zu den Aufgaben der Akademie heute Veranstaltungen wie das *Deutsche Olympische Jugendlager*, das den Sportnachwuchs an die Austragungsorte Olympischer Spiele bringt. Der jährlich wachsende *Olympic Day* in Köln begeisterte zuletzt über 3.000 Kinder, und die Kooperation mit *Jugend trainiert für Olympia / Jugend trainiert für Paralympics*, dem weltgrößten Schulsportwettbewerb, wurde über all die Jahre aufrechterhalten. Die Wiederauflage der *Biebricher Schlossgespräche*, die sich vor allem an ein interessiertes Fachpublikum richtet und seit kurzem auch Schauplatz der Verleihung des *Fair-Play-Preises des deutschen Sports* ist, ist darüber hinaus nur eines von vielen Beispielen für die gute und gewachsene Zusammenarbeit mit dem Land Hessen. Mit Publikationen wie den *Olympia ruft: Mach mit!* – Unterrichtsmaterialien und der Posterserie *Faszination Olympia* erreicht die DOA tausende Schulklassen und gibt gleichzeitig mit *Olympia kompakt* eine Informationsbroschüre für alle deutschen Athletinnen und Athleten bei Olympischen und Paralympischen Spielen heraus.

Auch im internationalen Umfeld ist die DOA unter Gudrun Doll-Teppers Vorsitz schnell zu einer festen Größe geworden. So nimmt die Akademie heute im europäischen Raum eine Vorbild- und Führungsrolle ein und wurde für ihr außergewöhnliches Engagement um die Olympische Bewegung und insbesondere die Olympische Erziehung im Jahr 2016 von der Internationalen Olympischen Akademie (IOA) mit dem Athena-Preis ausgezeichnet.

Einen wichtigen Anteil an Erfolgen wie diesem hat dabei auch die gute Zusammenarbeit zwischen der Geschäftsstelle der Deutschen Olympischen Akademie und ihrer Vorsitzenden. Gudrun Doll-Tepper ist für die Mitarbeiterinnen und Mitarbeiter in der Frankfurter Otto-Fleck-Schneise immer ansprechbar, sucht den persönlichen Kontakt und hat so von Anfang an eine positive Arbeitsatmosphäre geschaffen. Auch ihre stets enge und vertrauensvolle Zusammenarbeit mit dem DOA-Direktor Tobias Knoch sowie seinem Vorgänger Dr. Andreas Höfer hat die erfolgreiche Entwicklung der Akademie befördert.

Vor allem aber profitiert die Deutsche Olympische Akademie von der unerschöpflichen Energie, mit der Gudrun Doll-Tepper ihre zahlreichen Aufgaben angeht. Egal, aus welchem Flugzeug sie gerade steigt oder in welcher Zeitzone sie gerade noch unterwegs war – sie schafft es immer, sich sofort auf ihr aktuelles Gegenüber einzustellen und allen Menschen herzlich zu begegnen. Trotz ihres beeindruckenden Reisepensums, dem häufig auch die eine oder andere Stunde Schlaf zum Opfer fällt, vermittelt Gudrun Doll-Tepper stets das Gefühl, dass ihr jede ihrer Aufgaben gleichermaßen wichtig ist und dass sie sie von Herzen gerne wahrnimmt – sei es beim spielerisch-sportlichen *Olympic Day* mit Schulkindern, bei anspruchsvoll-kritischen Diskussionen mit dem Sportnachwuchs beim *Deutschen Olympischen Jugendlager* oder im fachlichen Austausch mit Kolleginnen und Kollegen aus aller Welt an der Internationalen Olympischen Akademie.

Wie wichtig der Pädagogin Gudrun Doll-Tepper vor allem die Begegnung und Beschäftigung mit jungen Menschen ist, wird auch an einem unumstößlichen Termin deutlich, der mittlerweile all ihren Kollegen und Mitarbeitern rund um die Welt bekannt sein dürfte: Der Mittwoch ist ihr heilig, ganz egal, welche Gremien oder sonstigen Verpflichtungen rufen. Aber wer an einen freien Tag bei all ihren Terminen denkt, hat weit gefehlt: Mittwochs ist sie ganz für ihre Studenten und Studentinnen an der Freien Universität Berlin da.

Die Deutsche Olympische Akademie und all ihre aktuellen und ehemaligen Mitarbeiterinnen und Mitarbeiter sind dankbar dafür, seit zehn Jahren mit Gudrun Doll-Tepper eine herzliche, engagierte und fachkundige Vorsitzende zu haben, und überbringen ihr die besten Wünsche zum 70. Geburtstag!

A Personal Thank You

Uri Schaefer
President ICSSPE

Dear Gudrun, dear ICSSPE Honorary President,
A *mazal tov* to a special day and to a special person. May you celebrate your birthday joyfully together with your family and friends.

Please let me first extend my thanks and appreciation for motivating and encouraging me and the ICCE to join ICSSPE way back in 2005. The rest, as they say, is history... I thank you very much in assisting and advising me whenever I reached out to you on many topics and issues. It gave me a unique opportunity and I was privileged to learn from you throughout the years.

What you have accomplished and contributed throughout your stellar career – for society in general and for so many individuals with special needs worldwide, by initiating and contributing to activities that are meant to make their lives healthier and happier – needs to be applauded by all. You did so whilst conducting and publishing numerous scientific research studies, holding many leading positions which have impacted leading organisations in Physical Education, Sport and Physical Activity with a special emphasis on Adapted Physical Activity. And, of course, we must not forget your outstanding presidency of ICSSPE.

Your integrity, wisdom, knowledge, your open, friendly and dynamic personality, your sense of humour and your respected leadership capabilities make you so very special to all those who had the opportunity to work with you, to the ICSSPE family, and to me, personally.

Dear Gudrun, I, also on behalf of the ICSSPE Executive Board, wish you good health and happiness for many more years to come. Continue doing what you like most – using Physical Activity as a vehicle to enhance people's quality of life, regardless of their religion, nationality, gender, race or political orientation.

Yours in friendship and respect,
Uri

Mauern überwinden und Knoten lösen

Guido Schilling
Chair ICSSPE Editorial Board 1997–2003

Liebe Gudrun,
ich konnte und durfte dich einige Zeit auf deinem Weg in die und in der ICSSPE Leitung begleiten. Zusammen haben wir viele Verbindungen geknüpft und manchmal auch Knoten lösen können.

In guter Erinnerung habe ich unsere erste persönliche Begegnung. Es muss beim wissenschaftlichen Kongress vor den Olympischen Spielen 1992 in Malaga gewesen sein. Der Lärm der Autobahn war in der Nacht sehr stressig, aber der Kongress war ein sehr wichtiger Schritt auf dem Weg zum gemeinsamen Vor-Olympischen Kongress aller Sportwissenschafterinnen und Sportwissenschafter.

Du hast mich dann zur Mitarbeit in der Redaktionskommission ermuntert. Es entstanden einige bemerkenswerte Publikationen.

Ein Meilenstein zur Entwicklung ICSSPEs war 1998 sicher die 58. Exekutivsitzung in Lausanne, bei der es vor allem um die Zukunft der Organisation ging. Gemeinsam – alle Sitzungsteilnehmerinnen und -teilnehmer waren per Computer miteinander verbunden – wurde ein Leitbild erarbeitet und auch visualisiert. Gleichzeitig wurden die Überarbeitung der Strukturen, eine neue Finanzstrategie und eine Revision der Statuten beschlossen. Es wäre prima, wenn auch andere Sportorganisationen solche Weitsicht hätten und sich ihre Mitglieder an der nötigen Weiterentwicklung so direkt beteiligen könnten.

In nasser Erinnerung habe ich eine Veranstaltung in Finnland an der Sporthochschule in Jyväskylä, wo wir nach einem sommerlichen Gewitterregen völlig durchnässt ins Hotel zurückkehrten.

Sehr gefreut hat mich, dass du im Sommer 2001 zu meiner Abschiedsvorlesung an der ETH nach Zürich kamst. Du hast in die Veranstaltung eingeführt und mir zudem auch die Urkunde mit meiner Ernennung zum ICSSPE Honorary Member überreicht.

Nimm meinen herzlichen Dank für unsere gute und erfolgreiche Zusammenarbeit über die vielen Jahre. Es freut mich, dass ich für die Festschtift zu deinem 70. Geburtstag einen Beitrag zum Eigenleben des Frauensportes in islamischen Ländern schreiben konnte. Frauen werden ausgegrenzt. Ich führte dazu ein Gespräch mit Shokouh Navabinejad, die wir beide sehr schätzen.[1]

Nicht nur Ausgrenzung, sondern Grenzen im umfassenden Sinn beeinflussen alle Bereiche unseres Lebens, sei es als Grenze zum Nachbarn oder als Kontrolle etwa beim Passieren einer Landesgrenze. Grenzen geben aber auch Halt und ermöglichen Identität. Auch mit dem Bau der Großen Mauer in China wollten Menschen dies erreichen. Heute sind wir offener und möchten Grenzzäune abbauen.

Leider werden in vielen Bereichen – auch im Sport – die Grenzen zu möglichen Partnern und Mitspielern nicht abgebaut, sondern zum Teil sogar neu befestigt, wie etwa mit dem Zaun des Todes in der Grenzwüste zwischen Mexiko und den USA.

Eine Welt ohne Grenzbefestigungen durch Mauern und Zäune und ganz ohne Überwachung durch Menschen oder mit technischen Hilfsmitteln wird es wohl nie geben. Oder doch? Wer sah die schnelle Öffnung der Mauer in Berlin zwischen den beiden deutschen Staaten im Voraus?

Herzliche Glückwünsche zum 70. Geburtstag!

---

1 Das Interview ist in Teil 2 dieser Publikation abgedruckt.

Eine Paralympische Siegeshymne

Wolfgang Schrödter
Geschäftsführer Fürst Donnersmarck-Stiftung

09. September 2016: Live-Schaltung nach Rio de Janeiro aus der sehr gut besuchten STATION Event-Location am Gleisdreieck.

Auf dem großen Saalbildschirm: Frau Professorin Gudrun Doll-Tepper, seit 20.06.2003 Kuratoriumsmitglied der Fürst Donnersmarck-Stiftung, der erste deutsche Olympiasieger der Paralympics 2016 im Kugelstoßen, Herr Niko Kappel, und der Präsident des Deutschen Behindertensportverbandes, Herr Friedhelm Julius Beucher, die uns stolz und begeistert die erste Goldmedaille der Paralympics in Rio für Deutschland präsentieren.

Großes Staunen, großes Hallo, großer Jubel, großer Beifall!

Der ehemalige Senator und Kuratoriumsmitglied, Herr Dr. Ehrhart Körting, gratuliert im regen Gespräch den Paralympioniken, die uns wiederum herzliche Grüße zum 100. Jubiläum der Fürst Donnersmarck-Stiftung übermitteln.

Gudrun Doll-Tepper, Niko Kappel und Friedhelm Julius Beucher

Diese Szene, so meine ich, schildert beispielhaft alle oder wenigstens viele der Gaben und Begabungen, der Persönlichkeit von Gudrun Doll-Tepper, die sich ohne Zögern für die Menschen in der Stiftung sowie für die Menschen im Sport einbringt und einsetzt und Großes damit erreicht.

Acht Wochen zuvor in der Vorbereitungsrunde wurde deutlich, dass unser Jubiläumsfest parallel zu den Paralympics in Rio de Janeiro stattfinden muss und schnell kam die Idee auf: Eine Liveschaltung nach Rio muss her!

Trotz vielfacher Bedenken rief ich Gudrun Doll-Tepper an und stieß sofort auf ungebremste Begeisterung: »Super Idee, das machen wir, rufen Sie mal den Geschäftsführer des Deutschen Behindertensportverbandes an.« Und so wurde aus einer *crazy* Idee rasch ein konkreter Plan mit überschaubaren Kosten, denn wir waren uns darin schnell einig: Wir machen das über Skype trotz vielfältiger technischer und anderer Einwände.

Und so geschah es dann.

Diese Szene zeigt beispielhaft Gudrun Doll-Tepper: Sie
- ist begeisterungsfähig,
- ist voll engagiert,
- kennt die richtigen Leute,
- ist unprätentiös,
- macht anderen klar, welche Erwartungen auf ihnen ruhen,
- kriegt die Prominenz vor die Kamera,
- ist gut gelaunt, aufgeräumt und lebendig,
- hat das Herz am rechten Fleck,
- kämpft für die Sache trotz aller Widerstände,
- ist verlässlich und professionell,
- ist jung und dynamisch,
- reißt die Leute mit,
- hat mit überflüssigen Konventionen nichts am Hut,
- wahrt Stil und Form und
- ist eine geistvolle Ästhetin.

Gudrun Doll-Tepper ist eine wunderbare Frau mit hoher Fachkompetenz in (sport-) pädagogischen Themen und eine echte Leitungsfrau, die weiß, wo es langgeht, und Studenten und Studentinnen, Mitarbeiter und Mitarbeiterinnen sowie Kollegen und Kolleginnen gleichermaßen für ihre Themen begeistern kann, ihnen den Weg weist und mit ihnen die angestrebten Ziele auch erreicht.

Wir gratulieren herzlich zu dem runden Geburtstag und sagen ein großes Dankeschön für das schöne, gute, beschwingende, aufregende Miteinander.

Herzlichen Glückwunsch!

An Encounter with Professor Doll-Tepper and the Development of Adapted Sports in Japan

Tomoyasu Yasui
Hokkaido University of Education, Japan

I first met Professor Gudrun Doll-Tepper at the 7th International Symposium of Adapted Physical Activity in Berlin in 1989 for which she served as the Executive Chairperson. As you may know, this conference was a wonderful symposium and is remembered by many stakeholders as a legendary success. Since at that time, I was only acquainted with closed academic societies, both, the operation and the atmosphere of the conference were quite enlightening for me. Besides the large scale of the convention, everything presented was fresh, including the overall positive mentality, enthusiasm for the physical activity of people with disabilities, and the candid discussions. I think that Professor Doll-Tepper's own feelings for the subject were projected onto the conference itself. Immediately I became aware that an academic conference is a free, intellectual gathering space wherein everyone can participate equally. At this conference it was also decided to hold the 1993 ISAPA in Yokohama, Japan. Since then, Gudrun Doll-Tepper is the pole star for many members of various Japanese adapted sports research organisations and individuals, including me.

As mentioned, the 9th ISAPA was held in Yokohama. Fortunately, I was given the opportunity to co-chair a poster session with Professor Doll-Tepper. I think that this encounter was fate. Three years later, I became a visiting professor at the laboratory of Professor Doll-Tepper at the *Freie Universität Berlin*, serving half a year in 1996, and again in 2005. During these years, I learned a lot from Professor Doll-Tepper.

I served as Chairman of the Japanese Society for Adapted Physical Education and Exercise for seven years from 2005 to 2012, and as Chairman of the Asian Society for Adapted Physical Education and Exercise from 2012 to 2013. During this period I organised numerous conferences and I was always conscious of the 1989 conference in Berlin and the way Professor Doll-Tepper handled it.

Professor Doll-Tepper visited Asia, including Japan, many times and she continued to influence people concerned with adapted physical education and other areas of research. In 2011, at a conference of the Japan Society for Sport and Gender Studies, the keynote speech *The International Situation and Trends on Women and Sport and Measures from the Viewpoint of the IOC* had great influence on researchers in this field. Some comments concluded that it was *very encouraging* and that participants were *able to find a direction for Japan's efforts* after this pivotal convention.

As Japan prepares for the 2020 Olympic and Paralympic Games in Tokyo, the most important question to consider is what legacy will remain after these events are over. In particular, for Japan, which tends to put emphasis on the infrastructure, such as athletic facilities, there is a need for changing both, the system and people's consciousness, in order to increase the opportunities for sports participation, regardless of one's disability.

In January 2016, Professor Doll-Tepper gave a lecture in Tokyo in front of stakeholders of the Paralympic Games and media correspondents about the possibilities and advantages of a multifaceted strategy for creating a sport environment for persons with a disability. In addition, in July 2016, we invited Professor Doll-Tepper to a joint congress of sports-related research involving persons with a disability in Hokkaido, including a keynote lecture and a symposium. The theme of the keynote lecture, *The Paralympics as a Vehicle for Change in Local Community Sport*, offered suggestions for many participants, coinciding with Japan's future direction in this area of research. Again, Professor Doll-Tepper offered *new challenges* for many of us. The content of the lecture was published in the Japanese Journal of Adapted Sports Science. We believe that the lectures of Professor Doll-Tepper will continue to transmit more and more information to the Japanese Society.

The 9th ISAPA in Yokohama, Japan 1993

Keynote Lecture in a congress in Hokkaido, Japan 2016

Gudrun with congress staff in Hokkaido, Japan 2016

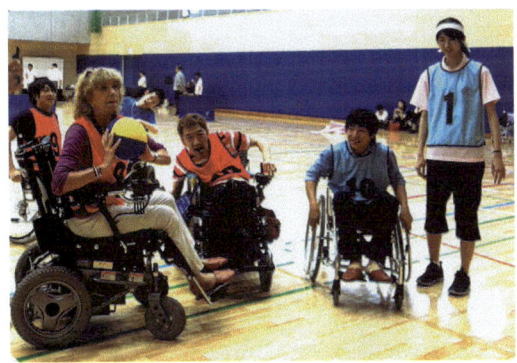

Gudrun loves to try something new in Hokkaido, Japan 2016

2. Changes and Challenges

Der Beitrag des (organisierten) Sports für die Entwicklung junger Menschen

Wolf-Dietrich Brettschneider und Erin Gerlach
Universität Paderborn und Universität Potsdam

Der Titel der Festschrift *Passionately Inclusive: Towards Participation and Friendship in Sport* spiegelt den Spagat wider, den Gudrun Doll-Tepper während ihrer gesamten ehrenamtlichen und beruflichen Karriere zu meistern hatte. In ihren Funktionen als Vertreterin des organisierten Sports machte sie sich stark für den Sport mit seinen vielfältigen Facetten und die Menschen, die in ihm aktiv sind. Als Mitglied der *scientific community* – national wie international – stand sie genauso engagiert und entschieden auf der Seite derer, die sich mit dem Sport wissenschaftlich auseinandersetzten. Der folgende Beitrag befasst sich daher mit beiden Aspekten.

Die Rolle sportlichen Engagements zwischen Wunsch und Wirklichkeit

Sportive Praxen in vielfältiger Form spielen im Alltag von Heranwachsenden in zweifacher Hinsicht eine herausragende Rolle. Zum einen zählt Sporttreiben für die überwiegende Mehrheit der heutigen Kinder und Jugendlichen zu den zentralen Freizeitaktivitäten; zum anderen erwächst dem Sport im Zuge der Entgrenzung von Bildungsprozessen offenbar eine neue Aufgabe. Auf diese Weise wird der Sport vor allem in seiner organisierten Form zu einem attraktiven Wegbegleiter der Heranwachsenden in einer entscheidenden Phase ihrer Entwicklung. Da kann es nicht verwundern, dass es für Vertreter und Vertreterinnen des organisierten Sports und auch für Sportpolitiker und -politikerinnen vor allem in der Vergangenheit kaum eine Grenze hinsichtlich der dem Sport zugeschriebenen Effekte gab – von der Stärkung der Gesundheit, der Bildung der Persönlichkeit, der sozialen Integration, der Prävention von Suchtmittelkonsum bis zur Entwicklung kognitiver Fähigkeiten. Nicht zuletzt das gebetsmühlenartige Wiederholen solcher Wirkungsversprechen hat im Alltagsbewusstsein wie auch in der Öffentlichkeit das Bild vom Sportverein als *Entwicklungsmotor* und *gesellschaftlicher Reparaturwerkstatt* geprägt.

Nun gibt es aber sowohl aus theoretischer wie auch empirischer Sicht gute Gründe den formulierten Wirkungsversprechen und Transferhoffnungen mit Zurückhaltung und Skepsis zu begegnen. Wenn etwa Entwicklung als aktive Auseinandersetzung zwischen genetischem Potenzial und Umwelteinflüssen verstanden wird, ist kaum anzunehmen, dass die Entwicklungsdialektik gerade im Zusammenspiel von Individuum und sportlicher Aktivität außer Kraft gesetzt wird. Ebenso ist es unwahrscheinlich, dass ein zeitlich eingegrenztes Sporttreiben im Verein derartige positive Wirkungen in den Entwicklungsbereichen entfalten könnte, für die dem Elternhaus und der Schule mangelnder Einfluss oder gar Versagen vorgeworfen wird. Und auch aus empirischer Sicht ist angesichts vorliegender nationaler wie auch internationaler Befunde Zurückhaltung gegenüber Wirkungsversprechen angebracht. Noch ist die Anzahl der Studien, die nicht nur Aussagen über korrelative Zusammenhänge zwischen Sport und jugendlicher Entwicklung treffen, sondern evidenzbasierte Befunde zur Wirkungsrichtung vorlegen können, begrenzt. Fundierte Aussagen zur entscheidenden Frage, ob nämlich – wie behauptet – tatsächlich Sport die Ursache für die Entwicklung von Heranwachsenden darstellt (Sozialisation) oder aber günstige Anlagen die Durchführung sportlicher Aktivitäten initiieren und forcieren (Selektion), also zwischen Ursache und Wirkung unterscheiden können, sind ausschließlich prospektiven Längsschnittuntersuchungen vorbehalten. In methodisch einwandfreier Form ist diese Untersuchungsvariante vor allem in der deutschsprachigen sportwissenschaftlichen Forschung eher selten anzutreffen.

Die Wirkungsversprechen und die damit verbundenen hohen Erwartungen der Bevölkerung an die positiven Effekte des Sporttreibens in organisierter Form einerseits und die uneinheitliche und unbefriedigende empirische Befundlage andererseits veranlassten die Autoren dieses Beitrags gemeinsam mit Kollegen den Zusammenhang zwischen Sportaktivität und ausgewählten Facetten jugendlicher Persönlichkeitsentwicklung in zwei Längsschnittuntersuchungen näher zu analysieren (Brettschneider & Kleine, 2002; Gerlach & Brettschneider, 2013). Während sich die erste Studie dezidiert Jugendlichen widmete und diese fast drei Jahre lang mit quantitativen und qualitativen Methoden untersuchte, analysierte die zweite Studie Heranwachsende zehn Jahre lang zwischen Kindheit und Adoleszenz, konkret: zwischen Grundschule und Abitur bzw. Ausbildung.

Fragestellungen und Befunde der Paderborner Längsschnittstudien

Im Folgenden werden nach der Darstellung der Fragestellung ausgewählte Befunde vorgestellt, bevor dann auf deren Rezeption in der Wissenschaft und in den Sportorganisationen eingegangen wird. Gefragt wird, ob und wie sich das sportliche Engagement im Verein auf die körperliche und psychosoziale Verfassung der Heranwachsenden auswirkt und ob durch Sporttreiben entwicklungsfördernde Ressourcen mobilisiert werden bzw. entwicklungshemmenden Risikofaktoren gemindert oder gar verhindert werden können. Dabei fungieren Vereinsstatus bzw. Gestaltung der Vereinskarrieren in der Phase des Aufwachsens als Differenzierungskriterien. Design, Datenerhebung und Auswertungsstrategien sind ausführlich in den genannten Studien beschrieben. Auf ihre Darstellung wird hier verzichtet.

Zunächst zu den Auswirkungen des sportlichen Engagements im Verein auf die motorische Entwicklung wie auch die physische Gesundheit von Heranwachsenden. Am Beispiel der Entwicklung von Übergewicht und Adipositas lassen sich – zur Überraschung vieler Funktionäre und Funktionärinnen sowie Politiker und Politikerinnen, aber im Einklang mit Befunden anderer Studien zur Gesundheit von Heranwachsenden – gesundheitliche Wirkungen des organisierten Sporttreibens nicht finden.

Eine Analyse psychosomatischer Beschwerdebilder wie etwa Kopfschmerzen und Schlaflosigkeit einerseits sowie Wohlbefinden und Lebensfreude andererseits zeigt, dass sportlich aktive Jugendliche stressresistenter und fröhlicher als ihre Altersgenossen sind, die Differenz zwischen den Gruppen im Verlauf der Sportkarriere aber unverändert bleibt. Sporttreiben im Verein sichert demnach ein unbeschwertes Aufwachsen – vor allem für Heranwachsende mit günstigen Voraussetzungen. Ein Mittel, um psychische Gesundheit nachhaltig zu fördern, ist es jedoch nicht.

Das Jugendalter markiert für viele eine Phase riskanten Verhaltens in zweierlei Hinsicht: Für den überwiegenden Teil der Jugendlichen ist Risikoverhalten Ausdruck eines zeitlich begrenzten Experimentierens ohne negative Auswirkungen auf die Entwicklung. Bei anderen wiederum drücken sich im riskanten Verhalten Unsicherheit und unbewältigte Belastungen mit möglichen negativen Auswirkungen auf den Übergang ins Erwachsenenalter aus. Zum (gesundheitlichen)

Risikoverhalten im Jugendalter zählt auch der Substanzmittelkonsum, in erster Linie das Rauchen und Trinken. Die Sichtweise auf die Kombination von Sport und Substanzkonsum ist ambivalent. Einerseits sieht man Sport als geeignetes Instrument zur Prävention risikoreichen Substanzkonsums, andererseits werden erhebliche Zweifel an seiner Präventionswirkung geäußert. Die empirischen Befunde unserer Studien sprechen eine eindeutige Sprache: Sportlich aktive Jugendliche rauchen eindeutig weniger als sportdistanzierte Jugendliche. Je intensiver Sport getrieben wird, desto weniger Nikotin ist im Spiel. Der Eintritt in den Sportverein markiert den Abschied vom Rauchen; umgekehrt steigt nach dem Verlassen des Sportvereins der Zigarettenkonsum an. Der Sport im Verein erweist sich gegenüber dem Rauchen als protektives Setting.

In entgegengesetzte Richtung weisen die Befunde zum Alkoholkonsum. Sportvereinsjugendliche trinken deutlich mehr als Vereinsabstinente. Beim Austritt aus dem Sportverein sinkt der Alkoholkonsum, wohingegen mit dem Eintritt in den Verein ein Anstieg des Konsums verbunden ist. Die Effekte sind zwar klein, aber eindeutig. Das Gefährdungspotenzial des Sports im Verein für Jugendliche ist evident. Aktuelle Studien im deutschsprachigen und internationalen Raum bestätigen die berichteten Befunde nachdrücklich (vgl. u. a. Gebert, Lamprecht & Stamm, 2017; Sallen, 2017).

Ob und in welchem Ausmaß mit dem Jugendalter verbundene chronische Belastungen bewältigt werden, hängt nicht zuletzt von der Quantität und Qualität von Schutzfaktoren resp. Ressourcen ab, die den Heranwachsenden zur Verfügung stehen. Aus dem Bereich der *personalen* Ressourcen wird beispielhaft auf das Selbstwertgefühl rekurriert, das als Kristallisationspunkt der Wahrnehmungen und Bewertungen der eigenen Person und vor allem bei Heranwachsenden als Schlüsselmerkmal für Zufriedenheit mit sich und der Welt gilt. Es strukturiert nicht nur die Wahrnehmung der jungen Menschen, sondern steuert auch ihr Verhalten entscheidend mit. Das Selbstwertgefühl ist bei sportlich aktiven Jungen und Mädchen positiver ausgeprägt als das der sportdistanzierten Jugendlichen. Im Verlauf des Entwicklungsprozesses bleibt das Selbstwertgefühl auf hohem Niveau relativ stabil, jedoch kommt es zu Annäherungen zwischen den Gruppen. Die Auswirkung der Sportaktivität auf das Selbstwertgefühl der Jugendlichen ist – variierend nach Alter und Geschlecht – nur gering ausgeprägt. Ein systematischer Einfluss in positiver Richtung kann nicht festgestellt werden.

Aus der Vielzahl der für Jugendliche wichtigen *sozialen* Ressourcen wie Eltern, Freunde und Freundinnen, Lehrer und Lehrerinnen, Übungsleiter und -leiterinnen sowie Trainer und Trainerinnen wird als Exempel die Sportgruppe gewählt. Die positive Wirkung, die von der Sportgruppe ausgeht, ist bemerkenswert: Ob sportliches Talent oder Teilnehmer am Kompensationssport, ob Dauermitglied im Sportverein oder Sportarten- und Vereinshopper – sie alle profitieren von ihrer Zugehörigkeit zu einer Sportgruppe. Wo es um die *sportbezogene Integration* geht, ist die Wirkung der Sportgruppe eindeutig nachweisbar. Effekte sind ebenso auf der Ebene sozialer Anerkennung auszumachen – interessanterweise bei denjenigen Heranwachsenden am stärksten ausgeprägt, die sich trotz begrenzter motorischer Kompetenzen dauerhaft einer Sportgruppe anschließen und dort die Anerkennung erfahren, die ihnen in anderen Bereichen ihrer jugendlichen Lebenswelt weitgehend verwehrt wird. Der wichtigste Effekt dieser Ressource ist jedoch auf der Ebene *sozialer Unterstützung* zu sehen. Wenn in kritischen Lebenssituationen – wie etwa beim Wechsel von der Grundschule ins Gymnasium oder von der Hauptschule in die duale Ausbildung – die ansonsten wirksamen Unterstützer und Unterstützerinnen wie Eltern oder Lehrer und Lehrerinnen wirkungslos bleiben, geht von der Sportgruppe insofern ein spürbarer Effekt aus, als diese offenbar als einzige Ressource in der Lage ist individuelle Belastungen zu mindern.

Fazit

Evidenzbasierte Wirkungsnachweise für das organisierte Sporttreiben auf den Entwicklungsverlauf von Kindern und Jugendlichen sind begrenzt. Ein systematischer kausaler Zusammenhang, wie er in den selbst formulierten Ansprüchen des organisierten Sports und in den Erwartungen der Sportpolitik zum Ausdruck kommt, lässt sich nicht nachweisen. Es scheint so zu sein, dass zunächst Selektionseffekte den Prozess des Aufwachsens und die Entwicklungsrichtung maßgeblich prägen, bevor dann der organisierte Sport in begrenztem Maße sozialisierend auf die Persönlichkeitsentwicklung der Heranwachsenden einzuwirken vermag.

Dieses Ergebnis entspricht zum einen theoretisch begründeten Erwartungen, zum anderen entspricht es der nationalen wie auch internationalen empirischen Befundlage (vgl. dazu Gerlach, Heim & Brettschneider i.V.).

Soviel zu den Ergebnissen der Studien. Nun zu ihrer Rezeption:

Rezeption der Studien

In ihrer inhaltlichen Ausrichtung und methodischen Anlage – Theorieorientierung, längsschnittliches Design (zwei und zehn Jahre), Kombination quantitativer und qualitativer Verfahren, Einbeziehung subjektiver und objektiver Variablen, mehrfaktorielle Varianzanalysen mit Messwiederholung als Auswertungsstrategie sowie Imputation als Methode zur Kompensation von Datenverlust durch längsschnittbedingte Mortalitätsrate – waren beide Studien innovativ und haben in der sportwissenschaftlichen Jugendforschung positive Spuren hinterlassen, werden vielfach rezipiert und haben Zustimmung erhalten.

Dem organisierten Sport missfielen allerdings einige der zentralen Ergebnisse, widersprachen sie doch den stetig geäußerten Wirkungs- und Transferversprechen. Die Einschätzung der Reaktionen auf die Studien fällt ambivalent aus. Nicht zuletzt die unterschiedliche Beachtung, die den Studien in der medialen Berichterstattung zuteil wurde, riefen bei den betroffenen Organisationen unterschiedliche Reaktionen hervor. Gleichwohl lässt sich ein gemeinsames Muster der Rezeption erkennen (das hier nur holzschnittartig dargestellt und daher den einzelnen Organisationen im Detail nicht gerecht werden kann).

Phase 1: Aufregung und Irritation

Weniger die empirische Befundlage als das von bestimmten Themenbereichen hervorgerufene mediale Interesse sorgte für erhebliche Irritationen und Aufregung in den Sportorganisationen und evozierte die Suche nach geeigneten Abwehrmechanismen.

Phase 2: Abwehr und Anfeindung

Als probates Mittel kamen zunächst Presseerklärungen zum Zuge, die die Befunde in Frage stellten. In einem zweiten Schritt wurden Gutachten in Auftrag gegeben, um die Seriosität der Studien, vor allem die zugrundeliegende Methodik, prüfen zu lassen. Im Fall unserer Studien lief diese Taktik ins Leere, weil entweder die Gutachten positiv ausfielen oder offenkundig wurde, dass die innovativen Aspekte etwa der Samplingstrategien oder Auswertungsstrategie die für die Presseerklärung Verantwortlichen schlichtweg überforderten.

»Brett« und Gudrun Doll-Tepper Vorbilder – Wolf-Dietrich Brettschneider und Erin Gerlach

Phase 3: *Business as usual*
Nachdem die Aufregung um die empirischen Befunde und deren Rezeption in der Presse verklungen war, wurde wieder zum *Daily Business* übergegangen. Erneut wurden die bekannten Wirkungsversprechen wiederholt und – wie gehabt – die alltagstheoretischen Deutungen ins Spiel gebracht. Erst nach und nach gelangten die Befunde wieder ins Bewusstsein und diffundierten in die Köpfe der Verantwortlichen, was zu Phase 4 überleitete.

Phase 4: Nachdenklichkeit und sachliche Auseinandersetzung
Hatte sich der erste Sturm gelegt, trat Nachdenklichkeit ein. Die Befunde der Untersuchungen wurden vorbehaltlos geprüft, festgestellte Defizite konstruktiv gewendet und neue Programme zur Optimierung der Jugendarbeit in den Vereinen entworfen. Evaluation der Programme und empirische Analyse ihrer Wirksamkeit der neuen Programme – diese zentrale Forderung wurde allerdings nur selten umgesetzt.

Die Rolle von Gudrun Doll-Tepper im Umgang mit den Studien war nicht einfach. Als Wissenschaftlerin wusste sie, dass Forschungsergebnisse so zu präsentieren sind, wie sie vorliegen und nicht nach Opportunitätsgesichtspunkten oder bestimmten Erwartungen manipuliert werden dürfen. Als Sportpolitikerin wiederum hatte sie die schwierige Aufgabe zu bewältigen, nämlich einerseits für eine sachlich angemessene Rezeption der Ergebnisse und für einen fairen Umgang mit ihnen in der Sportorganisation zu sorgen und anderseits eine sachliche Auseinandersetzung mit den Befunden und eine konstruktive Umsetzung in entsprechende Programme zu sichern. Diese Doppelaufgabe meisterte Gudrun Doll-Tepper souverän und (wie immer) charmant.

Als Kollegen und Freunde wissen wir das zu schätzen!

Literatur

Brettschneider, W.-D. & Kleine, T. (2002). *Jugendarbeit in Sportvereinen. Zwischen Anspruch und Wirklichkeit.* Schorndorf: Hofmann.

Gebert, A., Lamprecht, M. & Stamm, H. (2017). Die präventive Wirkung von Sport und Verein. Sportaktivität und Suchtmittelkonsum von Kindern und Jugendlichen in der Schweiz. *German Journal of Exercise and Sport Research,* (47) 2, 122–132.

Gerlach, E. & Brettschneider, W.-D. (2013). *Aufwachsen mit Sport. Befunde einer 10-jährigen Längsschnittstudie zwischen Kindheit und Adoleszenz.* Aachen. Meyer & Meyer.

Gerlach, E., Heim, R. & Brettschneider, W.-D. (2017). Zwischen Wunsch und Wirklichkeit – Wirkungen des Sportengagements auf die jugendliche Selbstkonzeptentwicklung. *Diskurs Kindheits- und Jugendforschung (i.V.).*

Sallen, J. (2017). *Leistungssportliches Engagement und Risikoverhalten im Jugendalter. Eine Studie zum Konsum von Drogen, Medikamenten und Nahrungsergänzungsmitteln.* Hamburg: Feldhaus.

The Effects of Technology Supported Brain Breaks on Physical Activity in School Children

Fatma Sacli Uzunoz; Ming-Kai Chin; Magdalena Mo Ching Mok; Christopher R. Edginton; and Hrvoje Podnar

Nevsehir Hacı Bektas Veli University, Turkey; HOPSports, Inc., USA; The Education University of Hong Kong, Hong Kong; University of Northern Iowa, USA; and University of Zagreb, Croatia

Abstract

The aim of the study was to examine the effects of technology supported brain breaks on attitudes towards, beliefs, self-efficacy, self-confidence and motivation on the physical activity of school children in the Cappadocia region of Turkey. The participants for this study included 300 elementary school students from two public schools, grades 3 to 5, consisting of 193 (64%) in an experimental group and 107 (36%) in a control group (Mage = 9.55 years, SD = .98 years). There were 139 (46%) males and 161 (54%) females among the participants. Convenience sampling was used in this study. The »Attitudes toward Physical Activity Scale (APAS)«, (Mok et al., 2015) was used as pre-test and post-test to measure the attitudes, beliefs, self-efficacy, self-confidence and motivation toward physical activity. The experimental group received the Brain Breaks® Physical Activity Solutions as an intervention for the duration of four months during each school day in three to five minute segments at various intervals. In this current study, the exploratory factor analysis revealed a six factor solution – *self-efficacy in learning with video exercises, exercise motivation and enjoyment, self-confidence on physical fitness, promoting the holistic health, importance of exercise habit, trying to do personal best* – explaining 48.7% of the variance with 51 items on being physically active. Internal consistency coefficients of each factor ranged from 0.93 to 0.71. The results indicated significant changes in measured APAS between the time points in the experimental group and differences in the changes between the experimental and the control group. As a conclusion, we may say that technology supported brain breaks have a positive impact on promoting physical activity in school children.

Keywords: obesity, children, technology, brain breaks, physical activity, Brain Breaks® Physical Activity Solutions

Introduction

The World Health Organization (2016) reports demonstrate that the worldwide prevalence of obesity has more than doubled between 1980 and 2014. Overall, about 13% of the world's adult population is obese, 39% of adults aged 18 years and over are overweight, and 42 million children under the age of five are overweight or obese. It has become increasingly clear that obesity and many of the chronic diseases we face today are associated fundamentally with the pervasive sedentariness of modern life. Reasons for the decrease in physical activity of children are ascribed to the effects of environmental factors, increasingly demanding school curriculum, programme objectives to be mastered and huge amounts of homework, coupled with excessive use of social networks and communication programmes in the internet, etc. With the increase in the amount of time children spend learning, watching television and sitting in front of the computer, resulting in the theoretical possibility for spending less time with physical activities, has increased in general.

As a part of modern life, technology has both, good and bad effects on active lifestyles of children. Study results showed that although playing computer games causes a sedentary life, technology can also be used effectively to promote an active lifestyle (González et al., 2016). Pedometers, accelerometers, and heart rate monitors have been heretofore used in promoting physical activity worldwide. However, with the age of technology, interactive video games and internet-based physical activity interventions became more attractive for children (Hall, & Bierman, 2015).

The school environment is ideal for implementing physical activity interventions due to the possibility to reach wide numbers of children who are spending most of their time in schools (Hills, Dengel, & Lubans, 2015). The present research on the implementation of school-based physical activity programmes indicates either positive or non-significant improvement of cognitive skills and attitudes, academic performance and behaviour with only few studies indicating a negative relationship (Mura et al., 2015). In this context, there is an important need for additional research on effects of school based physical activity to support the efforts of initiating policies to promote changes at decision making levels which aim at providing children with more regular access to physical activity in school settings. Another important need is to find new ways to promote physical activity and encourage behaviour change to increase participation in physical activity by making it interactive, fun and engaging. Children's participation in physical activity is influenced by the built, natural and social environments in which they live as well as by personal factors such as sex, age, ability, time and motivation. Government, university, community, schools and non-governmental organisations have a crucial role to play in creating environments that promote opportunities for physical activity and active living (Lewallen, Hunt, Potts-Datema, Zaza, & Giles, 2015). Without the help and support of parents and the community, it is not possible to initiate and maintain children's participation in regular physical activity.

One promising intervention to meet the above mentioned goals is a school-based, video-exercise intervention called Brain Breaks® Physical Activity Solutions by HOPSports® (HOPSports, 2014). Brain Breaks® Physical Activity Solutions are web-based structured physical activity breaks that stimulate students' health and learning. They are specifically designed for the classroom settings to motivate students to improve their performance in theoretical lessons and provide opportunities not only to be physically active during breaks, but also to learn new motor skills, languages, learn about art, music, and about different cultures (Chin, Edginton & Tang, 2013).

The present study explored the effects of implementing Brain Breaks® Physical Activity Solutions in classroom settings focussing on children to report on their physical fitness, self-efficacy, personal best goal orientation, interest in physical activity, their understanding of importance and benefits of physical activity and the contribution of physical activity to learning about health. It was hypothesised that regular participation in physically active breaks would have positive effects on measured beliefs and attitudes.

Method
Participants
A pre-test and post-test with a quasi-experimental design was used in this quantitative study. The participants for this study comprised 300 primary school students, grades 3 to 5, consisting of 193 (64%) in an experimental group and 107 (36%) in a control group (Mage = 9.55 years, SD = .98 years) from two public schools in the centre of the Cappadocia region of Turkey. There were 139

(46%) males and 161 (54%) females among the participants. A convenience sampling was used in this study. The percentages of students in grades 3 to 5 were 47.3%, 29.3%, and 23.3%, respectively. The sampling distribution across grade levels and their gender in groups is presented in Table 1.

Table 1: Distribution of participants (n = 300)

Grade	Group	n	Female	Male	Total
Grade 3	Experimental	88	44	44	142
	Control	54	31	23	
Grade 4	Experimental	61	36	25	88
	Control	27	17	10	
Grade 5	Experimental	44	22	22	70
	Control	26	11	15	
Total		300	161	139	300

Students completed the questionnaire on paper by themselves during class time before and after the four-month experiment. Before the start of the study, ethical approval was obtained from the university's institutional review board and the departmental review board. In addition, written and oral informed consent was obtained from both, parents and children in groups.

Instruments

The effects of Brain Breaks were measured by a Turkish version of the Attitudes toward Physical Activity Scale (APAS) (Mok et al., 2015). The scale was designed for a larger global project which included Turkey, Lithuania, Croatia, Poland, South Africa, Romania, Singapore, Serbia, and Zimbabwe to measure outcomes of Brain Breaks video exercise supported lessons. It consisted of a demographic section and seven sections, sharing a design focus on measuring children's attitudes and perceptions regarding various aspects of engagement in physical activity, with particular emphasis on physical activity using video games. Each APAS was made up of several four-point Likert-type items with the response categories for all items characterised as »Strongly Disagree«, »Disagree«, »Agree«, and »Strongly Agree«. The original version of the English questionnaire was translated into Turkish with back and forward translation, in order to ensure the conceptual and cultural equivalent to the original one. The translation process was supervised by Physical Education and English language experts comprising university professors, educators and field expert coaches.

Procedure

Technology supported brain-breaks intervention was carried out in two elementary schools in the centre of the Cappadocia region of Turkey. Twelve classes from grades 3 to 5 participated in the study. For grade 3, four classes were the experimental and two classes were the control group, while two classes were experimental and one class was the control group for both grade 4 and grade 5. In the beginning of the intervention all students in both groups completed the APAS as a pre-test measurement. Then, students in the experimental groups carried out the BB video exercises, three to five minutes during every school day for four months from September to December 2014 in their classrooms, supervised by their teachers, while the control groups did not participate in these exercises. At the end of the four-month-intervention, all students in both groups once more completed the APAS as a post-test measurement. Different movement-integrated learning opportunities with motor and fitness skills, performed by animated and real-life instructors, were provided at each brain breaks video, which included health and nutrition education, social learning, environmental protection, core curricular learning, character development, arts and culture. The main goal was to use the Brain Breaks once a day regularly throughout the week, either before or after the lesson, during lunch time, or subject transitions to refresh the brain of the students by moving. The students at third grade attended regular *games and physical activity* lessons determined by the national educational curriculum 45 min per day. However, it took place only twice a week for the students in grade 4 and grade 5, which was a limitation for this study.

Statistical Analysis

The exploratory factor analysis was used to establish a factor structure of the Turkish version of the APAS. Internal consistency coefficients were calculated by Cronbach alpha. The test for data normality using skewness and kurtosis indicated that factors were approximately normally distributed. Descriptive statistics were used. A repeated measure analysis of covariance (ANCOVA) with Time as the within subject factor and Group (experimental vs. control) as the between subject factors (2 × 2) was used to analyse the effects of video exercise intervention on APAS scores. Gender and age were included in the ANCOVA as covariates. The partial eta-squared (ή²) effect sizes for the tests were calculated to indicate the magnitude of the effect.

Results

To establish an initial factor structure for the Turkish version of the APAS, an exploratory factor analysis was conducted using a principal components method. Initially, 58 items were submitted for analysis. Factor criteria included: (1) items should correlate with the factor with the load >.40; (2) items should not cross-load on the other factors with the load >.30; and (3) each factor should be composed of not less than three items. Following priori criteria, seven items were deleted from further analysis for failure to match. These items were: »Being physically active helps to give me new experience every time« (1f), »Even if I have a lot of work to do, I still keep being physically active« (2e), »I achieve my physical activity goals even if I am tired« (5d), »I persuade my friends to join me in doing physical activity« (5e), »I feel more confident after physical activity« (5h), »I think my good friends enjoy doing physical activity« (5k), and »My target is to go beyond what I have achieved in physical activity« (7b). The procedure was then repeated. Six meaningful factors were finally retained with eigenvalues from 7.42 to 1.97. The six factors combined explained 48.7% of the variance. The Kaiser-Meyer-Olkin coefficient was .84, indicating the sample was adequate for factor analysis. Bartlett's test of sphericity led to the rejection of the null hypothesis ($p<.001$) which stated that the correlation matrix was an identity matrix. Internal consistency (Cronbach's alpha) of each factor ranged from 0.93 to 0.71 which was acceptable. The final factor structure was represented by 51 items (see Table 2).

Table 2: Factor structure of the APAS from the exploratory factor analysis (n = 300)

Items	Factors					
	1	2	3	4	5	6
Self-efficacy on learning with video exercises						
3e. I learned about language through video exercise.	.754					
3j. I learned about hygiene from video exercise.	.747					
3d. I learned about mathematics through video exercise.	.743					
4d. I know which is my favourite physical activity in video exercise.	.739					
3h. I learned about healthy lifestyle from video exercise.	.708					
4b. I know how to do physical activity if there is a video exercise to follow.	.706					
3c. I learned about art through video exercise.	.691					
4a. I know how to choose physical activity in video exercise that suits me.	.678					
3k. I learned about environmental protection from video exercise.	.673					
4c. I can follow physical activity in video exercise with minimal mistakes even without a teacher.	.671					
3f. I learned about writing through video exercise.	.662					
3a. I learned about culture through video exercise.	.656					
3b. I learned about music through video exercise.	.641					
3i. I learned about healthy diet from video exercise.	.620					
3g. I learned about composition through video exercise.	.781					
Exercise motivation and enjoyment						
5l. I think my classmates enjoy doing physical activity.		.743				
5m. I think other children enjoy doing physical activity.		.736				
5i. I think better after physical activity.		.718				
5j. I improve on my school work after physical activity.		.714				
5f. I feel better after physical activity.		.674				
5c. I enjoy doing physical activity with my classmates.		.659				
5b. I look forward to doing physical activity.		.658				
5a. I think physical activity is fun.		.652				
5g. I feel stronger after physical activity.		.588				
5o. I think my teachers enjoy doing physical activity.		.578				
5n. I think my good friends enjoy doing physical activity.		.555				
Self-confidence on physical fitness						
6b. I am confident with my endurance.			.794			
6h. I am confident in doing physical activity elegantly.			.760			
6f. I am confident with my rhythm.			.756			
6g. I am confident with my hand-eye coordination.			.653			
6a. I am confident with my strength.			.650			
6c. I am confident with my balance.			.621			
6d. I am confident with my agility.			.608			
6e. I am confident with my flexibility.			.578			

		F1	F2	F3	F4	F5	F6
Promoting the holistic health							
1e.	Being physically active helps to enhance my self-concept.	.742					
1i.	Being physically active helps to improve my sleep.	.696					
1g.	Being physically active helps to give me more willpower.	.689					
1c.	Being physically active helps to reduce my anxiety.	.648					
1d.	Being physically active helps to improve my analytic skills.	.612					
1a.	Being physically active helps to make me fit.	.605					
1j.	Being physically active helps to improve my school work.	.590					
1b.	Being physically active helps to refresh my thinking.	.587					
1h.	Being physically active helps to give me good health.	.515					
Importance of exercise habit							
2a.	It is important to spend time to be physically active.					.750	
2b.	It is important to form a habit of being physically active.					.732	
2c.	It is important to be physically active for my health.					.706	
2d.	Being physically active is something I would not give up in my life.					.658	
Trying to do personal best							
7d.	I do not compare with others but just do my personal best in physical activity.						.768
7c.	I keep striving for breakt throughs in physical activity.						.713
7e.	I seek to explore my best potential in physical activity.						.653
7a.	I try my best to engage in physical activity.						.768
Eigenvalues		7.42	5.60	4.34	3.37	2.11	1.97
Percentage of explained variance		14.6	10.9	8.5	6.6	4.1	3.9
Percentage of total explained variance		14.6	25.5	34.1	40.7	44.8	48.7
Internal consistency (Cronbach' Alpha)		.93	.88	.84	.82	.72	.71

The six scales represent: (1) ***Self-efficacy in learning with video exercises:*** A fifteen-item scale was constructed to measure children's perceptions of their self-efficacy (Bandura, 1986) in learning curriculum subjects, such as language, art, music, mathematics, culture, and health by using video exercises. Illustrative examples: »I learned about language through video exercise«, »I know how to do physical activity if there is a video exercise to follow«. (2) ***Exercise motivation and enjoyment:*** An eleven-item scale was designed to measure the motivation and enjoyments of participants to do physical exercise. An example is, »I think physical activity is fun«. (3) ***Self-confidence on physical fitness:*** An eight-item scale was constructed to measure children's self-perception of physical fitness. An example is, »I am confident with my strength«. (4) ***Promoting the holistic***

health: A nine-item scale was constructed to measure participants' attitudes toward the effectiveness of physical activities in promoting holistic health. An example is, »Being physically active helps to improve my analytic skills«, »Being physically active helps to make me fit«. (5) ***Importance of exercise habit:*** A four-item scale was designed to measure participants' attitudes toward the importance of doing exercise as a lifestyle. An example is, »Being physically active is something I would not give up in my life«. (6) ***Trying to do personal best:*** A four-item scale was constructed to measure participants' personal best goal orientation (Martin, 2006) in doing physical activity. An example is, »I try my best to engage in physical activity«.

Table 3: Pearson correlation coefficients between variables

Variables	1	2	3	4	5	6
1. Self-efficacy in learning with video exercises	1					
2. Exercise motivation and enjoyment	.036	1				
3. Self-confidence on physical fitness	-.028	.101	1			
4. Promoting the holistic health	-.020	.066	.143*	1		
5. Importance of exercise habit	-.021	-.017	.047	.255**	1	
6. Trying to do personal best	-.035	.311**	.041	-.029	-.015	1

**p<0.01, *p<0.05

Table 4: Pre-test and post-test mean scores, adjusted for gender and age, and effect sizes (partial ή²) of differences between time points and between experimental and control group

Variables on physical activity	Group	Pre-test M (SD)	Post-test M (SD)	Partial ή² (Time)	Partial ή² (Time x Group)
Self-efficacy in learning with video exercises	Experimental	2.12 (.65)	2.62 (.34)	.293*	.306*
	Control	2.11 (.62)	2.11 (.42)		
Exercise motivation and enjoyment	Experimental	2.11 (.54)	2.41 (.44)	.204*	.139*
	Control	2.12 (.57)	2.16 (.40)		
Self-confidence on physical fitness	Experimental	2.26 (.60)	2.58 (.47)	.171*	.113*
	Control	2.29 (.57)	2.34 (.45)		
Promoting the holistic health	Experimental	2.39 (.66)	2.78 (.50)	.253*	.202*
	Control	2.41 (.67)	2.44 (.47)		
Importance of exercise habit	Experimental	2.71 (.69)	3.05 (.47)	.112*	.102*
	Control	2.69 (.72)	2.70 (.47)		
Trying to do personal best	Experimental	1.92 (.55)	2.28 (.53)	.203*	.136*
	Control	1.90 (.56)	1.94 (.47)		

Note: *p<.01

A repeated-measures ANCOVA with a Greenhouse-Geisser correction identified statistically significant differences in the mean scores of Self-efficacy in learning with video exercises ($F(1, 298)=123.382$, $p<0.01$); Exercise motivation and enjoyment ($F(1, 298)=76.328$, $p<0.01$); Self-confidence on physical fitness ($F(1, 298)=61.677$, $p<0.01$); Promoting the holistic health ($F(1, 298)=100.743$, $p<0.01$); Importance of exercise habit ($F(1, 298)=37.663$, $p<0.01$); Trying to do personal best ($F(1, 298)=75.891$, $p<0.01$) scales between two time points with both the experimental and control groups considered as a composite. When the experimental and the control groups were considered as a composite, the post-test scores were significantly higher than the pre-test scores for each of the scales, indicating significant time effect. Based on the partial ή², magnitude of the effect of the time was the most salient for the scores on Self-efficacy in learning with video exercises (see Table 4).

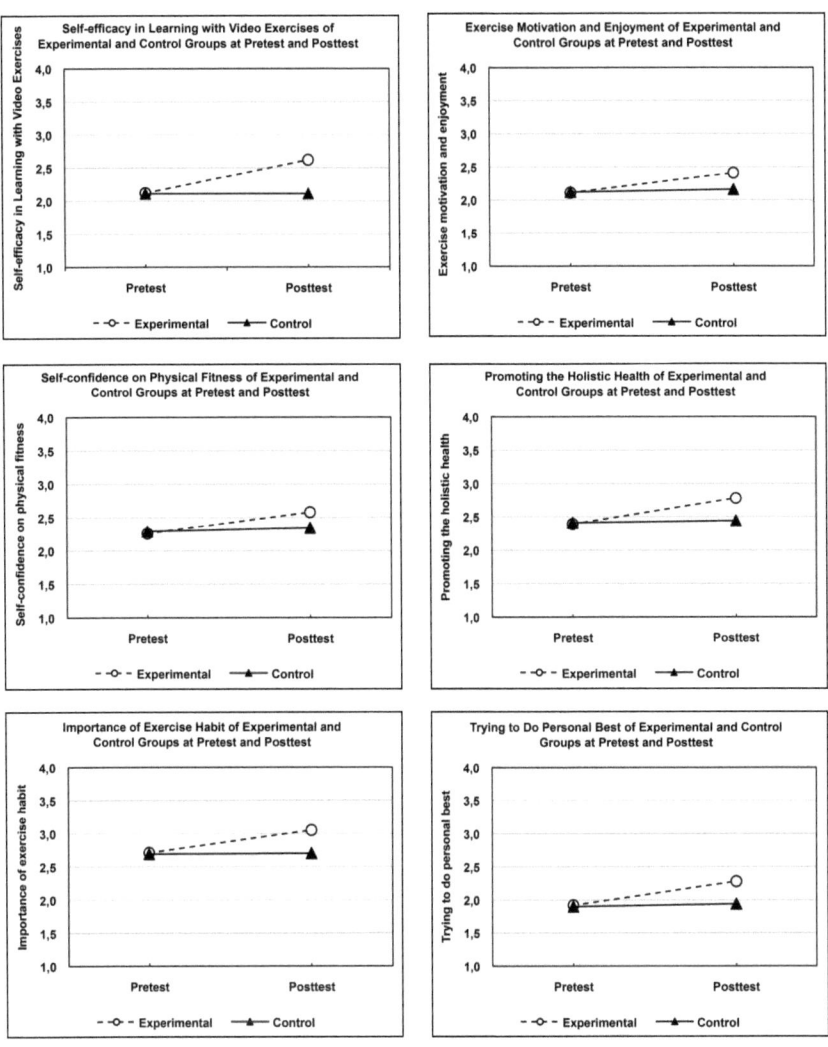

Figure 1: Distribution of scale scores for the Experimental and Control groups in pre-test and post-test

The repeated-measures of ANCOVA with groups (experimental vs. control) between subject factors showed a significant effect for the Time x Group interaction for each scale, indicating significant Time x Group interaction effects. The experimental and control groups had different gains from the pre-test to the post-test. As illustrated in Figure 1, whilst the experimental and control groups were similar in scores in the pre-test, the experimental group gained significantly more than the control group from the pre- to the post-test, resulting in the experimental group having substantially higher scores than the control group in the post-test. The Time x Group interaction effect was significant for all the APAS scales, namely, Self-efficacy in Learning with Video Exercises ($F(1, 298)=131.477$, $p<0.01$); Exercise Motivation and Enjoyment ($F(1, 298)=47.985$, $p<0.01$); Self-confidence on Physical Fitness ($F(1, 298)=38.138$, $p<0.01$); Promoting the Holistic Health ($F(1, 298)=75.595$, $p<0.01$); Importance of Exercise Habit ($F(1, 298)=33.804$, $p<0.01$); Trying to do Personal Best ($F(1, 298)=46.935$, $p<0.01$). Based on the partial $\acute{\eta}^2$, magnitude of the effect of the Time x Group interaction was the most salient for the scores on self-efficacy in learning with video exercises (see Table 4, Figure 1).

Discussion and Conclusion

Studies have demonstrated that physically active children are able to perform better academically than peers who lack physical activity (Ahamed et al., 2007; Donnelly et al., 2016; Fedewa & Ahn, 2011; Srikanth, Petrie, Greenleaf, & Martin, 2015). Also, additional research studies have reported that activity programmes including short amounts of exercise in the classroom have been found to increase children's overall physical activity, on-task behaviour, and academic outcomes (Bartholomew & Jowers, 2011; Dunn, Venturanza, Walsh, & Nonas, 2012; Hillman, Erickson, & Hatfield, 2017; Kibbe et al., 2011; Mahar, 2011).

The aim of the present study was to investigate the effects of implementing Brain Breaks® Physical Activity Solutions. To examine the effects of four-month implementation of 3 to 5 minutes of classroom-based physical activity daily the Attitudes toward Physical Activity Scale (APAS) was used. The APAS was developed based on Welk's (1999) Youth Physical Activity Promotion (YPAP) Model which included three groups of contributing factors to physical activity, namely enabling factors, predisposition factors and reinforcing factors (Mok et al., 2015). The researchers examined the effects on self-reported physical fitness, self-efficacy, personal best goal orientation, interest in physical activity, perceived importance and benefits of physical activity and contribution of physical activity to learning about health. The instrument addressed questions such as »Am I able?« and »Is it worth it?« These are two questions which children consider before engaging in physical activity (Welk, 1999). As this study was conducted with elementary school children in the Cappadocia region of Turkey, before starting the study, Attitudes toward *Physical Activity Scale (APAS)* was adapted to the native language of the participants. The Turkish version of the scale revealed valid and reliable results in elementary school children.

When the study was initiated, it was evident that the experimental and control group were equivalent according to pre-test scores on the APAS. When analysing the pre-test mean scores in each of the scales, the highest one was *importance of exercise habit, promoting the holistic health, self-confidence on physical fitness, exercise motivation and enjoyment, self-efficacy in learning with video exercises,* and *trying to do personal best,* respectively for both groups. These results showed that although elementary school children can comprehend most the relationship between physical activity and health, they did not realize their self-efficacy in learning with video exercises, and were not thinking about doing their personal best before the brain break interventions.

Comparing the post-test scores with pre-test scores, the experimental group showed more gains from the pre- to the post-test, and the control group showed only small gain from the pre- to the post-test on each scale. As one reviews the score changes from the pre- to the post-test, the most significant increases were seen for *self-efficacy in learning with video exercises, promoting the holistic health, trying to do personal best, importance of exercise habit, self-confidence on physical fitness,* and *exercise motivation and enjoyment,* respectively in the experimental group. Small point increments in each scale were not significant for the control group.

The findings which supported improvements for all the scales are encouraging, including self-efficacy, self-confidence and enjoyment and supported reports of related literature. Behaviour is moulded by the intellectual, affective, and gender of the person. The students' beliefs and feelings about themselves influence their physical activity habits. Equally, the students' physical activity behaviours influence their self-efficacy. Previous studies reported self-efficacy or physical activity confidence as being one of the most influential correlates of future continued participation in physical activity (Dishman et al., 2004; Dishman et al., 2005; Sallis, Prochaska, & Taylor, 2000; Sallis, Owen, & Fisher, 2015; Spruijt-

Metz, & Saelens, 2016; Van der Horst, Paw, Twisk, & Van Mechelen, 2007). Research indicates that higher levels of physical activity, self-efficacy and physical activity enjoyment correlate with higher levels of physical activity participation (Robbins, Pender, & Kazanis, 2003; Robbins, Pis, Pender, & Kazanis, 2004; Harmon et al., 2014; Babic et al., 2014).

In the experimental group, the Brain Breaks® Physical Activity Solutions interventions improved most in self-efficacy of children in learning with the video exercises scale. The Brain Breaks® Physical Activity Solutions intervention contributed to the children's development of health-related knowledge including health, healthy lifestyle, and healthy diet, and some specific academic knowledge in the areas of language, mathematics, art, writing, music, culture, composition, and environmental protection. With regard to the relationship with language, mathematics, art, music and culture, it can be concluded that children in the experimental group also improved their education in these areas.

This finding is very important as it shows that education in schools can be seen as a continuous process interchanging curricular education during classes and non-curricular education during short breaks. Both types of education contribute to the children's intelligence. Brain Breaks® Physical Activity Solutions also contribute to children's self-efficacy by letting them chose their favourite physical activity, following physical activity in the video exercise with minimal mistakes even without a teacher. An additional positive result of this study is the children's progress on promoting holistic health, the attempt to achieve one's personal best and the importance of building exercise habits.

The study results suggest that video exercise during the Brain Breaks® Physical Activity Solutions intervention programmes in primary school was effective, not only ensuring organised physical activity, but also enabling general education, continuity and forming a child towards a more confident, competent and responsible child to take care of its own health person. The results of this study indicate that online streaming may be an effective way to create a cognitive and motivational basis for physical activity among children, which in turn serves as empowerment for health related behaviours. The results of this study clearly support the positive effect of Brain Breaks® Physical Activity Solutions on children's perceptions, beliefs, knowledge towards physical activity for health purposes.

This study is unique as it focused not on physical activity itself, but on the underlying factors such as exercise motivation, exercise knowledge, physical self-confidence and specific outcomes.

On June 5, 2017, the Foundation for Global Community Health (GCH) and HOPSports Brain Breaks® Physical Activity Solutions signed a MoU with the United Nations Global Sustainability Index Institute (UNGSII) to promote the UN Global Sustainable Development Goals (SDGs) through Educational programmes for children from all 193 countries that signed to promote the 17 Sustainable Development Goals.

In conclusion, the Brain Breaks® Physical Activity Solutions intervention for the study period of four months demonstrated an improvement in children's attitudes towards and motivation for physical activity as well as for specific academic knowledge. It may be concluded that the Brain Breaks® Physical Activity Solutions intervention programme was effective and contributed to physical, health and general education of primary school children in the Cappadocia region of Turkey.

References

Ahamed, Y., Macdonald, H., Reed, K., Naylor, P. J., Liu-Ambrose, T., & Mckay, H. (2007). School-based physical activity does not compromise children's academic performance. *Medicine & Science in Sports & Exercise, 39*(2), 371–376.

Babic, M. J., Morgan, P. J., Plotnikoff, R. C., Lonsdale, C., White, R. L., & Lubans, D. R. (2014). Physical activity and physical self-concept in youth: systematic review and meta-analysis. *Sports Medicine, 44* (11), 1589–1601.

Bandura, A. (1986). *Social foundations of thought and action: A social-cognitive theory*. Englewood Cliffs, NJ: Prentice Hall.

Bartholomew, J. B., & Jowers, E. M. (2011). Physically active academic lessons in elementary children. *Preventive medicine, 52*, S51–S54.

Chin, M. K., Edginton, C. R., & Tang, M. S. (2013). School physical education and health: A model of best practice – Integrating local context with global trends. *The Global Journal of Health and Physical Education Pedagogy, 1*(4), 251–282.

Dishman, R. K., Motl, R. W., Saunders, R., Felton, G., Ward, D. S., Dowda, M., et al. (2004). Self-efficacy partially mediates the effect of a school-based physical activity intervention among adolescent girls. *Preventive Medicine, 38*(5), 628–636.

Dishman, R. K., Motl, R. W., Saunders, R., Felton, G., Ward, D. S., Dowda, M., & Pate, R. R. (2005). Enjoyment mediates effects of a school-based physical-activity intervention. *Medicine and science in sports and exercise, 37*(3), 478–487.

Donnelly, J. E., Hillman, C. H., Castelli, D., Etnier, J. L., Lee, S., Tomporowski, P., & Szabo-Reed, A. N. (2016). Physical activity, fitness, cognitive function, and academic achievement in children: a systematic review. *Medicine & Science in Sports & Exercise, 48*(6), 1197–1222.

Dunn, L. L., Venturanza, J. A., Walsh, R. J., & Nonas, C. A. (2012). An observational evaluation of move-to-improve, a classroom-based physical activity programme, New York City schools, 2010. *Preventing chronic disease, 9*, E146–E146.

Fedewa, A. L., & Ahn, S. (2011). The effects of physical activity and physical fitness on children's achievement and cognitive outcomes: a meta-analysis. *Research quarterly for exercise and sport, 82*(3), 521–535.

González, C. S., Gómez, N., Navarro, V., Cairós, M., Quirce, C., Toledo, P., & Marrero-Gordillo, N. (2016). Learning healthy lifestyles through active videogames, motor games and the gamification of educational activities. *Computers in Human Behavior, 55*, 529–551.

Hall, C. M., & Bierman, K. L. (2015). Technology-assisted interventions for parents of young children: Emerging practices, current research, and future directions. *Early childhood research quarterly, 33*, 21–32.

Harmon, B. E., Nigg, C. R., Long, C., Amato, K., Kutchman, E., Anthamatten, P., ... & Hill, J. O. (2014). What matters when children play: influence of social cognitive theory and perceived environment on levels of physical activity among elementary-aged youth. *Psychology of sport and exercise, 15*(3), 272–279.

Hillman, C. H., Erickson, K. I., & Hatfield, B. D. (2017). Run for your life! Childhood physical activity effects on brain and cognition. *Kinesiology Review, 6*(1), 12–21.

Hills, A. P., Dengel, D. R., & Lubans, D. R. (2015). Supporting public health priorities: recommendations for physical education and physical activity promotion in schools. *Progress in cardiovascular diseases, 57*(4), 368–374.

HOPSports website (2014). Interactive Youth Physical Education Training System. Retrieved 29 June, 2017 from: http://www.hopsports.com.

Kibbe, D. L., Hackett, J., Hurley, M., McFarland, A., Schubert, K. G., Schultz, A., & Harris, S. (2011). Ten Years of TAKE 10!®: Integrating physical activity with academic concepts in elementary school classrooms. *Preventive medicine, 52*, S43–S50.

Lewallen, T. C., Hunt, H., Potts-Datema, W., Zaza, S., & Giles, W. (2015). The Whole School, Whole Community, Whole Child model: a new approach for improving educational attainment and healthy development for students. *Journal of School Health, 85*(11), 729–739.

Mahar, M. T. (2011). Impact of short bouts of physical activity on attention-to-task in elementary school children. *Preventive medicine, 52*, S60–S64.

Martin, A.J. (2006). Personal bests (PBs): A proposed multidimensional model and empirical analysis. *British Journal of Educational Psychology, 76*, 803–825.

Mok, M. M. C., Chin, M. K., Chen, S., Emeljanovas, A., Mieziene, B., Bronikowski, M., & Phua, K. W. (2015). Psychometric Properties of the Attitudes toward Physical Activity Scale: A Rasch Analysis Based on Data From Five Locations. *Journal of applied measurement, 16*(4), 379–400.

Mura, G., Rocha, N., Helmich, I., Budde, H., Machado, S., Wegner, M., Nardi, A., Arias-Carrión, O., Vellante, M., Baum, A., Guicciardi, M., Patten, S., & Carta, M. (2015). Physical activity interventions in schools for improving lifestyle in European countries. *Clinical practice and epidemiology in mental health*: CP & EMH, *11*(Suppl 1 M5), 77.

Robbins, L. B., Pender, N. J., & Kazanis, A. S. (2003). Barriers to physical activity perceived by adolescent girls. *Journal of Midwifery & Women's Health, 48*(3), 206–212.

Robbins, L. B., Pis, M. B., Pender, N. J., & Kazanis, A. S. (2004). Exercise self-efficacy, enjoyment, and feeling states among adolescents. *Western journal of nursing research, 26*(7), 699–715.

Sallis, J. F., Owen, N., & Fisher, E. (2015). Ecological models of health behavior. In K. Glanz, B. K. Rimer, & K. Viswanath (eds.), *Health behavior: theory, research, and practice* (5th ed.) (pp. 43–64). San Francisco: Jossey-Bass.

Sallis, J. F., Prochaska, J. J., & Taylor, W. C. (2000). A review of correlates of physical activity of children and adolescents. *Medicine & science in sports & exercise, 32*(5), 963–975.

Spruijt-Metz, D., & Saelens, B. E. (2016). 14 Behavioral Aspects of Physical Activity in Childhood and Adolescence. *Handbook of Pediatric Obesity: Etiology, Pathophysiology, and Prevention*, 227.

Srikanth, S., Petrie, T. A., Greenleaf, C., & Martin, S. B. (2015). The relationship of physical fitness, self-beliefs, and social support to the academic performance of middle school boys and girls. *The Journal of Early Adolescence, 35*(3), 353–377.

Van der Horst, K., Paw, M. J. C. A., Twisk, J. W., & Van Mechelen, W. (2007). A brief review on correlates of physical activity and sedentariness in youth. *Medicine & Science in Sports & Exercise, 39*(8), 1241–1250.

Welk, G. J. (1999). The Youth Physical Activity Promotion model: A conceptual bridge between theory and practice. *Quest, 51,* 5–23.

World Health Organization. (2016). Obesity and Overweight. Retrieved June 29, 2017, from http://www.who.int/mediacentre/factsheets/fs311/en/

Organismus und Mechanismus

Gunter Gebauer
Freie Universität Berlin

Lange Jahre habe ich der Arbeit meiner Kollegin Gudrun Doll-Tepper zugesehen, ohne dass ich eine Beziehung zu meinen eigenen Überlegungen über Theorien des menschlichen Körpers hergestellt hätte. In meinen Reflexionen ging es, wie selbstverständlich, um *normale* leistungsfähige Körper in der menschlichen Entwicklung, im Sport, in Interaktionen mit anderen *normalen* Körpern. Das Thema der körperlichen Behinderung tauchte bei mir kaum einmal auf. Das änderte sich schlagartig, als ich vor kurzem einen meiner Doktoranden, B., besuchte, der bei einem Unfall beide Unterschenkel verloren hatte. Es war das erste Mal, dass ich B. nach seiner Operation wiedersah. Er wartete auf mich, im Rollstuhl sitzend, in der Cafeteria seines Pflegeheims, in dem man ihn nach der Rehaklinik untergebracht hatte. Der erste Anblick war ein Schock für mich, ihn so klein, so körperlich vermindert zu sehen. Er muss das gemerkt haben, denn er entschuldigte sich, dass er seine Prothesen nicht angelegt habe. Das sei ihm oft noch zu mühsam, aber es ginge von Tag zu Tag immer besser. In einem bemüht normalen Gesprächston sagte ich, das Wetter sei so schön, ob wir nicht einen Ausflug in die Umgebung des Heims machen könnten. Er freute sich auf »die Gelegenheit, sein Rollstuhlfahren zu trainieren«. »Wunderbar«, sagte ich, »dann kann ich Sie ein wenig schieben, wenn Sie Hilfe brauchen.« – B. brauchte keine Hilfe von mir. Er rollte in sein Zimmer, war gleich mit einem Rucksack wieder zurück, manövrierte sich durch die Gänge, in den Fahrstuhl, durch den Ausgang für Rollstühle, durch die Straßen des Wedding, überquerte eine Hauptverkehrsstraße und rollte dann neben mir durch einen kleinen Park. Wir redeten über einen Autor, den wir beide gut kannten, einen Wiener Schriftsteller. B. war in Wien aufgewachsen und hatte mich in den Seminaren immer begeistert mit seinen genauen, mit Witz grundierten Beobachtungen über seine Heimatstadt und ihre Einwohner. Sobald er anfing zu reden, vergaß ich seinen Unfall. Nur bei jeder Überquerung einer Straße mussten Techniken angewendet werden, um die Vorderräder über den Kantstein zu heben. Nach einigen Stunden gemeinsamen Rollens, Schiebens, Hebens waren mir die – für mich – neuen Bewegungen etwas vertrauter. Als ich kurz darauf einen Aufsatz (Gebauer, 2006) wiederfand, den ich vor einiger Zeit über die Normalität von Bewegungen geschrieben hatte, war ich über die Selbstverständlichkeit überrascht, mit der ich bei meinen Überlegungen ausschließlich den voll funktionierenden normalen Körper betrachtet hatte. Ich drucke im Folgenden einige Passagen des Textes ab und füge ihnen in einer anderen Drucktype einige Kommentare aus meiner heutigen Sicht hinzu, als eine selbstkritische Sicht auf meine Positionen in der Vergangenheit.

1.

Der Mensch ist der erste Freigelassene der Natur, schreibt Herder: er kann gehen (Herder, 1989). Seine Freiheit liegt in der Überwindung von Zwängen, die ihn auf vier Beinen am Boden festhalten. Frei von Instinkten, in seiner Entwicklung sich selbst und seinesgleichen überlassen, bringt er sich selber aus eigenen Kräften hervor. Er handelt nicht aus Notwendigkeit, sondern aus einer Chance heraus, die ihm gegeben ist. Es ist seine Chance, ein sich selbst entwickelndes Wesen zu sein, das die in seinem Organismus gegebenen anatomischen und physiologischen Möglichkeiten exploriert und schrittweise ausarbeitet: ein funktionierender Organismus, der die Fähigkeit besitzt, sich mit eigenen Mitteln selbst zu formen, sich zu erweitern und aus den neu gebildeten Eigenschaften wiederum neue Möglichkeiten zu gewinnen. Sein grundlegendes Merkmal ist es, aktiv zu sein, sich zu entwickeln und sich zu explorieren. Er bringt seine Zielsetzung aus sich selbst hervor; er bewegt sich, übt und erweitert seine Möglichkeiten aus eigenem Antrieb.

Eine wesentliche Besonderheit des lebenden Organismus ist seine Spontaneität. Wenn man von Zwang und Notwendigkeit spricht, so wirken diese nicht unmittelbar auf die menschlichen Bewegungen, sondern man konstruiert sie von einem späteren Zeitpunkt der Entwicklung aus und projiziert sie auf den Anfang zurück. Insofern ist Herder Recht zu geben: In der Spontaneität liegt ein Moment der Freiheit, die freilich nicht durch die Kraft des Geistes errungen wird. In der frühesten Periode der Entwicklung des menschlichen Wesens gibt es noch kein steuerndes Denken. Aber es findet sich hier der freie Gebrauch der Möglichkeiten des Organismus, der eine einmal gefundene Möglichkeit exploriert, diese festhält und, auf ihr aufbauend, wieder neue Möglichkeiten sucht. Nietzsche beschreibt den fluktuierenden, beweglichen Organismus als »das nicht festgestellte Wesen«. Diese Entwicklungs*offenheit* macht den Menschen zu einem der »unerwartetsten und aufregendsten Glückswürfe, die das ›große Kind‹ des Heraklit, heiße es Zeus oder Zufall, spielt« (Nietzsche, 1988). Es ist seine glückliche Chance, sich selbst feststellen zu können.

Man kann Nietzsches Ausdruck des Sich-Feststellens ganz wörtlich verstehen, als ein Sich-Fixieren, insofern der Mensch in seinen Tätigkeiten bestimmte Einstellungen findet und festhält. Auf diese Weise werden Elemente des Verhaltens definiert, an den Gelenkstellen zu stabilen Strukturen zusammengefügt, so dass Funktionszusammenhänge und Gebrauchsmöglichkeiten wie bei einem Werkzeug hergestellt werden. In diesem Prozess tritt an die Stelle der Spontaneität des Organismus ein instrumentelles Funktionieren. Aus ungeordneten, ungeregelten und unvorhersehbaren Bewegungen entsteht eine Mechanik.

Als Organismus ist der Mensch Teil eines dynamischen Lebensprozesses: Er kann in seiner ungesteuerten und entwicklungsoffenen Aktivität Ordnungen hervorbringen, diese aber auch wieder auflösen. Als festgestellte Mechanik kann er sich Festigkeit und Dauer verleihen. Seine schöpferische Kraft bildet also zwei unterschiedliche Zustände aus, die in Wechselwirkung miteinander treten können: Einerseits probiert der Organismus die ihm gegebenen Möglichkeiten aus und sucht, wenn er eine Struktur gefunden hat, wieder nach neuen Wegen, andererseits fixiert er bestimmte Lösungen und stellt mit einem mechanischen Gebrauch die Dynamik des Lebensprozesses still. Menschliches Handeln kann also immer unter den zwei Aspekten des Organismus und des Mechanismus betrachtet werden. Die Entwicklung des Menschen wird von beiden Gesichtspunkten aus je unterschiedlich eingeschätzt.

In diesen Absätzen werden zwar die Möglichkeiten aller Menschen beschrieben, aber es ist offensichtlich, dass ausschließlich an nicht behinderte Körper gedacht wird. Der Text erhält eine ganz neue Dimension, wenn man die Möglichkeit hinzudenkt, dass sich auch der beschädigte Körper *machen* muss. Er muss, wie im Fall von B., nicht nur seine Funktionsfähigkeit wieder herstellen, sondern sich neue Möglichkeiten schaffen, wie den Gebrauch der Prothesen, die Vorwärtsbewegung im Rollstuhl, die Neuorganisation seines Lebens insgesamt. Wenn man mit Herder und Nietzsche die nicht-festgestellte Situation des Menschen hervorhebt, wie viel mehr Erneuerungskraft ist für den Menschen notwendig, der seinen Stand, seine Fortbewegung, sein Umgehen mit gewöhnlichen Interaktionen verloren hat. Kurz, der eben zitierte Absatz muss nicht neu geschrieben, aber wesentlich erweitert werden. An der Situation von Menschen mit Behinderungen wird die Gewinnung von Freiheit, die Herder feiert, in ein neues Licht gestellt.

2.
Mit der Annahme eines Wechselspiels von Organismus und Mechanismus wird der Heraklitischen Vorstellung vom ständigen Fluss des Seins eine Wendung gegeben: Leben ist kein regelloses Fließen, sondern ein Hin und Her zwischen einer produktiven Aktivität, die Neues hervorbringt, und einem Festhalten des einmal erreichten Zustands. Es handelt sich um einen Prozess der Selbstkonstruktion, in dem grundlegende Fertigkeiten der frühen Entwicklung, wie das Stehen und Gehen, herausgebildet werden. Wie gelangen kleine Kinder dazu, dass sie sich irgendwann in ihrem Leben aufrichten, frei stehen und gehen können? Wenn man ihnen dabei zusieht, wie sie wochenlang probieren, sich aufzurichten, ihren Gleichgewichtssinn entwickeln, den Einsatz von Gliedern und Muskeln zu üben, mit denen sie Zieh- und Ausgleichsbewegungen vollziehen, wie sie immer wieder den festen Halt aufgeben und auf den noch ungeschickten Füßen schwankend um den freien Stand ringen, wenn man diese vielen verschiedenen, komplexen und miteinander koordinierten Tätigkeiten beobachtet, erkennt man, dass der aufrechte Stand und das freie Gehen eine Errungenschaft des Menschen sind. Für diesen Vorgang kann eine Instinktbasis wohl nicht angenommen werden, ebenso wenig ein genetisches Programm, das den gesamten komplexen Vorgang in kodierter Form enthalten würde. Angesichts des außerordentlichen Ausmaßes von Eigentätigkeit des Kinds haben beide Annahmen kaum einen Erklärungswert. Auch die Möglichkeit von Nachahmung oder regelgeleiteter Tätigkeit ist hier nicht gegeben: Niemand kann einem Baby zeigen oder vorschreiben, wie es seinen ungeübten Körper in eine aufrechte Haltung bringen, sein Gewicht auf beide Füße verteilen und sich gerade halten sollte.

Kinder regulieren sich selbst; sie finden von sich aus die regelhaften Verhaltensweisen, die sie fähig machen, unter allen möglichen Umweltbedingungen zu stehen. Wenn sie einmal die Möglichkeit sicher zu stehen, gefunden haben, erzeugen sie diese bei anderer Gelegenheit von neuem und können sie schließlich sicher reproduzieren. Mit den erfolgreichen Versuchen richten sie ihr Verhalten an immer neuen Orientierungsmarken aus, die wie Leitlinien für die Körperhaltung, die Arm- und Beinbewegungen wirken. Wenn man dieses Verfahren als *Trial and Error* kennzeichnete, erfasste man vielleicht den Aspekt des Ausprobierens, aber einem entgingen die menschlichen Leistungen der Konstruktion und Koordination, welche die vielfältigen Aktivitäten zu einer komplexen Gesamtbewegung zusammenfügen. Die Marken und Leitlinien werden in körperlichen Handlungen gefunden und werden vom Organismus für die weitere Orientierungen gespeichert. Hilfen von anderen Personen können diesen Prozess höchstens unterstützen. Während Tiere ein genetisches Programm für ihre artspezifischen Bewegungen, Reaktionen und Haltungen besitzen, bilden Menschen in Eigentätigkeit Normen heraus, mit denen sie ihr Handeln regulieren.

Ein Kind formt seine elementaren Bewegungen nicht nur beim Stehen und Gehen, sondern auch bei Akten, an denen andere Menschen beteiligt sind, beispielsweise beim gezielten Greifen, Festhalten und Loslassen von Gegenständen, die ihm gegeben werden. Seine Orientierungsmarken, an denen es sein Stehen, Gehen, Greifen etc. ausrichtet und kontrolliert, wirken als Normen, mit denen es diese Aktivitäten bestimmt. Eine Norm in dem hier verwendeten Sinn ist, »was so ist, wie es sein soll« (Canguilhem, 1977). Mit Hilfe der selbst gebildeten Normen unterscheidet das Kind den Normalzustand von allen Aktionen, die davon abweichen. Der Normalzustand ist selber Ausdruck der Norm. Ohne dass es etwas *über* die eigene Normalität weiß, bildet es eine implizite Normativität aus, die sein Stehen, Gehen, Greifen als *gesollte* Zustände kennzeichnet.

Die Überlegung, dass Menschen die Normen ihrer Bewegung selbst herausbilden müssen, gilt auch für Menschen mit Behinderungen. Bei ihnen kommt jedoch hinzu, dass sie sich nicht oder sehr selten an Vorbildern orientieren können, die ihre Umwelt strukturieren, wie es die Bezugspersonen von kleinen Kindern tun. Woher sollen sie die Normen nehmen? Sie müssen sie selbst aus den Bewegungen ihres behinderten Körpers bilden. Eine weitere Schwierigkeit ist, dass sie, wenn ihre Behinderung erst im Erwachsenenalter entstanden ist, noch die in ihrem früheren Leben ausgebildeten motorischen Schemata besitzen, die sie nun nicht mehr gebrauchen können. Sollen wir davon reden, dass sie diese gleichsam *überschreiben?* Vergessen kann man sie nicht, und eine einfache Umformung ist wahrscheinlich nur in wenigen Fällen möglich. Eher handelt es sich bei den meisten um ein völliges Umlernen, nicht nur der Beinbewegungen, sondern des gesamten Körpers, insofern die Körperhaltungen von Füßen und Beinen ausgehen.

3.

Die ersten, tiefsten Regulierungen des körperlichen Verhaltens entstehen nicht durch sozialen Zwang, sondern sind in der explorierenden Produktivität des Lebens begründet. Ohne eine solche Selbstschöpfung könnte der Organismus in der weiteren Entwicklung nicht von außen geformt werden. Das kleine Kind ist ständig auf der Suche danach, was die Normativität der Gesellschaft ausmacht, was das Normale ist. In seinen ersten Lebensphasen ist es offensichtlich bestrebt mit diesem überein zu stimmen. Wenn es die üblichen Körpertechniken, die es bei den Erwachsenen vorfindet, herausgebildet hat, wird seine Konformität mit der Gesellschaft evident. Es wird ein Mitglied seiner Gruppe, das sich in gleicher Weise wie andere Mitglieder in vergleichbaren Situationen verhält. Es weiß, wie es andere zu begrüßen, wie es zu antworten hat, wie man isst; es lernt gesittet dazusitzen, sich im Schulunterricht zu verhalten, es erwirbt die Techniken des Lesens und Schreibens (vgl. Gebauer & Wulf, 1998). Wenn es seinen Körper zu einem mechanischen Funktionieren gebracht hat, wird dieser selbst ein Bild der Normativität der Gesellschaft.

Mit den von Marcel Mauss beschriebenen *Techniken des Körpers* (Mauss, 1972) erwirbt der Mensch bestimmte Weisen des Verhaltens, die den Normen seiner Gesellschaft entsprechen. Er formt seinen Körper in der Weise, dass er die in seiner sozialen Umgebung vorgefundenen Mechanismen ausbildet. In diesem Prozess unterstellt er sich den Normen der Allgemeinheit; er bildet sich entsprechend den allgemeinen Normen seiner Gesellschaft um: Sein Körper wird zu einem verallgemeinerten Körper (vgl. Mead, 1968).[1] Ebenso wie das Kind in seiner sprachlichen Entwicklung eine Umgangssprache ausbildet, eine Sprache, in der es mit der Gesellschaft übereinstimmt, konstruiert es einen Umgangskörper, mit dem es sich als Mitglied seiner Gruppe darstellt. Über die vitalen Normen des Organismus lagert das Individuum ein Schicht gesellschaftlicher Normen ab, die es zum mechanischen Einsatz seines Körpers befähigen: einen *Umgangskörper*, der die gleichen Normen verwirklicht wie die anderen Mitglieder seiner Gesellschaft.

---

1 Mit diesem Ausdruck nehme ich George Herbert Meads Gedanken des Verallgemeinerten Anderen (Generalized Other) auf.

Bewegungen sind *das* Milieu, in dem Menschen Normalität bilden und entfalten. Mit den Aktivitäten des Festhaltens, Sicherns, Schematisierens werden Institutionen, Systeme, symbolische Formen (Sprache, Mythen, Kunst, Architektur) gebildet, die eine Tendenz zur Verewigung haben. Ein Festgehaltenes ist etwas, an dem sich Menschen festhalten können, ein gesicherter Stand der Entwicklung, seine zweite Natur; diese ist keine wiedergefundene Natürlichkeit, sondern eine Mechanisierung der ersten Natur.

Wenn eine Macht alte Normen brechen und neue Verhaltens- und Denkweisen einführen will, setzt sie gewöhnlich bei den Bewegungen ein. Diese werden gewaltsam mit dem Ziel umgeformt, die Umgangskörper gleichsam umzukodieren. Die Macht unterbindet die freie Bewegung, indem sie die alltäglichen Verrichtungen reguliert und bis in kleinste Einzelheiten vorschreibt. Auf diese Weise werden, wie Foucault gezeigt hat, neue Normen produziert (Foucault, 1977). Eine solche Strategie setzt auf die menschliche Tendenz zur Normerfüllung: Zum menschlichen Leben gehört offensichtlich das Streben danach, aus dem Organismus-Körper eine Mechanik herzustellen. Würde es diese Tendenz nicht geben, könnten Menschen wohl kaum die Sprache und die Fähigkeit erwerben, an komplexen sozialen Vorgängen teilzunehmen. Politische Macht, die in das Bewegungsrepertoire eingreift, zielt auf eine Veränderung der individuell herausgebildeten Normen und macht sich den Bereich zugänglich, in dem die Normalität von Individuen produziert wird. Was Foucault in *Überwachen und Strafen* beschreibt, geht über den beobachtenden Blick und die kontrollierende Einwirkung hinaus: Disziplinierungen greifen in jene Aktivitäten des Subjekts ein, in denen es seine eigenen Normen bildet, eine wegen der Instinktfreiheit von Menschen notwendige Aktivität, mit der sie ihr Verhalten bestimmen. Eine tiefer angelegte Form der Selbstbestimmung gibt es nicht. Wenn das Subjekt sein Gehen, Blicken, Sprechen und die für sein Geschlecht typischen Bewegungen verändert, wenn es also alles umbaut, was bis dahin als normal galt, dann ist es von der Macht besetzt, insofern diese sich jene Region des Subjekts verfügbar macht, in der es seine Stellung zur Welt bestimmt.

Dieser letzte Absatz rückt die soziale Problematik von körperlichen Behinderungen in ein scharfes Licht: Gesellschaft wird zu einem nicht geringen Teil durch die soziale Normativität von Bewegungen konstituiert. Mit einem beschädigten

Körper ist der Mensch darauf angewiesen, *eigene* Normen zu bilden, die jenen der Gesellschaft nicht oder nur zum Teil entsprechen. Wir haben schon festgestellt, welche große Leistung darin liegt, wenn Menschen mit Behinderungen eigene Bewegungsnormen bilden. Nicht-Übereinstimmung von Bewegungsnormen mit jenen der Gesellschaft sind nicht einfach nur *andere* Bewegungsnormen. Wie in dem zitierten Absatz gezeigt, bestimmt die Gesellschaft *soziale Normalität* mit Bezug auf den ›verallgemeinerten Körper‹. Abweichungen von diesem werden oft als eine Abweichung von der Gesellschaft angesehen. Diese äußerst problematische Auffassung entsteht aus der Dominanz des verallgemeinerten Körpers. Wie Foucaults Arbeiten zeigen, liegt in dieser Normierung die große Gefahr, dass – über die Menschen mit Behinderungen hinaus – ganzen sozialen Gruppen aufgrund ihrer ›abweichenden‹ Körperlichkeit die Zugehörigkeit zur Gesellschaft verweigert wird. Man kann sich nicht mit dem Gedanken beruhigen, dass dies im offiziellen Diskurs in Westeuropa nicht geduldet wird. Unterhalb der politischen Korrektheit öffentlicher Reden gibt es Strömungen, die den ›verallgemeinerten Körper‹ in seiner gemessenen und fotografisch dargestellten Form in den Rang einer fetischartigen Norm erheben. Gerade die neuen Entwicklungen zeigen, dass das Konzept der *Normalität*, insbesondere in seinen neuen Ausprägungen, die Integration von Menschen mit körperlichen Behinderungen zu gefährden drohen.

Literatur

Canguilhem, G. (1977). *Das Normale und das Pathologische*. Frankfurt a. M.: Suhrkamp.

Foucault, M. (1977). *Überwachen und Strafen. Die Geburt des Gefängnisses* (2. Aufl.). Frankfurt a. M.: Suhrkamp.

Gebauer, G. (2006). Organismus und Mechanismus. In: G. Gebauer, S. Poser, R. Schmidt, M. Stern (Hrsg.), *Kalkuliertes Risiko. Technik, Spiel und Sport an der Grenze*. Frankfurt a. M.: Campus, 159 – 175.

Gebauer, G. & Wulf, C. (1998). *Spiel – Ritual – Geste. Das Mimetische in der sozialen Welt*. Reinbek: Rowohlt Taschenbuch Verlag.

Herder, J. G. (1989). *Ideen zur Geschichte der Philosophie der Menschheit*. (Werke in 10 Bänden, VI). Frankfurt a. M.: Bollenbacher.

Mauss, M. (1972). *Die Techniken des Körpers*. In M. Mauss (Hrsg.), *Soziologie und Anthropologie (Band 2)*. Frankfurt a. M.: Ullstein.

Mead, G.H. (1968). *Geist, Identität und Gesellschaft aus der Sicht des Sozialbehaviorismus.* Frankfurt a.M.: Suhrkamp.

Nietzsche, F. (1988). *Genealogie der Moral, Kritische Studienausgabe.* Berlin: de Gruyter.

Zwei Seiten einer Medaille: Olympische Idee und Identität – Eine Gedankenskizze und ein Fragenkatalog

Andreas Höfer
Deutsches Sport & Olympia Museum

Wer dreimal hintereinander gewinnt, der ist ein schlechter Mensch.

Im Sinne dieses den uramerikanischen Lakota-Indianern zugeschriebenen Merksatzes könnte man sich – etwa im (Rück-)Blick auf die Olympischen Spiele in Rio de Janeiro – zu der Behauptung versteigen, dass im deutschen Spitzensport, namentlich in unserem Olympia-Team, allenfalls vereinzelt schlechte Menschen auszumachen sind.

So etwa Michael Jung und sein *reitbarer* Untersatz Sam. »Der Vielseitigkeitsreiter«, so ein dpa-Artikel vom 9. August 2016, »hatte wie schon vor vier Jahren mit zwei Medaillen den Bann gebrochen und im deutschen Olympia-Team für Erleichterung gesorgt. Silber mit dem Team, Gold im Einzel – der 34-Jährige aus Horb ist ein deutscher Olympia-Held. ›Großartig‹, schwärmte Michael Vesper, Chef de Mission, und wirkte dabei sehr erleichtert: ›Die Reiter haben wieder geliefert.‹«

Nun mag man – jenseits aller ironischen oder zynischen Zungenschläge – im Sinne unserer Thematik die Frage aufwerfen, ob »Olympia-Helden« eo ipso schlechte Menschen sind oder sein müssen. Oder umgekehrt: Ob gute Menschen keine Top-Athleten sind und gar dreimal hintereinander gewinnen können oder dürfen, wobei im olympischen Kontext ja schon *einmal* einen grandiosen Erfolg darstellt, der trotz größter Anstrengungen vieler nur vergleichsweise wenigen gegönnt ist.

Das liegt in der Natur der Sache und bestimmt in hohem Maße deren besonderen Reiz. Der Platz auf dem Treppchen, gerade ganz oben, ist ein knappes Gut, gleichsam Mangelware, und schon von daher äußerst wertvoll und begehrt, bei den Aktiven, deren Betreuern, Funktionsträgern und Politikern – und bei uns Daheimgebliebenen.

Olympische Kernsportart

Nun siegt mal schön, ist die Devise für Deutschland, also für uns! Das ist doch wohl unser gutes Recht, wenn wir schon so engagiert mitfiebern, uns die Nacht vor der Glotze um die Ohren schlagen und mit unseren Steuergeldern unseren Obolus entrichten. So ist das Zählen von Medaillen unsere ureigene olympische Kernsportart – ein Breitensport allenthalben, bei dem alle mitmachen können, ohne sich erst qualifizieren zu müssen.

Andererseits: So eng wollen wir die Sache ja auch wieder nicht sehen – und als gelernter Kölner weiß man: Man muss auch gönnen können! Im Sinne der olympischen Correctness konzedieren wir, nolens volens, dass auch die oder der Zweite, Dritte, Vierte, Fünfte oder Zwölfte zur Weltklasse zählt und ihren oder seinen unverzichtbaren Beitrag zur Statik des Ganzen leistet. Denn ohne Verlierer kann es keine Sieger geben.

Beim olympischen Original, den Spielen im griechischen Olympia, war die Sache klar und viel unkomplizierter. Hier galt: *The winner takes it all!* Es war wie ein unumstößliches Naturgesetz, dass der sportliche Wettkampf – neben der Reverenz an die Götter – allein und ausschließlich der Ermittlung des Siegers diente. Nur dieser wurde ausgezeichnet, nachdem sich der knapp geschlagene Zweite, von den *unter ferner liefen* Platzierten zu schweigen, längst wie ein geprügelter Hund aus der Arena geschlichen hatte.

Olympische Haltung

Mit der Etablierung der neuzeitlichen Variante durch den französischen Baron Pierre de Coubertin erhielt die olympische Sache Ende des 19. Jahrhunderts eine ganz andere Qualität. Denn neben dem Handeln wurde nun die Haltung zu einem zentralen Wesensmerkmal, ja zu einer Conditio sine qua non, erhoben. So gewann der Sport als soziales und kulturelles Konstrukt eine – bis dahin irrelevante – ethische Konnotation, die ihn über die Aura des netten Zeitvertreibs hinaushob. Auf dieser Basis entwickelte sich der Sport zu einem gesellschaftlich und politisch relevanten und entsprechend legitimierten Phänomen, das mit seiner alten neuen Premiummarke *Olympia* einen Siegeszug durch das 20. Jahrhundert antreten konnte.

Nur in Klammern sei angemerkt: Ob der Sport als eine solcherart herausgehobene Erscheinung des Zeitgeistes auch das 21. Jahrhundert überlebt, können wir letztlich erst so in etwa achtzig Jahren verlässlich sagen. Manche hegen diesbezüglich Zweifel.

Um es noch einmal zu betonen: Die vom olympischen Gottvater Coubertin definierte ethische Dimension verlieh seinem Projekt eine bis dahin unbekannte Bedeutung, Funktion und Legitimation – kurz: einen Sinn, der die Erfolgsgeschichte des Sports ganz wesentlich bestimmt und erklärt. Indem sich der Sport eben nicht nur durch ein – ebenso umfassendes wie überschaubares – Regelwerk, sondern auch durch – ebenso informelle wie verbindliche – Werte konstituiert, steht er für die globale Utopie einer friedlichen und besseren Welt, die Hans Küng »Weltethos« nennt und Pierre de Coubertin *Olympische Idee* nannte.

Olympische Idee

Die bahnbrechende Innovation des französischen Barons entsprang zum Ende des 19. Jahrhunderts eben nicht allein genuin sportbezogenen Motiven, sondern auch und zuerst einem humanen – sprich: pädagogischen – Impuls. Ihm ging es, unter anderem, um die *Jugend der Welt*, um eine neue weltweit wirksame Option für ihr Recht auf eine *gesunde* Bildung von Körper, Geist und Charakter, wobei der Sport nicht mehr und nicht weniger als ein Vehikel und Katalysator sein sollte.

Freilich zielte Coubertins Bemühen nicht nur auf das Wohlergehen des Individuums, vielmehr verfolgte er mit seinem – zu seiner Zeit ganz neuartigen und schon von daher vielfach kritisierten, teils vehement angefeindeten – Konzept einer Demokratisierung und Internationalisierung des Sports auch einen universalen Anspruch, den er in einem Vortrag 1894 wie folgt auf den Punkt brachte:
»Gesunde Demokratie und richtig verstandener, friedlicher Internationalismus werden in das erneuerte Stadion eindringen und hier den Kult der Ehre und der Uneigennützigkeit aufrechterhalten, der es dem Athletismus ermöglichen wird, neben der Entwicklung des Leibes das Werk moralischer Vervollkommnung und sozialer Befriedung weiterzuführen.«

A la bonne heure! Große Worte, die auf nicht weniger als auf ein friedliches, von Achtung und Respekt geprägtes Zusammenleben im Zeichen von Menschen-rechten und Gerechtigkeit abheben, auf eine Welt, die von gemeinsam wahrgenommener Verantwortung getragen wird und dem Einzelnen die Möglichkeit zur Entfaltung seiner je eigenen Möglichkeiten bietet – eine Utopie, die das Attribut *olympisch* wahrlich verdient.

Wurde der Sport, namentlich die Olympischen Spiele, auf diese Weise mit einem *guten Zweck* verbunden und zu einem wertvollen und schützenswerten Kulturgut, nach Sven Güldenpfennig gar in den Rang eines »Weltkulturerbes« erhoben, wurde mit dem mehr als ehrgeizigen Anspruch zugleich aber auch das Scheitern programmiert und die Diskrepanz von Anspruch und Wirklichkeit als ein geradezu konstituierendes Merkmal der olympischen Geschichte manifestiert.

So führten uns nicht erst die Spiele in Rio, die in Sotschi oder die in Peking, sondern schon die von 1972 in München oder die von 1936 in Berlin sowie mehr oder weniger auch alle anderen zuvor und danach immer wieder vor Augen, dass der Sport, auch und gerade seine olympische Variante, keine Bastion gegen äußere Anfechtungen und innere Verwerfungen, schon gar keine *Insel der Glückseligkeit* darzustellen vermag – wie schon der große Olympier Willi Daume dereinst ganz nüchtern formulierte. Schließlich wird er von Menschen gemacht und betrieben. Und selbst wenn es sich um Sportler handelt, sind Risiken und Nebenwirkungen programmiert.

Denken wir nur an das ewige und ewig leidige Problem des Dopings, das an dieser Stelle gar nicht vertieft, aber auch nicht ganz ausgeblendet werden soll und darf. Markieren die Olympischen Spiele doch gleichsam die Amplituden der Konjunkturschwankungen eines den Sport seit Jahrzehnten begleitenden Themas, das sich zuletzt auf die *Russland-Frage* fokussierte.

Nur um kein Missverständnis aufkommen zu lassen: Natürlich ist Doping verwerflich. Weil es gegen die Regeln und den Geist des Sports verstößt! Weil es andere, gerade auch junge Menschen zur Nachahmung animieren könnte! Weil entsprechende Mittel und Methoden gesundheitliche Schäden hervorrufen könnten! Und, auch das ist ja klar: Weil es die Geschäftsgrundlage des Sports und damit auch und vor allem der Olympischen Spiele gefährdet!

Im Blick auf den letzten Gedanken richtet sich der Argwohn mancher Experten auf den Umstand, dass trotz stetig steigenden Aufwands die *Dopingpolizei* stets gleiche Aufklärungsraten vermeldet, was den Zweiflern und Verzweifelten das Gefühl vermittelt, dass die Verantwortlichen nur *ihr Bemühen* glaubhaft machen und zugleich suggerieren wollen, dass die große Mehrheit und das große Ganze *sauber* seien. Dass dies nicht immer und überall funktioniert, belegt etwa der kürzlich erfolgte Ausstieg eines süddeutschen Schuhfabrikanten, der seine seit immerhin 1972 greifende Partnerschaft als Ausrüster der deutschen Olympiamannschaften im Kontext der Rio-Spiele mit dem Brustton der Entrüstung aufgekündigt hat. Nun, auch dieses Thema mag sich an anderer Stelle vertiefen lassen.

Gleichwohl sei der Hinweis erlaubt, dass negative Begleiterscheinungen, und seien es nur entsprechende Schlagzeilen, dem Ruf nicht gerade förderlich sind und den Kurs der olympischen Aktien ganz offensichtlich und ganz gravierend zu beeinflussen vermögen. Eine Binsenweisheit, die in den vergangenen Jahren auch und gerade hierzulande den Protagonisten der olympischen Sache Verdruss und Schlimmeres bereitet hat, da so manche olympischen Blütenträume mit Knalleffekt zum Platzen kamen.

Man denke nur an die Enttäuschungen von München und Hamburg, wo sich die Bürger mit Mehrheit gegen eine Bewerbung um die Olympischen Spiele ausgesprochen haben, jedenfalls solche, die die Gelegenheit zur Abstimmung wahrgenommen haben.

An dieser Stelle offenbart sich wohl ein vielleicht typisch deutscher Wesenszug, der einem erfolgreichen Werben um den olympischen Großauftrag bisher oft im Wege stand. Mehr als andernorts nämlich scheint Begeisterung an Bedenken zu scheitern, die ebenso selbstquälerisch wie genüsslich verfolgt werden und jede (Vor-)Freude im Keime zu ersticken drohen. Dabei wären die Chancen zuletzt weit besser gewesen als die der *deutschen Bewerbungen* seit Berchtesgadens Bemühen um die Winterspiele von 1992, das ebenso erfolglos blieb wie die Kandidaturen von Berlin und Leipzig für die Ausrichtung der Spiele in den Jahren 2000 und 2012. Erinnert man sich daran, dass das IOC im Blick auf die Winterspiele des Jahres 2022 zwischen nur zwei Bewerbungen entscheiden konnte und dabei Peking, wahrlich kein Mekka des Wintersports, gegenüber dem kasachischen Almaty, früher Alma Ata, den Vorzug gab, dann dürfte die These nicht allzu gewagt erscheinen, dass München mit einem (nicht nur) vergleichsweise hervorragenden Konzept beste Karten gehabt hätte.

Da auch für den Sport und sein exponiertestes Markenzeichen, die fünf Ringe, die Grundgesetze der Marktwirtschaft gelten, kann man sich den betreffenden Wahrheiten nicht verschließen: Wenn die Nachfrage sinkt, stellt dies die Qualität des Angebots in Frage. Auch für die im September 2017 anstehende Vergabe der Sommerspiele von 2024 sind nur zwei Kandidaten im Rennen geblieben, nachdem Madrid, Rom und Budapest ihre bereits eingereichten Reverenzen zurückzogen. Vor dem Hintergrund solcher olympischer Mangelerscheinungen, die an schlimmste Krisenzeiten denken lassen, beschloss das IOC – nach dem Vorbild der FIFA – eine historisch einmalige Doppel-Vergabe, die allein die Frage aufwirft, ob zuerst Paris und dann Los Angeles zum Zuge kommen wird oder ob es zur umgekehrten Reihenfolge kommen soll. Nochmals in Klammern: Los Angeles war Mitte der siebziger Jahre der weltweit einzige Kandidat für die Spiele von 1984 und das IOC hatte nur die Wahl zwischen Skylla und Charybdis – das hieß, »amerikanische Bedingungen« zu akzeptieren oder die Spiele ausfallen zu lassen. Eine Erinnerung und ein Szenario, das dem IOC und seinem Präsidenten Fragen von existenzieller Bedeutung stellt.

Der olympische Wert und die Werte

»Wir wollen den Wert des Sports auch mit seinen Werten steigern«, verkündete Thomas Bach am 20. Mai 2006 in der Frankfurter Paulskirche, nachdem er gerade zum Gründungspräsidenten des Deutschen Olympischen Sportbundes gewählt worden war. Inzwischen steht er als IOC-Präsident an der Spitze des olympischen Eisbergs und muss an vorderster Front den viel beklagten Ausverkauf der Werte verhindern. Wahrlich eine Herkulesaufgabe – um nicht das Bild des Augiasstalls zu bemühen.

So wie *wir* vor einigen Jahren *Papst waren*, sind wir nun seit geraumer Zeit IOC-Präsident. Und da mag es natürlich erscheinen, wenn der Amtsträger hierzulande umso mehr im Fokus kritischer Betrachtung steht. Im Übrigen spielte Thomas Bach auch schon vor der Amtsübernahme eine wichtige Rolle im IOC und wirkte nicht unwesentlich daran mit, dass die Prosperität des Unternehmens in Milliardenhöhe wuchs. Ein grandioser Erfolg, der auch eine gewisse Sicherheit gewährleistet, etwa für den *worst case* einer Absage der Olympischen Spiele, doch eben der fällt ihm nun auf die Füße. Hatte er mit seinem Reformvorhaben, der *Agenda 2020*, noch Punkte gemacht, sieht er sich, spätestens seit den Spielen in Rio, zunehmend mit heftigem Gegenwind konfrontiert.

Olympische Identität

Apropos Rio 2016: Denkt man an die *gerade eben* vergangenen Spiele zurück, was in unserer schnelllebigen Zeit ja fast schon aktiver Erinnerungsarbeit gleichkommt, dann verfestigt sich der Eindruck, dass am Fuße des Zuckerhuts *zwei* Veranstaltungen stattfanden. Durch die Brille von ARD und ZDF betrachtet, handelte es sich wieder einmal um großen Sport – faszinierende Wettkämpfe, auch in Sportarten und Disziplinen, deren Existenz man seit den letzten Spielen fast vergessen, jedenfalls nicht mehr vor Augen hatte, vor teils atemberaubender Kulisse, wenn auch vor nicht selten irritierend leeren Rängen.

Und wenn man die Zeitung aufschlug, Radio hörte oder sich im Internet umtat, dann sprang einem ein Festival von Betrug und Korruption, von Bau- und Umweltsünden, von sozialen und ökonomischen Verwerfungen ins Auge beziehungsweise ins Ohr, das man bestenfalls hätte ignorieren, wenn nicht vehement hätte verteufeln müssen.

Während sich scheinbar *business as usual* abspielte, begegneten sich eine krisengeschüttelte Bewegung und ein krisengeschüttelter Ort, gleichsam als Quadratur olympischer Misslichkeiten. Wenn man nun davon ausgehen darf, dass die Aktiven und die übrigen Beteiligten das Geschehen vor Ort wiederum auf eine andere, je eigene Weise wahrnahmen, dann sind im Blick zurück nach vorne Fragen aufgeworfen, die im Sinne und im Dienste der olympischen Zukunft eine Antwort verdienen.

Welche Olympischen Spiele haben in Rio und davor in Sotschi denn nun stattgefunden? Wie sind Verlauf und Wirkung zu bewerten? Was folgt daraus für die kommenden Spiele? Wie steht es mit dem Sinn des Ganzen oder dem Nutzen? Und damit: Welcher Aufwand rechtfertigt derselbe? Was soll so bleiben, wie es ist, und was muss sich ändern? Wie definiert und qualifiziert sich ein idealer Austragungsort? Und damit, um den Finger auch in diese Wunde zu legen: Wie wollen wir es hierzulande zukünftig mit der Frage einer olympischen Gastgeberrolle halten?

Olympische Meriten

Und dann bliebe, neben vielen anderen, ja auch noch die Frage nach den Medaillen. 42 sammelte die deutsche Mannschaft in Rio, zwei weniger als vier Jahre zuvor in London. Dafür sechs Goldene mehr. Bei 306 Entscheidungen bedeuten 16 Siege gute 5 %. Im Blick auf die Gesamtzahl der vergebenen Medaillen waren es 4,62 %. Ist das viel oder wenig? Oder zumindest *genug* oder doch *zu* wenig?

Wie viele Medaillen soll/kann/muss ein Land wie Deutschland bei den Olympischen Spielen für sich verbuchen? Und warum eigentlich? Wie groß ist der Wert oder der Mehrwert einer Medaille und wie viel darf sie kosten? Ist Platz fünf in der ebenso inoffiziellen wie bedeutsamen Nationenwertung okay oder nicht? Hinter den USA, Großbritannien, China und Russland. Vor Japan, Frankreich, Italien, Australien und den weiteren knapp 200 beteiligten Nationen!

Es war zu lesen, dass der eigentliche Gewinner der Spiele die Bahamas seien, auch wenn nur je einmal Gold und Bronze zu Buche schlugen. Eine auf den ersten Blick recht magere Bilanz, die aber gemessen an der Einwohnerzahl absolut top ist. Genauso viele, nämlich zwei Medaillen gewann auch Indien – pro 650 Millionen Einwohner eine! Olympische Rechenexempel, die das Herz passionierter Erbsen-, pardon, Medaillenzähler höher schlagen lassen mögen. Allein: Was sagen oder nutzen uns solche statistischen Aha-Effekte?

Natürlich: Medaillen sind das Salz in der olympischen Suppe oder, frei nach Innen-, also auch Sportminister Thomas de Maiziere, *die harte Währung des Sports*. Womit er zum Ausdruck bringen wollte, dass die Anzahl derselben eine *alternativlose* Bezugsgröße für die Berechnung und Rechtfertigung öffentlicher Zuwendungen an den Leistungssport darstelle. Während er, politisch korrekt, auch betont, dass die sportliche Leistung – gemeint ist eher der zählbare Erfolg – über jeden moralischen Zweifel erhaben sein muss.

Nun muss dies nicht a priori einer Quadratur der Ringe entsprechen. Oder ist es naiv zu glauben, dass ein Platz auf dem Treppchen auch völlig ohne unerlaubte Mittel und in fairem Wettkampf gewonnen werden kann, dass also beide Seiten der Olympischen Medaille zugleich glänzen können? Doch viel verlangt ist es schon. Vielleicht gar eine Zumutung? Schwer genug, wenn gute Sportler gute Sportler sein wollen oder sollen, doch noch viel schwerer, wenn sie – im Sinne der Lakota-Indianer – zugleich auch gute Menschen sein sollen. Sicher kann man beides haben, aber vielleicht nicht gleichzeitig. Oder doch?

Allemal einfach ist es, sich zu echauffieren, wenn *wir* vermeintlich zu wenig Kastanien aus dem olympischen Feuer holen, und sich in gleichem Maße zu entrüsten, wenn einer der *unseren* – oder auch einer der *Anderen* – gegen das *elfte Gebot* verstieß und sich erwischen ließ. Bisweilen hat man den Eindruck, dass wir unsere *Helden* nur oder vor allem auf den Sockel heben, um sie bei nächstbester Gelegenheit genüsslich vom selben zu stoßen. Boris Becker wäre ein Beispiel, um nicht Jan Ullrich zu nennen.

Natürlich sind die Aktiven auch moralisch in der Pflicht, schließlich werden sie gefördert und hofiert. In der Pflicht ist auch das Umfeld, Trainer, Ärzte und dergleichen. Verantwortung tragen naturgemäß auch diejenigen, die entsprechende Ämter und Funktionen übernahmen. Und natürlich sind neben der Politik, die eine zentrale Größe in der olympischen Verantwortungskette darstellt, auch noch die Medien zu nennen.

Bliebe noch der Blick auf den Endverbraucher. Schuld sind immer die anderen, könnte man sagen, während wir uns, hoch und trocken, am Dilemma delektieren. So muss die Frage erlaubt sein: Wie steht es um unsere eigene olympische Moral? Natürlich sind wir mit von der Partie, wenn der Sport das hohe Lied von Ethik und Moral anstimmt. Doch wie ist unsere Position in einer Gesellschaft, in der menschliche Arbeitskraft zu *Humankapital* degradiert und neben Fitness und Gesundheit, ständiger Erreichbarkeit und umfassender Kompetenz auch gutes Aussehen und mediengerechtes Auftreten zum allgemeinen Muss erhoben werden? In der Burnout und Herzinfarkt als Merkmale prototypischer Lebensläufe hingenommen werden und in der der Gebrauch von Medikamenten und der Missbrauch von Drogen als vielleicht bedauerliche, aber doch unvermeidliche Begleiterscheinung einer auf Leistung gepolten Zeit verharmlost werden. Ist der Sport, sind die Olympischen Spiele nicht (nur) ein Spiegel unserer Zeit?

Olympisches Dilemma

Fragt sich der Vater eines, sagen wir, elfjährigen Sohnes, ob er denselben der Obhut eines Kadertrainers oder eines Leistungszentrums anvertrauen möchte, um zugleich ein Loblied auf das humane Kapital des Sports und auf die Strahlkraft der Olympischen Idee zu singen, offenbart sich ein Dilemma, das sich auf andere, aber ebenso bezeichnende Weise in der Ambivalenz im Blick auf die Spiele ausdrückt. Viele Menschen wollen nämlich, wie Umfragen belegen, diese durchaus in der Nähe veranstaltet wissen, nur eben nicht vor der eigenen Haustür.

Denn steht *Olympia* als Metapher für eine großartige Innovation des 19. und beeindruckende Erfolgsgeschichte des 20. Jahrhunderts mit ihren vielfältigen sportlichen, politischen, sozialen, ökonomischen, ökologischen und manch anderen Implikationen in Rede, ist vorbehaltlose Begeisterung oder differenzierte Betrachtung oder distanziertes Schulterzucken zunehmend Zweifel, Bedenken und Ablehnung gewichen. Dies mag man mindestens insofern verstehen, als die Komplexität olympischer Identitäten vor dem Hintergrund sich stetig schneller wandelnder Koordinaten des Zeitgeistes widersprüchliche Gedanken hervorrufen und drängende Fragen aufwerfen muss. Schade nur, dass Gedanken und Fragen allein auch nicht weiterhelfen.

Willi Daume hat auch dieses schön gesagt: »Der Sport wird sein, was wir aus ihm machen.« Und um einen weiteren, um eine Nuance noch gewichtigeren Gewährsmann, nämlich Johan Wolfgang von Goethe, zu bemühen: »Es ist nicht genug zu wissen, man muss auch anwenden; es ist nicht genug zu wollen, man muss auch tun.«

Es fragt sich nur…

Jeder Sport hat (s)einen Preis...

Detlef Kuhlmann
Leibniz Universität Hannover

1 Einleitung

Zugegeben – die gewählte Überschrift zu meinem Beitrag ist gewöhnungsbedürftig. Ein Aussagesatz als Titel klingt per se komisch, sei aber in dieser Festschrift ausnahmsweise einmal gestattet. Er bedarf daher der Aufklärung. Diese will ich im Folgenden leisten: Ich bin gebeten worden einen kleinen Fachbeitrag für diese Festschrift beizusteuern. Der Beitrag soll sich auf ein Arbeitsgebiet beziehen, in dem sich Gudrun Doll-Tepper seit vielen Jahren engagiert. Ob und ggf. inwiefern ich diesen Anspruch tatsächlich erfüllen kann, sollen am Ende alle Leserinnen und Leser selbst entscheiden – am meisten und zuallererst aber die Jubilarin Gudrun Doll-Tepper, der ich hiermit zur Vollendung Ihres 70. Lebensjahres in langjähriger kollegialer und freundschaftlicher Verbundenheit sehr herzlich gratuliere. Sie wird für sich am besten nachvollziehen können, in welcher Hinsicht sie sich mit meinem kleinen Text berufsbiografisch im Sport mit seiner ganzen Vielfalt vom paralympischen Sport bis zum Schulsport verorten kann und an welche *schönen* Ereignisse sie sich womöglich dabei selbst am liebsten erinnert.[1] Soviel steht fest: Jeder Sport hat (s)einen Preis…

2 Preise im Sport – Einblicke in die Preisszene

Während der Arbeit an diesem Beitrag erhielt ich medial Kenntnis über die Ausschreibung bzw. die Verleihung etlicher (nationaler) Preise im Sport, darunter ein Werte-Preis der Stiftung Deutsche Sporthilfe (vgl. DOSB-PRESSE Nr. 18 vom 2. Mai 2017), der Inklusionstaler 2017 des DJK-Sportverbandes (vgl. DOSB-PRESSE Nr. 20 vom 16. Mai 2017), ein Wissenschaftspreis, der erstmals 2018

---

1 Gudrun Doll-Tepper hat in ihrem bisherigen Leben zahlreiche Auszeichnungen für ihr großes und breites akademisches Schaffen im Sport bzw. der Sportwissenschaft erhalten. Alle ihre Preise hier als »Fußnote« aufzuführen, würde allein dem Kriterium der guten Form zuwiderlaufen. Gudrun Doll-Tepper hat in ihrem bisherigen Leben aber auch zahlreiche Auszeichnungen an andere Menschen für besondere Leistungen im Sport verleihen dürfen. Eine Anspielung auf den Titel meines Beitrags ist darin allemal zu sehen – denn: Jeder Sport hat (s)einen Preis…

vom Sportbund Pfalz ausgelobt wird (vgl. DOSB-PRESSE Nr. 13 vom 28. März 2017), der Nachwuchspreis des Verbands Deutscher Sportjournalisten (vgl. DOSB-PRESSE Nr. 22/23 vom 30. Mai 2017) sowie der Award als Deutscher Fußball-Botschafter im Ausland (vgl. DOSB-PRESSE Nr. 21 vom 23. Mai 2017). Diese Notierungen zeigen beispielhaft: Ständig werden im Sport irgendwo irgendwelche Preise vergeben. Der Sport reiht sich damit in eine Preisszene ein, die auf anderen Gebieten Bambis und Echos genauso einschließt wie die verschiedenen Nobels und zahllose andere Auszeichnungen, die im Gedenken an herausragende Persönlichkeiten benannt sind. Überall gibt es Preise. Gibt es überhaupt einen gesellschaftlichen Bereich, der heutzutage (noch) nicht bepreist wird?

Dieser Frage geht seit kurzer Zeit übrigens eine Forschergruppe der Universität Bielefeld nach. Im Sonderforschungsbereich (SFB 1288) zum Thema *Praktiken des Vergleichens* sollen Geschichte, gesellschaftliche Ursachen sowie die Funktionen und Wirkungen von allen möglichen Ratings und Rankings, von Wettbewerben und Castings erforscht werden. Dabei soll die an sich ganz einfache Frage beiläufig beantwortet werden: Was tun die Akteurinnen und Akteure, wenn sie (sich) vergleichen? Der Sport ist – sofern der Internetauftritt dieses Sonderforschungsbereichs aktuell und vollständig ist – dabei (noch) nicht vertreten. Die Dauer der angestrebten Förderung des SFB beträgt zwölf Jahre. Das lässt hoffen, dass der Sport vielleicht später doch noch aufgenommen und darin integriert wird.

2.1 Sport als doppelseitige Preisofferte

Warum sollte der Sport zu den *Praktiken des Vergleichens* gehören? Jeder Sport hat (s)einen Preis... Die Überschrift meines Beitrags könnte thesenartig diese Praktik des Vergleichens unterfüttern, aber zugleich verdeutlichen, dass der Sport gleichsam prinzipiell über zwei *Preisschilder* des praktischen Vergleichens verfügt. Der Sport unterscheidet sich demnach wesentlich von allen anderen Preissegmenten durch eine doppelseitige Preisofferte. Denn soviel steht fest: Seit es Sport gibt, werden im Grunde immerzu Preise vergeben. Das sind solche für (vorwiegend körperliche) Leistungen in Form von Punkten und Platzierungen bzw. in Form von Tafeln und Tabellen, oder sei es in Form von Pokalen, Prämien und Preisgeldern. Das ist aber nur die eine Seite. Sie wohnt dem Sport originär inne (vgl. dazu Darstellungen zum Wesen des modernen Sports wegweisend z.B. bei Guttmann, 1979, ferner Lenk, 1983, Grupe, 2000, daneben auch Kuhlmann, 1998).

Offenbar gibt es über diese dem Sport innewohnenden Preisvergaben hinaus auch noch weitere originelle Möglichkeiten, Sport mit Preisen zu preisen. Das sind dann nämlich jene Preise, die nicht direkt durch das *harte* originäre Bewertungssystem des Sports über Tore, Punkte, Meisterschaften etc. vergeben werden, sondern wo der Sport auf ganz andere Weise mit Preisen gewürdigt wird. Es spricht sogar einiges dafür, dass dieses *weiche* Belohnungssystem des Sports gerade in den letzten Jahren an Umfang und Form mächtig zugelegt hat (vgl. dazu Kommentare über die Preislandschaft im Sport bei Kuhlmann, 2014, bes. S. 136–141 sowie Kuhlmann, 2011, auf den dieser Beitrag aufbaut).

2.2 Zur Konjunktur im sportbezogenen Preisaufkommen

Am Institut für Sportwissenschaft der Leibniz Universität Hannover ist seit geraumer Zeit ein stetig größer werdendes Archiv entstanden, in dem alle bundesweit ausgelobten Sportpreise dokumentiert werden. Niemand weiß bislang, ob diese Sammlung schon annähernd vollständig ist. Derzeit lässt sich nur festhalten, dass es in Deutschland weit über hundert Sportpreise allein von nationaler Reichweite gibt. Man mag den Zahlenwert für hoch oder niedrig halten, er ist so oder so noch mit einer unbestimmten Dunkelziffer zu addieren – ganz abgesehen von all den Preisen im Sport, die nur landesweit in den einzelnen Bundesländern oder lokal vor Ort in Solingen oder Reutlingen, in Brandenburg und Neubrandenburg ausgeschrieben werden. Sieht man sich die Entstehungsgeschichte aller bislang schon erfassten Sportpreise etwas genauer an, dann fällt auf, dass die meisten erst in den letzten ca. zehn bis fünfzehn Jahren erstmals ausgelobt wurden. Preise im Sport haben offenbar gerade kolossale Konjunktur. Das 21. Jahrhundert könnte das Preisjahrhundert des Sports werden – vorausgesetzt, die Preise im Sport werden tatsächlich alle auf Dauer gestellt, also in einem bestimmten zeitlichen Rhythmus immer wieder neu vergeben.

Zu den Preis-Dinosauriern im Sport gehört neben einigen anderen beispielsweise auch der erstmals 1967 als Wanderpreis der Deutschen Olympischen Gesellschaft (DOG) vergebene Wilhelm-Garbe-Preis, benannt nach dem Mitbegründer der DOG, damals auch mitverantwortlich für den *Goldenen Plan* zum Bau von Sportstätten und langjähriger Förderer des organisierten bzw. des olympischen Sports in Deutschland, speziell in seiner Heimatstadt Hannover: Wilhelm Garbe (1893 bis 1967) war selbst im Rudern, Rugby und in der Leichtathletik aktiv und im Hauptberuf Manager bei den Continental Gummiwerken in Hannover. Heute verleiht die DOG den Willi-Garbe-Preis jährlich in Form einer Geldprämie an die drei Zweigstellen, die im Jahreszeitraum die meisten neuen Mitglieder aufnehmen konnten.

Branchenführer, was die Anzahl der national ausgelobten Preise im Sport anbelangt, ist – wer hätte das nicht auf Anhieb gewusst – der Deutsche Olympische Sportbund (DOSB), dem die Jubilarin Gudrun Doll-Tepper seit seiner Gründung im Jahre 2006 als Vizepräsidentin für Bildung und Olympische Erziehung vorsteht.[2] Derzeit vergibt er allein 26 Preise, teilweise zusammen mit der Deutschen Sportjugend (dsj), an weiteren Preisen ist er kooperativ beteiligt. Zu den Top Ten beim DOSB gehören jährlich die *Sterne des Sports*, die zusammen mit den Volks- und Raiffeisenbanken vergeben werden, und das Grüne Band, ursprünglich in Zusammenarbeit mit der Dresdner Bank. Der Deutsche Schulsportpreis von DOSB und dsj, der im Jahre 2002 geboren wurde, ist sogar älter als sein *großer Bruder*, der Deutsche Schulpreis. Auf der langen Preistafel des DOSB stehen dann aber auch noch der Wettbewerb *Mission Olympic*, der die sportlichste Stadt auszeichnet, neben der Auszeichnung *Eliteschule des Jahres*, dem *Trainer des Jahres* und dem Förderpreis *Pro Ehrenamt* etc. In den letzten Jahren neu hinzugekommen ist der Wettbewerb *Klimaschutz im Sportverein* mit dem Bundesumweltministerium als Förderer, der erstmals an den Hannoverschen Sport-Club von 1893 wegen der besonders umweltfreundlichen Sanierung des Klubhauses und der intensiven Umweltbildung für Kinder überreicht wurde.

Die Festakademie mit Gudrun Doll-Tepper als Festrednerin für den alle zwei Jahre ausgeschriebenen Wissenschaftspreis des DOSB fand zuletzt gerade Anfang des Jahres 2017 (erstmals in den neuen Räumlichkeiten beim Deutschen Olympischen Sportbund in Frankfurt) statt, als dessen Vorläufer die 1953 erstmals

---

2 In diesem Zusammenhang ließe sich die Jubilarin Gudrun Doll-Tepper sogar als Zeitzeugin befragen: Wie viele Preise durfte sie aus welchen Anlässen in ihrer bisherigen Amtszeit als zuständige Vizepräsidentin des DOSB selbst schon überreichen bzw. in welchen Jurys durfte sie mit ihrer Expertise bis dato selbst mitwirken? Stellvertretend sei wenigstens hier der Deutsche Schulsportpreis erwähnt, der alle zwei Jahre vom DOSB bzw. der Deutschen Sportjugend vergeben wird und wo Gudrun Doll-Tepper regelmäßig bei der Preisverleihung (auch mit einer Laudatio) dabei ist, was wiederum der Autor dieses Beitrags als »Zeitzeuge« bestätigen kann (vgl. speziell zum Deutschen Schulsportpreis auch Kuhlmann, 2013 und 2015).

vergebene Carl-Diem-Plakette gilt. Sie ist die mit Abstand älteste Auszeichnung in der Preischronik vom DOSB bzw. seinem Vorgänger, dem Deutschen Sportbund. Das Preiskarussell beim DOSB dreht sich aber auch anders herum: Der DOSB selbst ist nämlich schon im Jahre 2009 für sein großes umweltpolitisches Engagement mit dem erstmals vergebenen *IOC-Award for Sport and the Environment* ausgezeichnet worden.

2.3 Preise im Sport ausloben – warum und wie?

Versucht man das immer größer werdende Ausloben von Preisen im Sport irgendwie zu verorten, dann kann die Darstellung über ein Koordinatensystem weiterhelfen. Das sieht dann auf der Horizontalen etwa so aus: Wer Preise auslobt, erhofft sich davon positive Wirkungen, die sowohl nach innen als auch nach außen gehen. Der Preisgeber zeichnet in aller Regel besondere Leistungen von Menschen bzw. Gruppen im Sport (*intern*) aus und kann diese öffentlichkeitswirksam bzw. medial (*extern*) präsentieren.

Die vertikale Koordinate ließe sich dann etwa so darstellen: Wer Preise auslobt, verfolgt damit bestimmte Ziele: Man kann damit bisherige Verdienste in einer (zeithistorischen) Rückschau würdigen und werten, aber auch zukunftsorientiert zur (perspektivischen) Entwicklung von Innovationen und Modellen im Sport und für den Sport auffordern und anspornen. Egal, wo ein Preis dann ganz genau angesiedelt ist: Entscheidend für die Preisvergabe ist die eingehende Beurteilung auf der Basis von vorher festgeschriebenen Kriterien der Exzellenz. Um die Feststellung dieser Exzellenz kümmert sich in aller Regel eine mehrköpfige Jury. Sie bringt selbst jene Expertise mit, die notwendige Voraussetzung ist, um aus preisverdächtigen preisgekrönte Leistungen zu küren. Was Kampfrichter beim Geräteturnen sind, beäugen Juroren bei Preisen – nicht nur, aber auch im Sport. Allerdings arbeiten sie meist unerkannt hinter verschlossenen Türen. Es kommt selten vor, dass die Namen der (oftmals prominenten) Jury und dazu noch deren Voten im Einzelnen bekannt gegeben werden, wie das vor einiger Zeit allerdings beim Sven-Simon-Preis für Sportfotografie (ausnahmsweise) der Fall war, der im Sport und Olympia Museum Köln zum zwölften Male vergeben wurde und wo z. B. Boris Becker und Franz Beckenbauer die meisten Punkte für das spätere Siegerfoto (*Ein Tor für die Ewigkeit* von Markus Gilliar) vergeben hatten, während u. a. Heiner Brand und Katarina Witt als Jury-Mitglieder ganz andere Motive vorn auf ihrer Liste nominiert hatten…

Apropos Jury: Das Preisthema außerhalb des Sports hat längst literarische Facetten gefunden. Im Roman *Preisverleihung* des Berliners Günter de Bryun[3] geht es beispielsweise um die Frage, ob es moralisch verantwortbar ist, auch eine schlechte Leistung derart hochzuloben, dass es zur *Preisverleihung* kommt. Und der österreichische Skandal-Schriftsteller Thomas Bernhard hat in seinem Selbstporträt als Preisempfänger die Auszeichnungen, die ihm zuteil wurden, prosaisch mit seinem Werk *Meine Preise*[4] kritisch unter die Lupe genommen. Da gerinnt dann auf einem Jahrmarkt der Eitelkeiten die Preisverleihung zur Peinlichkeit: »Ich hasste die Zeremonien, aber ich machte sie mit, ich hasste die Preisgeber, aber ich nahm ihre Geldsummen an«. Apropos Geldsummen: Die schwanken im Sport natürlich auch und fangen bei jenen ideellen Preisen an, bei denen kein Bargeld, sondern *nur* eine künstlerisch wertvolle Trophäe vergeben wird. Der derzeit *teuerste* Preis im Sport dürfte *Mission Olympic* mit 75.000 Euro sein. Aber diese Summe erhält dann auch nicht eine einzelne Person, sondern gleich eine ganze Stadt. Der Preis wurde von 2008 bis 2014 jährlich vom DOSB (zusammen mit Coca Cola) vergeben.

3 Prüfsteine für einen Preisskeptizismus

Preisgelder hin oder her – Preise sind so oder so ein geradezu selbstverständlicher Teil unserer Gegenwartsgesellschaft. Der Sport ist darin gleichsam involviert – Tendenz steigend! Ist gar eine *Verpreisung des Sports* in Sicht? Diese Frage sollten am besten diejenigen beantworten, die sich immer wieder um Preise bewerben. Versucht man jedoch diese gegenwärtige Preiskonjunktur im Sport für eine zukünftige Preiskultur zu festigen und weiter zu pflegen, dann sind dabei mindestens die folgenden vier Prüfsteine als ein konstruktiver Preisskeptizismus in Anschlag zu bringen:

3.1 Exzellenz

Der erste Prüfstein lautet Exzellenz und meint: Mit der stetig steigenden Anzahl der ausgelobten Preise muss nicht zwangsläufig die Qualität der Leistungen steigen, die ausgezeichnet werden (sollen). Anders und pauschal: Wer immer mehr und irgendwann alles bepreist, der missachtet am Ende das Kriterium der

---

3 Günter de Bruyn (1993). *Preisverleihung. Roman.* Frankfurt: Fischer Taschenbuch Verlag.
4 Thomas Bernhard (2009). *Meine Preise.* Frankfurt: Suhrkamp.

Exzellenz, das den Preisen per se den unaustauschbaren Stempel aufdrückt. Die Gefahr des Exzellenzverlustes bedroht so gesehen nicht nur die Vergabe eines neuen Preises, sie lauert im Grunde auch bei jeder neuen Vergabe eines schon etablierten Preises.

3.2 Sättigung

Der zweite Prüfstein lautet Sättigung und meint: Mit der stetig steigenden Anzahl der ausgelobten Preise muss nicht zwangsläufig die Anzahl derjenigen ansteigen, die sich dem Wettbewerb um die Vergabe von Preisen immerzu stellen. Anstatt andauernd in der Erarbeitung von aussagekräftigen Bewerbungsunterlagen zu versinken, kann man auch den Entschluss fassen, auf eine Bewerbung schlicht und einfach zu verzichten – zumal dann, wenn das Verhältnis von Bewerbungsaufwand und der Chance, den Preis hinterher zu erhalten, von vornherein nicht unbedingt erfolgversprechend erscheint.

3.3 Instrumentalisierung

Der dritte Prüfstein lautet Instrumentalisierung und meint: Mit der stetig steigenden Anzahl der ausgelobten Preise wächst die Anzahl derjenigen, die solche per se ausloben bzw. als Partner und Unterstützer auftreten. Viele Preise im Sport werden inzwischen von mehreren Organisationen und Unternehmen gemeinsam ausgeschrieben. Sie verbinden damit bestimmte und teilweise durchaus berechtigte Interessen. Damit einher geht prinzipiell jedoch die Gefahr der Instrumentalisierung von Preisen. Am Beispiel: Wer Kinder und Jugendliche über gesunde Ernährung aufklären will, der muss sich fragen lassen, ob es dazu notwendig und sinnvoll ist, einen Preis zusammen mit einer Fast-Food-Kette auszuloben, oder ob es andere und bessere Maßnahmen und Möglichkeiten dafür gibt.

3.4 Nachhaltigkeit

Der vierte Prüfstein lautet Nachhaltigkeit und meint: Mit der stetig steigenden Anzahl von ausgelobten Preisen hierzulande und im Sport geht auch eine Kehrseite einher: Es scheint nämlich gleichzeitig die Anzahl derjenigen Wettbewerbe zu steigen, die nach kürzester Zeit wieder vom Preismarkt verschwinden. Ein Preis, der nur ein einziges Mal ausgelobt wird, bringt sich selbst um das Etikett der Nachhaltigkeit – zumal dann, wenn ausdrücklich mit der Preisvergabe *vorbildliche Leistungen* oder *modellhafte Projekte* ausgezeichnet werden, die andere zur Nachahmung animieren sollen. So hat sich – und dies als *schmutziges*

Sahnehäubchen ganz zum Schluss oben drauf – der Fotowettbewerb *Die marode Sportstätte* im Jahr 2009 selbst schnell als marode erwiesen. Er wurde nur ein einziges Mal vergeben: Wer hat denn schon Lust sich Jahr für Jahr Bilder von (den gleichen) baufälligen Sportanlagen anzusehen und die aktuell schlimmsten für einen Preis auszuwählen. Ganz im Ernst: Da hilft nur noch Sanierung. Jeder Sport hat (s)einen Preis …

Literatur

Grupe, O. (2000). *Vom Sinn des Sports. Kulturelle, pädagogische und ethische Aspekte.* Schorndorf: Hofmann.

Guttmann, A. (1979). *Vom Ritual zum Rekord. Das Wesen des modernen Sports.* Schorndorf: Hofmann.

Kuhlmann, D. (1998). *Wettkampfsport: Domäne in der Defensive? Theoretische Ansätze und empirische Befunde.* Schorndorf: Hofmann.

Kuhlmann, D. (2011). Den Sport mit Preisen preisen … Eine inflationäre Entwicklung. *Olympisches Feuer, 1*, 32–34.

Kuhlmann, D. (2013, unter Mitarbeit von E. P. Büchner). *Deutscher Schulsportpreis des DOSB und der dsj. Eine Zwischenbilanz.* Frankfurt: dsj.

Kuhlmann, D. (2014). *Querpässe zwischen Sport und Sportwissenschaft.* Hildesheim: Arete.

Kuhlmann, D. (2015). Der Deutsche Schulsportpreis – eine Zwischenbilanz. *sportunterricht, 64*(9), 258–263.

Lenk, H. (1983). *Eigenleistung. Plädoyer für eine positive Leistungskultur.* Osnabrück; Zürich: Fromm.

Für den Erhalt des *Youth Leadership Programmes*

Wilfried Lemke
Ehemaliger UN-Sonderberater für Sport im Dienst von Entwicklung und Frieden

Sport ist ein globales Phänomen, das historisch gesehen in jeder Gesellschaft einen außerordentlichen Stellenwert genießt und nach wie vor weltweit große Beachtung findet. So verfolgten beispielsweise eine Milliarde Zuschauer die Eröffnungsfeier der Olympischen Spiele in London 2012 vor dem Fernseher. Erfreulicherweise sind wir in den vergangenen fünfzehn Jahren ebenso Zeuge der wachsenden Rolle des Sports als treibende Kraft für positive soziale Veränderungen in der Welt geworden. Aufgrund seiner besonderen Fähigkeit Menschen unterschiedlicher Herkunft, Geschlechts, Hautfarbe, Sprache, ethnischer Zugehörigkeit und Religion zusammenzubringen, leistet der Sport einen wichtigen Beitrag zur internationalen Völkerverständigung. Durch seine universelle Sprache, Kosteneffizienz und grundlegenden Werte wie Respekt, Teamwork, dem Einhalten von Regeln und Disziplin trägt Sport zu Toleranz bei, sorgt für den Abbau von Vorurteilen und vermittelt Fähigkeiten, die für ein friedliches, harmonisches Miteinander notwendig sind. Insbesondere mit Bezug auf junge Menschen kann

Gudrun Doll-Tepper, Wilfried Lemke, Tegla Loroupe und Jonas Burgheim

Sport diese in ihrer persönlichen Entwicklung stärken und ihr Potenzial als führende Vorbilder und zukünftige Vordenker in ihren Gemeinden entfalten.

In diesem Zusammenhang möchte ich von einem Programm berichten, auf das ich persönlich mit Freude blicke. Im Rahmen meines kürzlich abgelegten Mandats als *Sonderberater des Generalsekretärs der Vereinten Nationen für Sport im Dienst von Entwicklung und Frieden* von 2008 bis 2016 hatte ich die Gelegenheit auf meinen UN-Missionen und Dienstreisen in wirtschaftlich strukturschwache Länder mit niedrigem oder mittlerem Einkommen viele *Sport-für-Entwicklung*-Projekte auf Basisebene zu besuchen und näher kennenzulernen. Während dieser Reisen habe ich unzählige junge Menschen getroffen, die sich mit ganzem Herzen für die Entwicklung ihrer Gemeinden durch Freiwilligenarbeit in diesen Projekten einsetzen.

In Deutschland mag es selbstverständlich sein als Mitglied eines Sportvereins irgendwann von einem Abteilungsleiter gefragt zu werden: »Willi, hast du nicht Lust, Pressereferent der Leichtathletik-Jugendabteilung zu werden?«. Damals war ich ganz stolz und habe beim Hamburger Sportverein mein erstes Ehrenamt übernommen. Das ist jedoch nicht selbstverständlich für einen Jugendlichen aus benachteiligten Verhältnissen, der morgens mit sieben Geschwistern und nur der Mutter zu Hause in einer kleinen Hütte aufsteht, die vielleicht acht Quadratmeter groß ist. Obwohl er Schwierigkeiten hat seine eigenen Grundbedürfnisse zu erfüllen, geht er nachmittags trotzdem ins Sportprojekt und sagt: »Hier bin ich, ich möchte jetzt die Kinder aus meiner Nachbarschaft trainieren und ihnen dabei helfen durch den Sport ihre sozialen Fähigkeiten zu stärken«.

Viele dieser jungen Menschen verfügen oftmals nur über eine geringe Schulbildung, haben keine Mittel zur Durchführung ihrer Projekte und kein geeignetes Forum, um bewährte Anwendungsmethoden in diesem Feld zu erlernen oder ihre Führungsqualitäten zu entwickeln. Nichtsdestotrotz weisen sie einen enormen Enthusiasmus auf und gelten als vertraute sowie respektierte Vorbilder in ihren Nachbarschaften.

Dieses Engagement und diesen Enthusiasmus wollte ich gemeinsam mit meinem Büro, dem *United Nations Office on Sport for Development and Peace (UNOSDP)* fördern. Seit Beginn meiner Amtszeit als UN-Sonderberater gab es Bestrebungen ein Programm für junge Menschen ins Leben zu rufen, die in Ihren Heimatorten in allen Winkeln dieser Erde den Sport für Frieden und Entwicklung nutzen. Die Grundidee war diese jungen hochmotivierten Menschen mit solch vielversprechendem Potenzial zusammenzubringen, ihre Führungskompetenzen weiterzuentwickeln und ihnen die Möglichkeit zu geben sich sowohl untereinander als auch mit internationalen Experten aus dem Bereich Sport im Dienst von Entwicklung und Frieden auszutauschen. Die wertvollen Erfahrungen und neu erlernten Fähigkeiten sollten sie dann wirkungsvoll zur Optimierung ihrer *Sport-für-Entwicklung*-Projekte sowie zu ihrer eigenen professionellen Entwicklung einbringen, um zu führenden Vorbildern von morgen zu reifen. Aus diesen Bestrebungen heraus wurde dann schließlich im Januar 2012 mit Zustimmung des Generalsekretärs der Vereinten Nationen das *Youth Leadership Programme (YLP)* der Vereinten Nationen ins Leben gerufen, das zum ersten Mal im *Aspire Dome* in Doha, Katar stattfand.

Im Rahmen eines rund zweiwöchigen Aufenthalts in einem *Youth Leadership Programme* erhielten diese Vorbilder Zugang zu theoretischem und praktischem Training, um ihre persönlichen Fähigkeiten und ihre Projekte auszubauen bzw. zu verbessern und um ihnen die richtigen Werkzeuge und Methoden an die Hand zu geben, wenn sie in ihre Gemeinden zurückkehren. Wir konzentrierten uns dabei auf benachteiligte Gemeinden: Slums, Townships, Flüchtlingslager und Favelas. Da, wo die Not wirklich am größten ist, identifizierten wir über Nichtregierungsorganisationen Projekte für junge Menschen und nahmen sie dann ins Programm auf. Dabei legten wir besonderen Wert auf eine ausgeglichene Anzahl von weiblichen und männlichen Teilnehmern sowie die Einbindung von jungen Menschen mit Behinderungen. Die Nachfrage nach Plätzen im Programm war groß. Potenzielle Teilnehmerinnen und Teilnehmer wurden über ihre jeweiligen Vereine und Organisationen empfohlen und erhielten bei Teilnahme Stipendien, sodass ihnen keinerlei Kosten entstanden. Zu unserem breiten Feld an erstklassigen Implementierungspartnern gehörten Trainer und Fachexperten aus internationalen Sportdachverbänden in Sportarten wie Volleyball, Judo, Tischtennis, Basketball, Badminton und Taekwondo, aus international renommierten Sportvereinen und Stiftungen wie dem *Liverpool Football Club, InterCampus (Inter Mailand)* und der englischen *Football Association* sowie UN-Institutionen, bilateralen Entwicklungsorganisationen und Nichtregierungsorganisationen, welche auf die Durchführung von *Sport-für-Entwicklung*-Projekten spezialisiert sind.

Mit dem großartigen Erfolg des Pilot-Camps und mit Hilfe unserer Förderer sowie langfristigen Partnerschaften gelang es uns, seit dem Start des ersten Camps in Doha insgesamt 21 Camps in Europa, Asien, Nord- und Südamerika bis Ende des Jahres 2016 durchzuführen. Allein in Deutschland konnte UNOSDP dank der Unterstützung des Bundesministeriums für wirtschaftliche Zusammenarbeit und Entwicklung (BMZ) und der Gesellschaft für Internationale Zusammenarbeit (GIZ) vier äußerst erfolgreiche *Youth Leadership Camps* in Berlin, Hamburg und Hennef in den letzten vier Jahren ausrichten. Bei den begleitenden *High-Level Dinnern* in Berlin und Hamburg konnten sich die hochrangigen Gäste aus Politik und Sport von dem Konzept unseres Programms endgültig überzeugen und sich dabei von dem Enthusiasmus unserer Teilnehmer anstecken lassen. Weitere *Youth Leadership Programmes* fanden bisher in internationalen Ausrichterstädten wie Florida (Vereinigte Staaten), Gwangju (Südkorea), Magglingen (Schweiz), Medellín (Kolumbien), Stockholm (Schweden) and Tokio (Japan) statt.

Insgesamt gaben wir rund 760 Jugendlichen aus über 70 Ländern der Welt Methoden und Werkzeuge an die Hand als Multiplikatoren in ihren Gemeinschaften den Sport für Entwicklung und Frieden noch besser zu nutzen. Dabei gaben 90 % der *Youth Leaders* an, dass sie die Teilnahme an dem Programm weiter darin bestärkt und motiviert hat ihre Aktivitäten im Bereich Sport für Entwicklung in ihren Gemeinden ausbauen und Veränderungen in ihren methodischen Ansätzen herbeiführen zu wollen.

In der inhaltlichen Konzipierung unserer *Youth Leadership Programmes* fanden sich ebenso die fünf Prioritäten wieder, die ich während meiner Amtszeit als UN-Sonderberater festgelegt hatte: Sport als Beitrag zur Konfliktlösung, Inklusion von Menschen mit Behinderungen, Gleichstellung der Geschlechter, Jugendförderung auf Basisebene und ein besonderer Fokus auf den afrikanischen Kontinent. So stellte beispielsweise die Zusammenarbeit mit der Agitos Foundation des Internationalen Paralympischen Komitees bisher eines der Kernelemente des Trainingsprogramms dar, um die Bedeutung der Einbindung junger Menschen mit Behinderungen in den jeweiligen Sportprojekten der Teilnehmerinnen und Teilnehmer hervorzuheben.

Die Teilnehmerinnen und Teilnehmer kamen aus allen Teilen der Welt und hatten ganz verschiedene Hintergründe. Ich denke dabei zum Beispiel an einen unserer ersten *Youth Leader*, Lloyd Birungi, der die Experten des Internationalen Tischtennisverbands (ITTF) bei unserem *YLP* in Doha im Rahmen des *ITTF Dream Building Programms* mit viel Eigeninitiative und einer innovativen Idee davon überzeugen konnte seinem Projekt Tischtennismaterialien in mehreren Grundschulen in den ländlichen Gegenden Ugandas zur Verfügung zu stellen, um dort die sozialen Fähigkeiten der Kinder mit Hilfe von Tischtennisaktivitäten zu stärken. Eine andere Absolventin des *YLP*, Nomawethu Sokoyi, war aktive Fußballtrainerin in einem Township im südafrikanischen Kapstadt. Ihr Ansatzpunkt war es die Jugendlichen mit kostenlosem Fußballtraining von der Straße zu holen. Mitmachen durften allerdings nur diejenigen, die vorher an einem Aufklärungsseminar zum Thema HIV/AIDS teilgenommen hatten. Unsere Teilnehmerin aus Kathmandu, Romee Giri, setzte mit Leidenschaft und ihren Kenntnissen im Taekwondo Projekte zur Bewältigung der Erdbebenkatastrophe in Nepal um. Für ihre außerordentlichen Leistungen wurde sie zu den Feierlichkeiten anlässlich des Internationalen Tages des Sports für Entwicklung und Frieden sowie des Olympischen Geistes im April 2016 zu den Vereinten Nationen in Genf eingeladen und hielt dort in einer Reihe mit dem UN-Generalsekretär und dem IOC Präsidenten eine Rede zum sozialen Nutzen des Sports als Mittel zur Jugendförderung auf Basisebene.

Auch nach Ende ihrer *YLP*-Teilnahme begleiteten wir die Jugendlichen und verfolgten ihren weiteren Lebensweg. Dabei bin ich besonders stolz auf einen jungen Teilnehmer unseres Berliner Camps von 2014: Maclean Dzidzienyo, ein paralympischer Athlet aus Ghana, inspirierte viele der anderen Teilnehmerinnen und Teilnehmer, weil er eindrucksvoll unter Beweis stellte, dass jeder Mensch beim Sport die gleiche Ausgangslage hat. Nicht nur war er in seiner Gemeinde als Trainer und Vorbild anerkannt – durch sein Streben eines Tages bei den Paralympischen Spielen dabei sein zu können, trug er aktiv zum Abbau von Vorurteilen gegenüber Menschen mit Behinderungen bei. Seine Mitmenschen erlebten eindrucksvoll zu welch Leistungen er im Stande war. Seine Gemeinde unterstützte ihn aktiv bei seinen Vorhaben, und er erhielt einen neuen Rennrollstuhl. Er war Vorbild für Kinder und Athleten gleichermaßen und lebt ihnen die Wichtigkeit der Ausdauer zum Erreichen von Träumen unabhängig von physischen Einschränkungen vor.

Ich könnte die Liste der beeindruckenden Beispiele unserer Teilnehmerinnen und Teilnehmer endlos fortführen, um den enorm positiven Einfluss weiter zu unterstreichen, den das *Youth Leadership Programme* auf ihren weiteren Werdegang für sie und ihre Gemeinden genommen hat. Nicht ohne Grund fand das *YLP* in der Resolution der UN-Generalversammlung vom Oktober 2014 zu *Sport as a means to promote education, health, development and peace* Erwähnung und Anerkennung. Es kann somit als das Flaggschiff meiner Amtszeit als UN-Sonderberater bezeichnet werden.

Doch auch auf *Policy*-Ebene hat sich seit der Einführung des UNOSDP viel im Bereich des Sports im Dienst von Entwicklung Frieden getan. So wurde 2014 erstmals der Internationale Tag des Sports für Entwicklung und Frieden eingeführt und verlieh diesem wichtigen Thema weitere Anerkennung auf globaler Ebene. Im September 2015 beschlossen die Vereinten Nationen auf einem historischen Gipfeltreffen in New York die *Agenda 2030 für Nachhaltige Entwicklung.* Die in der Agenda enthaltenen 17 Ziele für nachhaltige Entwicklung (*Sustainable Development Goals, SDGs*) lösten die 8 Millenniums-Entwicklungsziele (*MDGs*) ab, die Ende 2015 ausliefen.

In der Resolution der Generalversammlung der Vereinten Nationen zur neuen Agenda 2030 erhielt der Sport in einem eigenen Paragraphen ausführliche Anerkennung als *ein wichtiger Wegbereiter [enabler] nachhaltiger Entwicklung,* insbesondere in Hinblick auf die Förderung von Toleranz und Respekt sowie seinen wachsenden Beitrag zur Stärkung von Frauen, jungen Menschen, Individuen sowie Gemeinden in der Verfolgung von Zielen zur Verbesserung der Gesundheit, Bildung und sozialen Inklusion. Sie bekräftigt somit die Verbindung der Vereinten Nationen mit der Welt des Sports zur sozialen Nutzung für Kinder und Jugendliche weltweit.

Das Hervorheben der entwicklungs- und friedensfördernden Wirkung des Sports in der Agenda 2030 stellt einen großartigen Erfolg für den Sektor Sport für Entwicklung im Allgemeinen dar und legitimiert überdies die Anstrengungen der mittlerweile mehr als 800 weltweit agierenden Organisationen in diesem Bereich auf globaler Ebene. Diese hohe politische Anerkennung und Bestätigung der Arbeit vieler kleiner und mittelgroßer Nichtregierungsorganisationen, welche Sport zum Erreichen der Nachhaltigkeitsziele einsetzen, ist gleichzeitig von hoher Bedeutung für diese, um Zugang zu den ohnehin wenigen Fördermitteln aus den Töpfen von Regierungen sowie anderen möglichen Geldgebern zur Finanzierung ihrer Projekte zu bekommen.

Umso mehr hat mich die am 4. Mai 2017 verkündete Entscheidung des neuen UN-Generalsekretärs António Guterres überrascht das Büro der Vereinten Nationen für Sport im Dienst von Entwicklung und Frieden infolge einer neuen, direkten Partnerschaft zwischen den Vereinten Nationen und dem Internationalen Olympischen Komitee zu schließen. Das UNOSDP führte seit seiner Entstehung im Jahr 2001 den globalen Diskurs zum Thema Sport für Entwicklung und Frieden an und verlieh diesem seine Existenzberechtigung, Legitimität und Glaubwürdigkeit auf höchster politischer Ebene im Kontext der internationalen Entwicklungszusammenarbeit. Es fungierte darüber hinaus als Sprachrohr für viele kleine, auf Basisebene agierende *Sport-für-Entwicklung*-Organisationen.

Insbesondere die Förderung von Projekten wie dem *UNOSDP Youth Leadership Programme* verlieh der Arbeit dieser Organisationen Wertschätzung und internationale Anerkennung. Das Interesse an einer Fortführung des *Youth Leadership Programmes* ist sowohl auf Seiten der Entsendeorganisationen von Teilnehmern als auch auf Seiten der Ausrichterstädte und Kooperationspartner nach wie vor eindeutig vorhanden und wächst ständig weiter. Erst Ende des Jahres 2016 wurde dies noch einmal durch die Unterzeichnung weiterer Absichtserklärungen mit verschiedenen Implementierungspartnern wie z. B. der englischen *Football Association* und den Veranstaltern des *Norway Cups* verdeutlicht. Für das Jahr 2017 waren bereits fünf weitere YLPs geplant. Ich setze mich daher ausdrücklich für eine Fortführung des *Youth Leadership Programmes* ein und hoffe, dass das IOC die Nachhaltigkeit dieses Projektes in der Zukunft sicherstellt.

Der Sektor Sport für Entwicklung und Frieden darf zukünftig nicht nur auf den Elitesport oder bestimmte Sportarten reduziert werden, sondern muss nach wie vor seine Existenzberichtigung auf der praktischen Arbeit der vielen, auf Basisebene erfolgreich operierenden Organisationen fundieren. Lassen Sie uns nicht den Fehler machen, das unglaubliche Verbreitungspotenzial dieser außerordentlich motivierten, vor allem jungen Menschen als Vorbilder in ihren Gemeinden zu ignorieren. Wir müssen diese Anführer von morgen weiter fördern, ihre Anstrengungen wertschätzen und ihnen die Möglichkeit zum Austausch von *Best-Practice*-Ansätzen geben, so dass der Sport auch in Zukunft weltweit einen wichtigen Beitrag zur sozialen Entwicklung und zu einem friedlichen Zusammenleben leisten kann.

Empowerment and Inclusion through Sport – A Universal Language

Marianne Meier
University of Bern

Gudrun Doll-Tepper would probably still agree with the statement made in 2004 by former UN Secretary General Kofi Annan who declared sport to be a universal language that brings people together. His conviction was also reflected in the UN Resolution 58/5 which labelled sport »as means to promote education, health, development and peace« (2003)[1]. The same resolution also paved the way for 2005 to be the *International Year of Sport and Physical Education (IYSPE)*.

Given Gudrun's outstanding career and multifaceted spectrum of involvement, this article is offering selected spotlights on some of her core working areas such as sport linked to development contexts, women in sport, empowerment, and inclusion – with no claim of being complete.

1 Sport in Crisis and Post-disaster Situations

Within the framework of the IYSPE, a conference held in Bad Boll, Germany, in February 2005 focussed on the opportunities and limits of sport for development from economic and cultural perspectives. At this occasion, the author of this article met Gudrun Doll-Tepper for the first time. This conference took place shortly after the disastrous Tsunami which had hit numerous parts of Southeast Asia. That is why many discussions dealt with the potential of sport providing relief and instilling hope in such disaster situations. Gudrun Doll-Tepper was convinced that sport has a role to play through rehabilitation measures and adequate interventions, thus providing new perspectives for the survivors.[2] With this mind-set, the first edition of the seminar *Communities and Crisis – Inclusive Development through Sport* was organised by ICSSPE in Rheinsberg, Germany,

---

1 See https://www.un.org/sport2005/resources/resolution.html (accessed 24-06-2017).
2 See http://www.bmw-berlin-marathon.com/news-und-media/news/2005/01/25/thomas-bach-und-gudrun-dolltepper-sport-soll-wiederaufbau-in-ueberflutungsgebieten-stuetzen.html (accessed 27-06-2017).

in 2007. Since then, eight other editions of this interactive international seminar were held; the most recent one in 2016. More than 450 participants from all over the world attended these seminars over the last decade gaining insights into the use of sport and physical activity for inclusive community building, particularly in areas affected by crisis. These kinds of crisis include natural disasters such as earthquakes and floods, as well as man-made crises like e.g. wars and vulnerable communities.[3] ICSSPE remained the main engine of *Communities and Crisis*, especially with regard to training opportunities for facilitators, and Gudrun Doll-Tepper was personally present in all those years to provide input.

Within the IYSPE framework 2015, she also promoted co-operation between key stakeholders with regard to post-disaster relief. Gudrun and ICSSPE were the driving forces to set up the project *Rehabilitation through Adapted Physical Activity and Sport in the Tsunami Affected Area of Southeast* Asia in Bangkok, supported by the German government.

In many of her presentations on the international scene, Gudrun demonstrated how sport reflects changes in society. Thereby she observed an increasing focus on opportunities for women, children and youth, ageing and elderly people, as well as persons with a disability. Despite the observed progress for women in sport, Gudrun emphasised that barriers still exist around the globe inhibiting female sport activity. Such inhibiting factors involved, for example, traditional gender roles, body image, and dress regulations. Therewith she described the multiple discrimination of women with a disability as additional barrier. Gudrun also talked about international initiatives that strive for more female participation in sport.[4] The following sub-chapter will provide a historic and institutional overview of some of these initiatives and movements.

2 Historic Overview of the *Women in Sport* Movement

Origins of the international *women in sport (WIS) movement* go back to 1949 when the *International Association of Physical Education and Sports for Girls*

---

3 See http://www.icsspe.org/content/communities-crisis-1 (accessed 24-06-2017).
4 Presentation held by Gudrun Doll-Tepper at the seminar ›Communities and Crisis‹ in Rheinsberg 2008.

and Women (IAPESGW)[5] was founded. On a regular basis, IAPESGW organises international networking meetings and scientific congresses mainly concentrating on sport-related topics taking a rather »middle-class, elitist character and white, western, educational and cultural hegemonic stance« (Hargreaves, 1999, p. 461). The first IAPESGW World Congress was held in Copenhagen in 1949. Since then, IAPESGW Congresses took place every four years in different countries and continents. The most recent 18th World Congress 2017 was held in Miami, USA, where IAPESGW committed to contribute to the UN *Sustainable Development Goals* (SDGs) for 2030, especially emphasising the SDGs on health and well-being, education as well as gender equality and empowerment.[6] The 19th consecutive IAPESGW Congress is scheduled for 2021 in Tokyo (Japan).

At the beginning of the 1970s, regulatory frameworks came into effect to foster female sport. A milestone in women's sport history was the famous *Title IX*, introduced in the USA. This 1972 revised *Education Amendments Act* guaranteed gender equality in the education sector and in all publicly funded federations. A major impact in Europe was reached in 1975 through the British *Sex Discrimination Act* (Eitzen, 1996).

The actual international *women in sport movement* emerged in the 1990s, but kept a rather conservative and elitist European, North American and Australian focus (Saavedra, 2005). However, these pioneers mainly worked on voluntary basis and steadily increased their international outreach. With the exception of IAPESGW, efforts to promote female sport in the early 1980s mainly focussed on regional or national levels. Influential players in this field were the *Canadian Association for the Advancement of Women and Sport and Physical Activity* (CAAWS)[7], founded in 1981 and the British Women's Sports Foundation (WSF)[8], established in 1984.

Although IAPESGW aimed at global memberships, it was difficult to reach out to women from *developing countries*, as for example, even members in some

---

5 See http://www.iapesgw.org/ (accessed 15-06-2017).
6 See http://www.iapesgw.org/ (accessed 24-06-2017).
7 See http://caaws.ca (accessed 08-06-2017).
8 See http://www.womenssportsfoundation.org/ (accessed 08-06-2017).

African countries, seemed to be privileged women. This led to an increasing dissatisfaction of women who wanted to address global gender and sport issues with a more critical approach. Out of these motives, a new organisation called *Women Sport International* (WSI)[9] was launched in 1994 (White, 1997; Hargreaves, 1999), perceiving themselves as a »global voice of research-based advocacy for women and sport«. WSI furthermore openly tackled, among other topics, *sensitive issues* such as homophobia or sexual harassment in sport.[10]

The 1994 Brighton Conference in the United Kingdom was the starting point for the famous *Brighton Declaration on Women and Sport*. This key document claimed »equality for women in sport throughout the world embodying a visionary sporting culture that would enable and value the full involvement of women in every aspect of sport« (Hargreaves, 1999, p. 465). Thereby, it paved the way for female sport to appear on political and institutional agendas also in places like Egypt and the Caribbean, and of federations like the IOC (White, 1997). Another Brighton outcome was the establishment of the *International Working Group on Women and Sport* (IWG) which committed inter alia to organise quadrennial *World Conferences on Women and Sport*. The vision of the IWG is »a sustainable sporting culture based on gender equality that enables and values the full involvement of girls and women in every aspect of sport and physical activity«.[11]

After Brighton, the 2nd IWG *World Conference* was held in Namibia in 1998 producing the *Windhoek Call for Action* which went beyond pushing for women's participation in sport and promoted sport as a means of achieving broader goals in health, education, elimination of violence and human rights. The *Montreal Tool-kit* was the output of the 3rd edition in Canada in 2002. This practice-oriented instrument is valuable to integrate sport within community development projects, health information campaigns, etc. (White & Scoretz, 2002). The 4th IWG Conference entitled *Participating in Change* took place in Kumamoto, Japan, in 2006, assembling 700 delegates. The legacy of the 5th *World Conference* in Australia in 2010 was the *Sydney Scoreboard* which claimed an »increase [of]

---

9 See http://www.sportsbiz.bz/womensportinternational (accessed 08-06-2017).
10 See http://www.sportsbiz.bz/womensportinternational (accessed 08-06-2017).
11 See http://www.iwg-gti.org (accessed 14-06-2017).

women's representation on sport boards globally«.[12] The 20th birthday of the Brighton Conference and its Declaration was celebrated in Helsinki, Finland, in 2014 together with 800 participants following the theme *Lead the Change, Be the Change*.[13] The 7th IWG World Conference is scheduled for 2018 in Gaborone, Botswana.

Next to these international initiatives, there have been also regional events organised by groups such as the *European Women and Sport* (EWS) and the *Asian Women and Sport* (AWS). In 2005, Gudrun Doll-Tepper attended the 3rd AWS Conference in Sanaa and contributed to the *Yemen Challenge* which advocated for an increased collaboration between the Olympic movement and the AWS for the promotion of women's rights.

The Mexican hurdler Enriqueta Basilio Sotel was the first woman entitled to light the 1968 Olympic Cauldron in Mexico-City with the Olympic flame.[14] Despite this powerful symbol, providing women access to organisational structures and leadership positions of the Olympic movement was a long haul. Only in 1981 the first two women were nominated as IOC members. More than thirty years later, in 2014, only twenty-four out of one hundred six IOC members were female. In 1990, the first woman was elected into the Executive Board, and in 1997 the first female IOC Vice-President was appointed (IOC, 2016). Currently, only four out of fifteen members of the IOC Executive Board are women (IOC, 2016). A milestone was set in 1995, when the *Women and Sport Working Group* was established, which was finally transformed into an official Commission in 2004. Gudrun Doll-Tepper accepted an invitation by IOC President Jacques Rogge in 2008 to join this *Women and Sport Commission*.[15] Many women in sport organisations accelerated and influenced this process through activism (White, 1997; Hargreaves, 1999). A major break-through happened in 1996 when advocacy for female sport was actually included in the Olympic Charter: »The IOC strongly

---

12 See http://www.sydneyscoreboard.com (accessed 14-06-2017).
13 See http://iwg-gti.org/common_up/iwg-new/files/Helsinki-calls-the-world-of-sport-to-LEAD-THE-CHANGE-BE-THE-CHANGE(1).pdf (accessed 14-06-2017).
14 See http://www.olympic.org/ioc (accessed 14-06-2017).
15 See http://www.germanroadraces.de/24-1-4705-prof-dolltepper-joins-ioc-women-and-sport.html (accessed 28-05-2017).

encourages, by appropriate means, the promotion of women in sport at all levels and in all structures, particularly in the executive bodies of national and international sports organizations with a view to the strict application of the principle of equality of men and women« (1996, p. 10).

Parallel to IAPESGW's and IWG's events, the IOC between 1996 and 2012 organised five world conferences on women and sport. Thereby, the main objective was »to analyse the progress made in this field within the Olympic Movement and to define a prioritised line of action to improve and increase the participation of women in sport« (IOC, 2011, p. 3). The first IOC gathering was held in Lausanne (1996) followed by conferences in Paris (2000), Marrakech (2004), Jordan (2008), and Los Angeles (2012). The conference in Jordan was held under the Patronage of King Abdullah II and Queen Rania with more than 600 delegates from NOCs, Organising Committees of Olympic Games, UN agencies and (non-)governmental organisations (IOC & NOC Jordan, 2008). Gudrun Doll-Tepper joined the IOC *Women and Sport Commission* after the Jordan Conference in 2008 and commented: »Instead of declarations, it's important to have concrete action plans to ensure gender equality in all areas of the Olympic Movement. We have committed to have a mandatory requirement for National Olympic Committees to have women on their Executive Boards, as well as to support the development of female sport journalists who can bring in another perspective on sport in their media reports.«[16]

In terms of the IOC, the number of women who are chairing commissions is slowly increasing, but still at a low level. Today, only seven out of twenty-six IOC commissions have female chairs.[17] In 2015 Gudrun Doll-Tepper also joined the *Commission* for *Olympic Education* with addresses youth education through sport.[18]

One of the first results of Thomas Bach's IOC presidency was the launch of the *Agenda 2020* in 2014 which represents the strategic roadmap for the Olympic movement. The 11th recommendation adresses *gender equality*. Despite this ex-

---

16 See http://www.germanroadraces.de/24-1-4705-prof-dolltepper-joins-ioc-women-and-sport.html (accessed 21-06-2017).

17 See https://www.olympic.org/women-in-sport/background/statistics (accessed 21-06-2017).

18 See https://www.olympic.org/olympic-education-commission (accessed 21-06-2017).

plicit statement, the two proposed measures remain rather vague and superficial: »The IOC to work with the International Federations to achieve 50 percent female participation in the Olympic Games and to stimulate women's participation and involvement in sport by creating more participation opportunities at the Olympic Games«. The second suggestion promotes »the inclusion of mixed-gender team events«.[19]

However, *Agenda 2020* enabled considerable progress in terms of human rights by strengthening the 6th Fundamental Principle of Olympism: The IOC finally included non-discrimination based on *sexual orientation*. The incidents linked to homophobia related to the 2014 Sochi Olympic Winter Games, for example, have demonstrated the need for such an amendment (Lenskyj, 2014; Van Rheenen, 2014).

At the end of the day, *Agenda 2020* will only be valuable and the IOC credible, if the words on paper are implemented and monitored for real. This implies more transparency in the future and would, for example, also include cooperation with independent research institutions necessitating unlimited access to data linked to Olympic Games (Coakley & Souza, 2013).

Continuing to be European based and active in certain advocacy domains, new players appeared in the WIS landscape over the recent years with innovative organisational concepts. One of them is *Women Win*, founded in 2007 which uses »sport as a strategy to advance women's rights«.[20] Next to organisations that support female sport activities mainly through global advocacy, national initiatives – especially in development settings – are of utmost importance. The Zambian *National Organisation for Women in Sport, Physical Activity and Recreation* (NOWSPAR)[21] is an example of regional and nation-wide advocacy and activism.

Summing up, the international WIS movement started almost seven decades ago and substantially gained momentum from the *Brighton Conference* in 1994

---

19 See https://stillmed.olympic.org/Documents/Olympic_Agenda_2020/Olympic_Agenda_2020-20-20_Recommendations-ENG.pdf (accessed 24-06-2017).
20 See http://www.womenwin.org (accessed 14-06-2017).
21 See http://www.nowspar.org (accessed 14-06-2017).

until today. In addition to various national organisations and initiatives as well as global efforts by IAPESGW, WSI, the IWG and subsequently the IOC, are promising for female sport enhancement around the world. However, two major concerns still need to be tackled: First of all, there are parallel cycles of international conferences striving for the same cause. On the one hand, this accumulated efforts lead to the fact that the common issue *women and sport* is constantly on the agenda somewhere in the world with specific thematic priorities. On the other hand, the existing substance and power of this international movement and its key messages are diluted. Thus, some individuals believe that the full potential of combined and well-managed international strategies remains untapped.

Another concern relates to sender-recipient relationships in the context of specific target groups. Who is promoting opportunities and addressing risks for whom? Is envisaged *empowerment* of others not a contradiction in terms? Saavedra emphasised that »WIS is rooted in the development of women's sport, and not primarily in women and development through sport« (2005, p. 3). Even though more and more conferences are taking place, fostering participation from the *Global South,* marginalised people from the grassroots level are often insufficiently involved. Those representatives of *developing countries* who can afford to spend leisure time away from family duties often belong to the social elite or at least middle-class (Hargreaves, 1999). Despite recent efforts, many actors of the WIS movement – who mostly work on voluntary basis – still follow *Western* patterns of reasoning and operating. Howsoever, a more fundamental structural and strategic change would require specialised knowledge and additional resources that exceed the possibilities of these voluntary organisations.

Meanwhile, reliable partnerships with like-minded entities and individuals in *developing countries* – including local stakeholders from academia, sport federations, NGOs, governments, etc. – need to be built and strengthened. Such a local embeddedness is essential to assure ownership and sustainability.

3 Gender Empowerment

Empowerment is one of Gudrun's favourite words. The term is used in various fields such as social work, education, sports science, psychology, economics, politics, and development cooperation. Despite broad international approval and application, explicit definitions of *empowerment* remain vague. Kabeer describes the use of the notion as »bewildering (...), from the mundane to the profound, from the particular to the very general« (1999, p. 2). Discourse on *empowerment* commonly adopts a sectoral approach in terms of economic, social, political or cultural empowerment (Luttrell et al., 2009), but this concept transcends this basic structure and »can help to focus thought, planning, and action in development« (Rowlands, 1995, p. 106).

An immediate association between *empowerment* and gender issues is very common. Some major development agencies and organisations such as SIDA[22] or USAID, use the term *empowerment* exclusively for gender topics (Luttrell et al., 2009). However, this article supports a holistic concept that is not automatically related to female *empowerment*, but may apply to any person who is, for example, unemployed, illiterate, abused, living in poverty or with a disability. Generally speaking, *empowerment* aims at strengthening and further developing existing resources. It calls upon the development potential through personal responsibility of human beings who are disadvantaged, neglected or deprived for whatever reason. One commonly shared perception of *empowerment* is the strong focus on a resource-oriented perspective and rejection of a deficit-oriented approach. Thus, with regard to female *empowerment*, one crucial feature is the rejection of traditional images of women and girls as incomplete *victims by nature* and weakened by deficits (Herriger, 2006). This approach has been nurtured by a recent ideological shift in psychology that is contemporarily focussing on *positive psychology-building strengths* rather than amendable deficiencies and weaknesses (Gould & Carson, 2008, p. 58).

According to UNIFEM & UNGC (2010) *empowerment* »is both a process and an outcome«. This hybrid approach is very important as it does directly affect the planning and management of any intervention. Moreover, the status of *being fully empowered* is by definition never completely accomplished, as it does involve a lifelong learning process. *Empowerment* defined by UNIFEM & UNGC means that »people – both women and men – can take control over their lives: set their own agendas, gain skills (or have their own skills and knowledge recognised), increase self-confidence, solve problems, and develop self-reliance« (2010, p. 9).

---

22 The ›Swedish International Development Cooperation Agency‹.

Another relevant *empowerment trait* is its interdependence of individual, collective and societal levels, thus dissolving the idea of unilaterally driven *outside* in or *top down* approaches (Rowlands, 1995).

Despite a broad acceptance of the transformational implications of *empowerment* (Sen & Grown, 1985; Batliwala, 1994; Kabeer, 2001; Bisnath, 2001; Malhotra et al., 2002; Mosedale, 2003), its *Northern* strategic targets have been criticised by feminist activists from the *Global South*. This discontent led to the establishment of the network DAWN (mid-1980s) which finally articulated the needs of poor women in developing regions and reshaped the *empowerment* discourse. Considering these indigenous voices, Moser (1993) differentiated between *practical gender needs* and *strategic gender needs* in her influential book *Gender planning and development*. While practical needs refer to prescribed gender roles (being a wife, mother, etc.), strategic gender needs may challenge existing unbalanced power relations. Thus, Moser's approach combines both needs by utilising the practical needs »as the basis on which to build a secure support base, and as a means through which strategic needs may be reached« (1993, p. 77).

The *empowerment approach* – elaborated by scholars, politicians, feminists, and NGO activists from the *Global South* – acknowledged the existence of female oppression, but emphasised »that oppression of women takes a variety of forms and different power hierarchies subordinate women simultaneously«. Depending on geography, politics, ethnicity, age, etc. experiences of discrimination and/or oppression can happen differently and coincidentally. Women living in poverty, for example, primarily need food, shelter, water, etc. This struggle which many people in developing contexts are facing every day, has been »historically (…) discarded as non-feminist as their actions do not challenge the power relations that subordinates them as women« (Kvinnoforum, 2001, p. 22). Thus, claiming a compulsory and substantial transformation linked to *empowerment* relates to an ethnocentric *Northern* or *Western* ideology that ignores the bitter reality of poverty.

Related to the development setting and the *Millennium Development Goals* (MDGs) which were envisaged until 2015, Grown et al. stated that »the concept of *empowerment* is related to gender equality but distinct from it. The core of *empowerment* lies in the ability of a woman to control her own destiny« (2005, p. 33). This claim involves much more than access to resources and participation (Oxaal & Baden, 1997; Kabeer, 1999; Malhotra et al., 2002; Mosedale, 2003). This means that »to be empowered women must not only have equal capabilities (such as education and health) and equal access to resources and opportunities (such as land and employment), but they must also have the agency to use those rights, capabilities, resources, and opportunities to make strategic choices and decisions (such as is provided through leadership opportunities and participation in political institutions). And for them to exercise agency, they must live without the fear of coercion and violence« (Grown et al., 2005, p. 33).

Even though the goal *gender equality and the empowerment of women* was notably represented in the MDGs, the 2010 evaluation report stated – despite many efforts – that »progress has been sluggish on all fronts – from education to access to political decision-making« (UN, 2010, p. 4). In the new millennium, most influential entities such as e.g. the World Bank explicitly identified »gender equality [as] a core development issue – a development objective in its own right« (2001, p. 1). It seems that this topic found its way from marginalised arenas to the central stage, but persistent critical queries from scholars, media, practitioners, and policy-makers are necessary to move beyond slogans, romanticism, political correctness, window-dressing, and marketing strategies. The UN Sustainable Development Goals (SDGs) and its Development Agenda 2030 succeeded the MDGs in 2015. Gender and *empowerment* are – particularly (SDG 5) and transversally – solidly embedded in the 17 SDGs and its targets. Paragraph 37 of the SDGs declaration even mentions *sport* explicitly as »an important enabler of sustainable development«. Moreover, it specifies the »growing contribution of sport to the realization of development and peace in its promotion of tolerance and respect and the contributions it makes to the empowerment of women and of young people, individuals and communities as well as to health, education and social inclusion objectives«.[23] This can be considered a major milestone, but again, governments, sport governing bodies, and all other international stakeholders need to walk the talk and live up to their promises.

---

23 See http://www.un.org/en/ga/search/view_doc.asp?symbol=A/RES/70/1 (accessed 10-07-2017).

4 Sport as an Inclusive Pedagogical Tool

Inclusiveness and participation are main characteristics of sport and development (S&D) programmes. They should reach out to anybody who wants to be involved regardless of demographics and abilities. Thus, the term *development* does not only refer to economically deprived and socially marginalised locations, but means human development in its broadest sense involving individual, community, and societal levels. Promising S&D programmes strive for human development which is defined by Flammer as »sustainable alterations of competences« (2009, p. 22). From a humanitarian and educational perspective, S&D interventions which involve, for example, a systematic talent scouting for elite sport as a *spin-off product* are worrisome. This social Darwinistic approach of fostering performance clashes with the core concepts of S&D such as participation, cooperation, and inclusion. The sport pedagogical concept of *multiple perspectivity* forms the basis of any S&D activity. Tackling gridlocked structures and perceptions, this concept claims that human motives for being physically active transcend excellence and performance (Kurz, 1995). Additional motivational interpretations of sport activities involve health, experience or adventure, expression, suspense as well as a sense of belonging and community (Kuhlmann, 2006). Thereby, the main focus lays on *development through sport* by using sport as a vehicle for human development. This approach contrasts with *development of sport* that mainly targets sport skills, culture, and infrastructure. Rather than concentrating on one approach, ideal sport interventions should strive for a complementary *double mandate* that combines *education towards sport* – in the sense of *sport culture*, and promoting lifelong physical activity – and *education through sport*. This *multiple perspectivity* approach does not exclude the support and promotion of talented young athletes who want to compete, but acknowledges the fact that this is only one out of several focus areas. From a pedagogical perspective, sport activities are of utmost value, if knowledge and skills are systematically interwoven with general education in terms of personality development (Prohl, 2010). Basically, claiming such a *double mandate* is relevant regardless of different socio-cultural contexts, but of course with altered emphases.

This *double mandate* also implies an inclusive approach. Gudrun Doll-Tepper was in numerous positions in which she advocated for *inclusion* among many other topics. She served inter alia as President of the *International Federation of Adapted Physical Activity* (IFAPA) and acted as chairperson of the *International*

Paralympic Committee Sports Science Committee (IPC SSC).[24] On a political level, considerable progress was made at the 5th UNESCO International Conference of Ministers and Senior Officials Responsible for Physical Education and Sport (MINEPS V) held in Berlin in 2013. Gudrun Doll-Tepper presented the results of the expert commission *Access to Sport as a Fundamental Right for All*. Thereby, she clearly mentioned that access to sport for girls and women and persons with disabilities should be emphasised. Gudrun took the opportunity in front of this high-profile audience to recall the importance of the following four legal documents: The UNESCO International Charter of Physical Education and Sport, the UN Convention on the Elimination of all forms of Discrimination against Women (CEDAW), the UN Convention on the Rights of the Child, and the UN Convention on the Rights of Persons with Disabilities.[25] At the end of the day, the governments need to ratify, implement, and monitor progress linked to these key documents to really enable each and every person to benefit from the potential sport and physical activity have to offer. Development also depends on political will and decisions, whether appropriate measures are taken to facilitate access to sport both in schools and recreational settings.

In an interview with Ken Black[26], Gudrun mentioned participation, opportunity, and free choice of the individual as key aspects with regard to sport and inclusion. Referring to the educational sector, Gudrun stated: »Since we have the UN Convention on the Rights of Persons with Disabilities, we are now trying to change our school system so that children with disabilities have an opportunity to participate in regular schools which also means in regular physical education. It's a dramatic change in the philosophy. We don't separate these young people anymore. We really give them the opportunity to participate like anybody else with choices, and this is not only true for the education system but for all areas in society, including sport.«[27]

---

24 See https://d1wjxwc5zmlmv4.cloudfront.net/fileadmin/downloads/2013/WHS_2013/CVs/Doll-Tepper_Gudrun_CV.pdf (accessed 11-07-2017).
25 See http://mineps2013.de (accessed 11-07-2017).
26 Ken Black is initiator of ›The Inclusion Club‹, see http://theinclusionclub.com (accessed 11-07-2017).
27 See https://www.icsspe.org/content/gudrun-doll-tepper-sport-and-inclusion (accessed 06-07-2017).

5 Closing Words

Besides the many prestigious *hats* she is wearing and the hard work linked to sport, inclusion, adapted physical activity, gender, and empowerment, Gudrun remains a sport fan delighted by athletes' passion, fair-play, and emotions. Personally invited by the influential Eunice Kennedy-Shriver, she attended her first Special Olympics World Games 1983 in Baton Rouge (USA). Since then, she visited this event at various occasions. Witnessing the Special Olympics 2015 in Los Angeles, USA, more than thirty years after her first attendance, Gudrun was still impressed and touched by the opening ceremony, the professional organisation, and the engagement of the large number of volunteers.[28]

With her academic work and numerous positions on international boards, she paved the way for substantial structural change. At the same time, she never lost touch with *the ground*. She always had and still has an authentic interest and fascination for the athletes and continues to celebrate their diversity around the globe. Over many decades, Gudrun's enthusiasm, care, and energy increased the quality of many lives in many ways. But there is still work to be done… Thank you!

References

Batliwala, S. (1994). The Meaning of Women's Empowerment: New Concepts from Action. In G. Sen, A. Germain, & L. C. Chen (Eds.), *Population Policies Reconsidered: Health, Empowerment and Rights* (pp. 127–138). Boston: Harvard University Press.

Bisnath, S. (2001). *Globalization, poverty and women's empowerment*, United Nations Division of the Advancement of Women (DAW), from http://www.un.org/womenwatch/daw/csw/empower/documents/Bisnath-EP3.pdf (accessed 05-07-2017).

Coakley, J., & Souza, D. L. (2013). Sport mega-events: Can legacies and development be equitable and sustainable? *Motriz: Revista de Educacao Física, 19*(3), pp. 580–589.

Eitzen, S. D. (1996). *Sport in contemporary society. An Anthology*. New York: St. Martin's Press.

---

28 http://specialolympics.de/aktuelles/alle/2015/07/doll-tepper-emotionen-und-leidenschaft-der-athleten-sind-einmalig/ (accessed 06-07-2017).

Flammer, A. (2009). *Entwicklungstheorien. Psychologische Theorien der menschlichen Entwicklung*, 4th ed., Bern: Verlag Hans Huber.

Gould, D., & Carson, S. (2008). Life skills development through sport: current status and future directions. *International Review of Sport and Exercise Psychology, 1*(1), pp. 58–78.

Grown, K., Gupta, G.R., & Kes, A. (2005). *Taking Action: Achieving Gender Equality and Empowering Women*. Task Force on Education and Gender Equality, UN Millennium Project, London/Sterling Va.: Earthscan.

Hargreaves, J. (1999). The ›Women's International Sports Movement‹: Local-Global Strategies and Empowerment. *Women's Studies International Forum, 22*(5), pp. 461–471.

Herriger, N. (2006). *Empowerment in der Sozialen Arbeit. Eine Einführung*. 3rd ed., Stuttgart: Kohlhammer-Verlag.

International Olympic Committee (1996). *Olympic Charter*, from: https://stillmed.olympic.org/Documents/Olympic%20Charter/Olympic_Charter_through_time/1996-Olympic_Charter.pdf (accessed 11-07-2017).

International Olympic Committee (2011). *Women in the Olympic Movement*. Olympic Studies Centre, Lausanne/Switzerland: IOC.

International Olympic Committee (2016). *Factsheet Women in the Olympic Movement Update – January 2016*, from https://stillmed.olympic.org/Documents/Reference_documents_Factsheets/Women_in_Olympic_Movement.pdf (accessed 14-06-2017).

International Olympic Committee, & National Olympic Committee of Jordan (2008). *Report on 4th World Conference on Women and Sport ›Sport as a Vehicle for Social Change‹*. Dead Sea/Jordan: International Cooperation and Development Department.

Kabeer, N. (1999). *The Conditions and Consequences of Choice: Reflections on the Measurement of Women's Empowerment*. UNRISD Discussion Paper No. 108, Geneva: UNRISD.

Kabeer, N. (2001). Resources, Agency, Achievements: Reflections on the Measurement of Women's Empowerment. In Sida, *Discussing Women's Empowerment: Theory and Practice*. Stockholm: SIDA, pp. 17–57.

Kuhlmann, D. (2006). Welche besonderen Möglichkeiten bietet die Sache? Sport im weiteren Sinne. In Balz, E., & Kuhlmann, D. (Eds.), *Sportpädagogik. Ein Lehrbuch in 14 Lektionen, 1*, 2nd ed. (pp. 81–96). Aachen: Meyer & Meyer.

Kurz, D. (1995). Handlungsfähigkeit im Sport – Leitidee eines mehrperspektivischen Unterrichtskonzepts. In Zeuner et al. (Eds.), *Sport unterrichten – Anspruch und Wirklichkeit* (pp. 41–48). St. Augustin: Academia.

Kvinnoforum/Foundation of Women's Forum (2001). *Measuring Women's Empowerment*. Report on a pilot project on methods for measuring women's empowerment in Southern Africa, partnering with Organisation of Rural Associations for Progress in Zimbabwe, Namibia National Association of Women in Business, Women's NGO Coalition in Botswana, Community Development Foundation in Mozambique, New York: UNDP.

Lenskyj, H. (2014). *Sexual diversity and the Sochi 2014 Olympics: No more rainbows*. Basingstoke: Palgrave Macmillan.

Luttrell, C., Quiroz, S., Scrutton, C., & Bird, K. (2009). *Understanding and operationalising empowerment*. Results of ODI research presented in preliminary form for discussion and critical comment, Working Paper 308, London: Overseas Development Institute.

Malhotra, A., Schuler, S. R., & Boender, C. (2002). *Measuring Women's Empowerment as a Variable in International Development*. Background Paper Prepared for the World Bank Workshop on Poverty and Gender: New Perspectives, from http://siteresources.worldbank.org/INTGENDER/Resources/MalhotraSchulerBoender.pdf (accessed 02-07-2017).

Mosedale, S. (2003). *Towards A Framework For Assessing Empowerment, Impact Assessment Research Centre*. Working Paper Series, No. 3, Paper prepared for conference ›New Directions in Impact Assessment for Development: Methods and Practice‹ in Manchester/UK, November 2003, Manchester UK: Institute for Development Policy and Management.

Moser, C.O.N. (1993). *Gender planning and development: theory, practice, and training*. London: Routledge.

Oxaal, Z., & Baden, S. (1997). *Gender and empowerment: definitions, approaches and implications for policy*. BRIDGE development – gender, Report No. 40, Brighton: Institute for Development Studies, University of Sussex.

Prohl, R. (2010). *Grundriss der Sportpädagogik*. 3. Aufl., Wiebelsheim: Limpert Verlag.

Rowlands, J. (1995). Empowerment examined. *Development in Practice*, 5(2), pp. 101–107.

Saavedra, M. (2005). *Women, sport and development, International Platform on Sport and Development.* from https://www.sportanddev.org/sites/default/files/downloads/56__women__sport_and_development.pdf (accessed 05-07-2017).

Sen, G., & Grown, C. (1985). *Development, Crisis, and Alternative Visions: Third World Women's Perspectives.* New Dehli: Development Alternatives with Women for a New Era (DAWN).

UN (2010). *The Millennium Development Goals.* Report 2010, New York: United Nations Department of Economic and Social Affairs (DESA).

UNIFEM, & UNGC (2010). *Women's Empowerment Principles: Equality means business.* New York: UNIFEM.

Van Rheenen, D. (2014). A skunk at the garden party: the Sochi Olympics, state-sponsored homophobia and prospects for human rights through mega sporting events. *Journal of Sport & Tourism, 19*(2), pp. 127–144.

White, A. (1997). *The growth of the international women and sport movement.* In Proceedings of The Second Scientific International Conference for Woman's Sport: Woman and Child, a Future Vision from a Sport Perspective (pp. 3–11). Alexandria/Egypt: University of Alexandria.

White, A., & Scoretz, D. (2002). *From Windhoek to Montreal.* Women and Sport Progress Report 1998–2002, International Working Group on Women and Sport (IWG).

World Bank (2001). *Engendering Development: Through Gender Equality in Rights, Resources, and Voice.* World Bank Policy Research Report, Oxford: Oxford University Press.

Olympic Education: History, Theory and Practice

Roland Naul and Deanna Binder
Willibald Gebhardt Research Institute and Education Design International

Section 1: Historical Roots and Contemporary Concepts of Olympic Education

Although the term Olympic Education only has a historical record of less than 50 years, pedagogical aims and objectives linked with Olympic Education can be dated back more than 200 years to the early time of Johann Christoph Friedrich GutsMuths and his philanthropic boarding school in Schnephenthal (Thuringia) and to his famous education book *Gymnastic for Youth* (1793; 1804) published in German and translated into all leading world languages at that time in only one decade. Interestingly, GutsMuth already demanded in his renewal of a balanced education of body and mind in reference to Greek antiquity:

»Our gymnastics adheres closely to the culture of the intellect; walks harmoniously hand in hand with it and thereby ideally resembles the pedagogical skills that were practised by the young men in the Academy of Athens« (GutsMuths, 1804, p. 176).

Of course, the inauguration of the Olympic Games one century later with the Olympic Congress at Paris in 1894 was another important step which designed the roadmap for Olympic Education. All members of the first International Olympic Committee were either involved as skilled teachers in school-based education of young people (Guth-Jarkovski, Kemeny) or worked as officers in military academies (Balk in Stockholm; Boutovski in St. Petersburg) to physically train future military personal and gymnastic teachers. Also, the Greek and first IOC President, Dimitrios Vikelas, as well as Pierre de Coubertin himself became strong supporters of games and sports for young people to reform secondary schools in their countries before and after the year 1900. Very often and until today this linked educational part is unknown as the real backside of the Olympic Games movement. It took some years when Pierre de Coubertin himself evaluated the development and outcome of the early Olympic Games Movement in his well known, so called *Lausanne Olympic letters*, published in the newspaper La Gazette in 1918. Coubertin assessed:

»The Olympic pedagogy which I recently said was based at once on the cult of effort combined on the cult of eurhythmy – and consequently on the love of excess combined with the love of moderation – is not sufficiently served by being glorified before the world once every four years in the Olympic Games. It needs permanent factories. The Olympic factory for the ancient world was the gymnasium. The Olympiads have been renewed, but the gymnasium of antiquity has not – as yet. It must be.« (Coubertin, 2000, p. 217).

This demand for the reestablishment of the antique gymnasium fits perfectly into the former position of GutsMuths. But surprisingly, for his IOC members but consequently for himself, Coubertin left his office as IOC President at the Olympic Congress in Prague 1925 and directed his interest and further working activities to rebuild this modern type of the gymnasium in his last ten years of life. Arnd Krüger (2009) documented in detail Coubertin's pedagogical efforts including his different steps and committees he set up to realise – after his successful inauguration of the Olympic Games – also his inauguration of the gymnasium of modern time – it should be established in each town and community. In the late 1920s and early 1930s all efforts by Coubertin and his supporters failed to set up this type of an Olympic gymnasium in Greece. The *International Olympic Institute* established only after Coubertin's death as a testimony of him at Berlin (1938–1943) may be assessed as an early version of this kind of gymnasium. It was headed by Carl Diem for some years. However, it was Carl Diem himself again who became active with his friend Ketseas after World War II to build up an International Olympic Academy (IOA) in Ancient Olympia with support of the IOC. Finally, the IOA started its educational purpose and teaching with different efforts to spread the Olympic idea to the youth of the world after 1961 (Georgiadis, 1995; Müller, 1995).

Section 2: German Contributions to the Development of Olympic Education

From the early days of the Olympic Movement educational principles of the Olympic idea were promoted in Germany. A first impulse was already set by Dr Willibald Gebhardt in 1904 in his talk on *The Olympic movement and the schools*, just before the St. Louis Olympic Games. Gebhardt (1904) recommended physical and moral education through sports, and teaching healthy lifestyles with good nutrition and avoiding alcohol and tobacco intake. He demanded regular physical health measurements at schools and daily physical exercises in the afternoon in fresh air as a part of health education. However, there was no impact of his ideas in real school life before WWI. With the curriculum shift in German physical education from *Spieß-gymnastics* into *Austrian natural gymnastics* in the 1920s, a reform decade started. It included a variety of games and sports at school which gave a belated impact of Gebhardt's reform ideas when some reform schools implemented daily physical activities, and some measurements about the positive outcome were reported, not restricted to motor performances but also about cognitive function of daily young school gymnasts (Rosenbaum & Schulze, 1928).

A first impact after Gebhardt's vision on Olympic Education development became visible with the Berlin Olympic Games in 1936. First brochures and booklets were published to help children and adolescents at school to become acquainted with some historical developments of the Olympic movement, types and records of different sports and games. After WW II, it was the German Olympic Society (DOG) which started the propagation of educational materials related to the Olympic ideals in the early 1950s. From 1952 up to the Olympics in 1964 the DOG produced film documentations about each of the Olympic Games with special emphasis on the pedagogical aims of the Olympic Movement to be presented in schools and sport clubs.

Schools in the state of Bavaria (where Munich is located) picked up the topic of the Munich Olympic Games (1972) and a famous German publishing house for school books published a first text book with a selection of poems and short writings of sports and the Olympics from famous authors. It was a few years earlier (1966) when the West German Olympic Committee (NOK=NOC) became active in educational matters related to the Olympic Games.

The term *Olympic Education* goes back to Norbert Müller, a well-known German Olympic historian, who published a first article with the topic of *Olympic Education* in German (Müller, 1975). However, the real turning point was the International Olympic Congress of Baden-Baden in 1981 when Willi Daume, the President of the West German NOC, launched the idea to establish an official sub-committee (Kuratorium Olympische Akademie und Olympische Erziehung) which served as an informal National Olympic Academy (NOA) dedicated to Olympic Education. In spring 1988 this committee published a first small booklet on the topic and purpose of the Seoul Olympic Games with educational tasks in different school subjects. From the year 1988 onwards up to the shift of this committee into the German National

Olympic Academy (2007) school materials were produced for each Olympic Games (Naul, 2007, pp. 93–100). These materials were published for ages 6 to 12 years and focused on an enlarged concept of Olympic Education, including the history of the ancient and modern Olympic Games movement, facts and findings about the German part and contribution to the Games movement, including relevant information about the respective country and city which was hosting the Olympic Games. But the real breakthrough for Olympic Education, in terms of academic concepts, teaching studies at higher learning institutes of physical education and sport science as well as teaching at primary and secondary schools, started in the 1990s after the so called *German unification in sports and the Olympic movement*. Another item for this development was the reestablishment of an Olympic Institute in Berlin, the German Olympic Institute (DOI), which opened doors in 1993 but was dismantled in 2006/07 before the new German Olympic Academy was founded and named after Willi Daume. Now for about 10 years, Gudrun Doll-Tepper is the President of this German Olympic Academy Willi Daume.

Section 3: Olympic Education – International Concepts

After early attempts in Russia (Stolyarov & Rodichenko, 2017), Canada (Binder, 2017) and Germany (Naul et al., 2017) in the late 1980s, the early 1990s welcomed the real beginning of academic discussion on various Olympic Education concepts in Germany and other countries and in particular with the different working sessions at the International Olympic Academy at Olympia (Naul, 2010, pp. 64). The school-based publications of the German NOC Education Commission, which continued after the first release in 1988, were developed with a typical *knowledge-oriented* approach (Naul, 2010, pp. 117), focusing on the ancient and modern Olympic Games, with international and national highlights, including dates and facts about the German contribution as well as first text materials published in Russia and Canada at that time. This concept was launched by many other National Olympic Academies (NOA) world-wide and it still is the most popular concept of Olympic Education to this date (Binder & Naul, 2017).

This concept changed slightly in Germany in the 1990s up to the year 2000. Ommo Grupe (1993, 1997) with his references to Coubertin and Carl Diem's works identified five tasks as objectives of an Olympic pedagogy. He set targets as Olympic objectives for general sport education to achieve (cultural tasks for school sports): the unity of the body, will and mind for a balanced, harmonious development; striving for self-perfection, ideal of amateurism, sports commitment to ethical rules and principles like fairness and chivalry, and the contribution of the Games to promote the idea of peace. Norbert Müller (1998), who served as a chairperson of the German NOC Education Commission between 1988 and 1998, picked up Grupe's aims and objectives but in recent years after his final publication of the collection of writings of Pierre de Coubertin (2000) he strived for a different approach of Olympic Education. Müller reshaped his concept (2004, 2006) by a clear historical reference to Pierre de Coubertin's principles of Olympism including principles of *religio athletae*, idea of peace and the principle of eurhythmics. This second concept of Müller highlights activities such as inter-cultural meetings and exchanges and the dimension of beauty as components of Olympic education. When Müller left the NOC Education Commission his further interest focused on the development of a global school network on Olympic Education in the spirit of Coubertin's Olympism – the Pierre de Coubertin School Network (Nikolaus, 2014).

Another concept of Olympic Education occurred in the 1990s with Rolf Geßmann (1992, 2002) in Germany. He emphasised the so-called *physical achievement approach*, and described Olympic Education as a part of teaching physical education. His approach focused on *performance*, *fair play*, and *respect* and the overlapping of these principles as the focus for the purpose and objective of Olympic Education. Olympic Education for Geßmann was limited to personal, continuing efforts to strive for the best individual record of physical performance in sports, based on fair play behaviour and respect of the opponent. The opponent is needed as a person for the individual to strive against for the best personal outcome in exercise and competition. For Geßmann just doing any sports without continuous training for the individual's best record has nothing to do with the message of Olympic values. Aspiration to improve as much as possible in physical terms is the baseline of this concept because psycho-social values of fair play and respect in behaviour come out of this context through the striving for permanent self-perfection.

In this respect Geßmann tackles the Olympic principle of Coubertin as well as the second concept of Olympic Education which Norbert Müller has proposed. Both concepts of Müller and Geßmann became the leading concepts for the educational work of the German NOC Olympic Education Committee after 1998 and for the newly founded German Olympic Academy Willi Daume (DOA) after 2007 until 2014. Only recently, the so called *integrative concept* of Olympic Education was implemented by the DOA prior to the Olympic Games of Rio de Janeiro (Naul, 2016).

Theoretically, the understanding of Olympic Education was enhanced by the analysis of the field when five different approaches to the teaching of Olympic Education became structured (Naul, 2010, pp. 102) Besides the traditional *knowledge-oriented* approach of most Olympic Education initiatives prior to the 1990s and later, three more concepts derived up to the year 2000 and dominated the discussion: the *experience-oriented* approach, featuring school festivals, youth camps and similar interactive and social-cultural experiences (Müller); the *physical achievement* teaching approach, emphasising athletic performance (Geßmann) with three main Olympic principles (performance, fair play and respect); and a *lifeworld-oriented* approach of Olympic Education, featuring holistic engagement with a collection of Olympic values based on physical activities. This approach was developed by Deanna Binder in Canada and was applied for the first time by a commissioned work she did on behalf of the *Federation of Olympic and Sport Education* (Binder, 2000) based in Greece when Athens was elected to became again the host city of the Olympic Games of 2004. The fifth, so called *integrative concept*, the Olympic learning approach which included all four basic principles of the previous Olympic Education concepts for teaching physical education at school (formal, curricular) and physical activities outside school in other social settings (informal, extra-curricular) was developed between 2002 and 2007 via the *White Book of Olympic Education* (Naul, 2007, pp. 101–116; Naul, 2016; Naul et al., 2017, pp. 184).

Section 4: The Development of the Lifeworld Approach and Olympic Values Education

This approach evolved in the late 1980s in Canada and through the 1990s (Binder, 2012, 2017) as educators began to leverage interest in the spectacle of the Olympic Games and the *sporting values* that they communicated in order to enhance a more broadly-based educational mandate for children and youth.

Curriculum development in the field of four Olympic-education related projects will be explored both, through their theoretical underpinnings and through the understandings that evolved from their practical applications in classrooms, gymnasiums, out on the playing field or in a coaching session = lifeworld of children. Each of these curriculum projects was informed by specific fields of relevant educational theory and, through application, reflection and interpretation, produced educational insights that then guided the next project.

Connecting to Curricula – Project #1 – The Calgary 1988 Olympic Winter Games Olympic Education Programme

Because the Canadian/Calgary public was uninformed about the history and traditions of the Olympic Games and about many sports of the Winter Games, the Organising Committee of the Games thought that providing information and activities through the schools would provide an Olympic experience for children, inform them and thus their families about Olympic Games and thus help to increase enthusiasm for the Games. Key questions that guided the development of *Come Together: the Olympics and You*, three 400-page binders (elementary, junior and senior high school activity manuals) were:

- What is the best way to present information about the Olympic Games, for example, ancient and modern Olympic Games history, sports, traditions and ideals to school children?
- How can this information be integrated into school-based curricula and presented so that teachers would find it useful?

According to Naul (2010), this project would be categorised as a knowledge-oriented approach with the added challenge that this *knowledge* needed to be integrated in the school curricula in such a way that it would help to promote learning in a variety of school-based subject areas. To accomplish this, volunteer teacher committees at all three levels of the Alberta school system were formed and invited to use Olympic and sport information as a context for the development of activities to accomplish learning outcomes in their various subject areas. The manuals were intended to be used as a resource and not as a textbook. Teachers were encouraged to pick and choose and adapt learning activities according to the objectives and needs of their own programmes.

In an evaluation carried out by the Canadian Olympic Committee two years after the Games, 97% of the teacher respondents said that they would use the materials again, confirming that the materials seemed to be useful in their flexible, off-the-shelf formats for the target groups. Historically the *Come Together* project was the first comprehensive school-based initiative sponsored by an Olympic Games Organising Committee; its legacy lived on in the mandate for Olympic Education adopted and carried on by the Canadian Olympic Committee, and in the educational programmes of Organising Committees of Olympic Games such as Lillehammer (1994) and Sydney (2000), which modelled their Olympic Education programmes on the basis of the Calgary initiative.

As a *first effort* in school-based Olympic Education curriculum development however, the programme had a number of shortcomings. It lacked a strong orientation to sport and physical activity, which, according to the aims of the *Olympic Charter* is the underlying rationale for the Olympic Games and for the Olympic Movement. From one perspective, using sport as a context for learning activities does raise the profile of *body* in other subject areas. However, as successful as the cross-curricular aspects were, learning activities were mostly classroom-based. At the time, the physical education curriculum was undergoing reconceptualisation; articulating activities to develop skills in the *kinaesthetic domain* seemed an elusive endeavour, even for physical education specialists. This aspect of curriculum development in Olympic Education projects continues to challenge curriculum specialists in the Olympic Education field.

Teaching Values – Project #2 – The Canadian Commission for Fair Play Manual for Schools

Following the revelations of an inquiry into the Ben Johnson doping scandal of the 1988 Seoul Olympic Games the Canadian government established an independent, non-profit Canadian Anti-Doping Agency, and the Ministry of Sport invited a group of sport leaders to participate in a Commission for Fair Play with an educational mandate. Building on the understandings from the Calgary project it was decided to create a manual that would infuse fair play concepts into activities to promote learning outcomes from school curricula. A review of the literature on the topic focussed on two key questions:
- How do children and youth learn fair play behaviours and values?
- What teaching methodologies support this sport-oriented interest in the definitions and descriptions of fair play to a focus on HOW – How, exactly, do you actually teach fair play attitudes and behaviours?

The dominant theory in values education in North America at the time, particularly in the field of sport and physical education, was moral development theory – an orientation most closely associated with the work of Lawrence Kohlberg (1981) and Norma Haan (1985). Kohlberg, a psychologist influenced by the cognitive development model of Jean Piaget (1975), postulated the hierarchical development of certain abilities with respect to abstract moral reasoning. The model emphasises the cognitive processes involved in moral reasoning. The current emphasis on rules, principles and penalties comes from the same kind of thinking about moral action. Moral development theory postulates stages in the development of ethical/moral judgment as part of a maturation process. *Fair Play for Kids* was grounded in this theory. Two learning processes that are recommended to help young people *rise* to the next level of moral development were highlighted throughout in *Fair Play for Kids* (4):

- Identifying and resolving moral conflicts. Talk is a very important component of the process of conflict resolution and moral decision-making. Most of the activities in this programme are accompanied by a *Let's Talk* section (4).
- Changing roles and perspectives. Children at this age tend to see their world from an egocentric point of view. Games, simulations, role plays etc. provide them with opportunities to put themselves in someone else's shoes (4).

Understandings that evolved from the processes of researching, developing and implementing *Fair Play for Kids* include: Fair play is a learned behaviour; it does not happen automatically because someone participates in a sport. Secondly, educational interventions improve fair play behaviours; and thirdly, dialogue (*Let's talk*) is a foundational methodology for teaching values. These understandings were confirmed in a study by Gibbons et al. (1995) who used selected educational activities from *Fair Play for Kids* in a study to test the effects on the moral development of children in physical education. They note that: »... implementation of a specially designed educational program can effect changes in several facets of moral development... [and that] These results support theory and empirical research that enhancing moral growth is not an automatic consequence of participation in physical activity, but rather that systematic and organized delivery of theoretically grounded curricula is necessary to make a difference.« (1995, p. 253)

Addressing Cultural Diversity – Project #3 – *Be a Champion in Life*:
A Project of the Athens Foundation of Olympic and Sport Education

Be A Champion in Life (Binder, 2000) began in 1997 with a vision (in Greek, an *orama*) of the President of the Athens Foundation for Olympic and Sport Education (FOSE), Antonio Tzikas. He was convinced that an educational programme focused on the positive values of Olympism and distributed to all of the schools in the world would eventually change the behaviours of human society. It is an outrageously unrealistic vision, but he had the resources and the influence within the sport system of Greece to bring together people from around the world to try and make some progress towards his vision. Dr Margaret Talbot, a former president of ICSSPE was one of the members of the Steering Committee, and Dr Doll-Tepper attended a number of the FOSE events.

The theoretical orientation for the programme was the *Olympic Charter* (2015) which espouses universal values and includes references to educational and pedagogical objectives. The curriculum developers, however, had several key questions with respect to the universality of Olympism. For example:
- Do the Olympic values have relevance in cultural contexts other than the ones based on Euro-American traditions?
- Are the methodologies proposed for teaching values in Euro-American contexts appropriate in other cultural contexts?
- How can international Olympic Education and fair play initiatives represent global cultural perspectives?

The Fundamental Principles of the *Olympic Charter* are grounded in Euro-Western philosophy, values and sport traditions – and specifically in the idealistic, optimistic ideas of 19th century humanism. For two hundred years these ideas, traditions and values – including the Euro-American systems of organised sport and the Olympic Games – were exported, for better or worse, to non-Western cultural lifeworlds. Post-modern educational and sport theorists critique the educational and sport legacies of colonialism, including its negative impact on traditional and indigenous sport. Others suggest, however, that Olympism may be attractive globally to the more than two hundred countries that have signed the *Olympic Charter* because it offers a general framework from within which the nations and regions that organise and participate in the Olympic Movement can represent their own cultural and ethical traditions.

With the tensions created by these considerations in the foreground, the curriculum framework for *Be A Champion in Life* evolved into five themes:
- Body, Mind and Spirit: Inspiring Children to Participate in Physical Activity,
- Fair Play: The Spirit of Sport in Life and Community,
- Multiculturalism: Learning to Live With Diversity,
- In Pursuit of Excellence: Identity, Self-Confidence and Self-Respect,
- The Olympics Present and Past: Celebrating the Olympic Spirit.

Curriculum development was informed by (a) the understanding from the Calgary project that Olympic Education curriculum materials for use in schools needed to be integrated with school-based learning outcomes, and (b) from the *Fair Play for Kids* project that values such as fair play can be encouraged through the implementation of specific values-based activities. With respect to basic pedagogy, *constructivism* was the dominant educational theory, whereby students were encouraged to use active and experiential techniques to create knowledge and understanding, and then to reflect on and talk about what they are doing and how their understanding is changing. This was consistent with the Calgary approach. With respect to a values-based pedagogy, the ten years since 1990 and *Fair Play for Kids* had introduced significantly different approaches to ethical and values-based developmental theory. New approaches highlighted helping young people to explore their emotional as well as their intellectual responses to ethical issues – through narratives, art, music and drama, and to practise care and compassion for others. Moral development theory with its focus on cognitive-based abstract discussions of moral dilemmas and its emphases on rules, enforcement and penalties no longer dominated the literature on values-based teaching and learning.

Based on the critique of the Calgary programme, the physical activity components of the FOSE manual were strengthened through the addition of a theme titled *Body, Mind and Spirit*. This theme highlighted the foundational idea of Olympism that young people develop physical, intellectual and moral capabilities when they challenge themselves in physical endeavour. To address concerns about cultural diversity, narratives and learning activities in the manual featured content from other cultural contexts, and learner tasks frequently required learners to explore the traditions and teachings of their own cultures. Five educational values – adapted from the vocabulary of the *Olympic Charter* were articulated for the programme: joy of effort in sport and physical activity, fair play, respect for others, pursuit of excellence and balance between body, will and mind.

Would this new curriculum conceptualisation help to make the manual relevant and useful for both Euro-American and non-Euro-American cultural and educational situations? Two reviews of drafts of the manual were implemented to answer this question. In the first review, educators from multiple cultural backgrounds gave the draft a *surface review* and engaged in discussions on the content and format. The second review took place in five classrooms on five continents: in China, in Brazil, in Australia, in South Africa and in England. Teachers who led the classroom trials in all of the different regions of the world seemed to connect Olympic values such as fair play and respect for others with ethical concepts from their own cultural traditions. Non-European and Non-American teachers, however, seemed to be uncomfortable with activities that focused students on self-awareness and self-development (for example in the theme *Pursuit of Excellence*) rather than on community unity and participation. This tension is most evident in faith-based traditions, and is a topic that requires further exploration. In general, however, the classroom trials of the initial drafts of *Be A Champion in Life* contributed the following understandings:

- Learning activities based on the Olympic values seemed to have relevance in classrooms in different cultural contexts.
- Learning activities based on the principles of *constructivism*, i.e., active, experiential learning seemed to contribute to improved attitudes and behaviour on the playgrounds and in school classrooms.
- Activities that explored emotions and attitudes, stimulated the imagination, and emphasised caring and compassionate behaviours were highlighted as favourites by teachers.
- The most used activities seemed to be in the *fair play* and *respect for others* themes.
- Some teachers, particularly in Asian and African contexts, were not comfortable with some of the activities in the *pursuit of excellence* theme. Since the Olympic values are grounded in Western concepts of SELF, Olympic values education initiatives must be sensitive to this cultural difference.
- Sport, physical activity and physical education concepts and learning activities need expansion and appropriate articulation in Olympic Education materials. It was suggested that the concept of *physical literacy* (Whitehead, 2001)

and its focus on developmentally appropriate skills and games might offer theoretical support for a more enriched focus on sport and physical activity.

Olympic Values Education – Project #4 – The OVEP Programme of the International Olympic Committee

With *Be A Champion in Life*, the conceptualisation of a *lifeworld* approach to curriculum development in the field of Olympic Education had global outreach. Ten years later, this approach inspired the development of an IOC initiative to promote the Olympic values. *Teaching Values: An Olympic Education Toolkit* (Binder, 2007), was published by the IOC as a tool »to maintain young people's interest in sport, encourage them to practise sport, and promote the Olympic values« (http://www.olympic.org/education-through-sport/ovep-sport-as-a-school-of-life). Curriculum development was based on the understandings drawn from the three projects previously discussed in this section. Through the five themes the Olympic values are highlighted:
- Introduction,
- Celebrating the Values Through Symbol and Ceremony,
- Sharing the Values Through Sport and the Olympic Games,
- The Five Educational Values: Joy of Effort, Fair Play, Respect for Others, Pursuit of Excellence, Balance between Body, Will and Mind,
- Implementation Tools.

Olympic-related information and the five educational values are continually reinforced through activities that inspire learning. Released, distributed and workshopped around the world from 2007 to 2017, the OVEP programme is now in its second version, complete with new materials to assist with implementation and delivery and a new emphasis on its *sport-based* mandate (https://www.olympic.org/olympic-values-and-education-program). OVEP 2 includes the following new materials:
- The Fundamentals of Olympic Values Education,
- Delivering OVEP – an implementation manual,
- OVEP Activity Sheets – classroom handouts and exercises.

A workshop programme to train people to deliver OVEP 2 is also in the planning stages.

References

Binder, D. (1986). *Come together: The Olympics and you* (Elementary, Junior High School and Senior High School Resource Manuals). Calgary: OCO'88.

Binder, D. (1992). *Fair play for kids: A handbook of activities for teaching fair play* (revised 1995). Ottawa: Fair Play Canada.

Binder, D. (2000). *Be a champion in life: An international teacher's resource manual*. Athens: Foundation for Olympic and Sport Education.

Binder, D. (2001). »Olympism« revisited as context for global education: Implications for physical education. *Quest, 53*, 14–34.

Binder, D. (2007). *Teaching values: An Olympic Education toolkit*. Lausanne: International Olympic Committee.

Binder, D. (2012). Olympic values education: evolution of a pedagogy. *Educational Review, 64 (3)*, 275–302.

Binder, D. (2017). Canada. Olympic Education programmes as legacies of Olympic Games. In R. Naul, D. Binder, A. Rychtecky, & I. Culpan (Eds.), *Olympic Education. An international review* (pp. 104–118). London/New York: Routledge.

Binder, D., & Naul, R. (2017). Olympic Education as pedagogy: terminology, pedagogical orientations and Olympic values education In R. Naul, D. Binder, A. Rychtecky, & I. Culpan (Eds.), *Olympic Education – an international review* (pp. 331–337). London/New York: Routledge.

Coubertin de, P. (2000). *Olympism. Selected writings*. Lausanne: IOC.

Gebhardt, W. (1904). Die olympische Bewegung und die Schule. In P. Schubert (Ed.), *Bericht über den I. Internationalen Kongress für Schulhygiene*. Band III (pp. 108–116). Nürnberg: Schrag.

Georgiadis, K. (1995). International Olympic Academy: the history of its establishment, aims and objectives. In IOA (Ed.), *2nd joint international session for directors and national Olympic academies, and staff of national Olympic committees and international sport federations* (pp. 15–21). Athens: IOA.

Geßmann, R. (1992). Olympische Erziehung und ihre schulische Umsetzung (in engl. Olympic Education and its application at school). In NOK für Deutschland (Ed.), *Olympische Erziehung in der Schule unter besonderer Berücksichtigung des Fair play-Gedankens* (pp. 33–43). Frankfurt: NOK.

Geßmann, R. (2002). Olympische Erziehung in der Schule. Zentrales und Peripheres. *Sportunterricht, 51 (1)*, 16–20.

Gibbons, S., Ebbeck, L., & Weiss, M. (1995). Fair play for kids: Effects on the moral development of children in physical education. *Research Quarterly for Exercise and Sport, 66*(3), 247–255.

Grupe, O. (1993). Olympisches Menschenbild und olympische Erziehung (in engl. Olympic human manner and Olympic Education). In R. Pohl (Ed.), *Facetten der Sportpädagogik. Beiträge zur pädagogischen Diskussion des Sports* (pp. 31–38). Schorndorf: Hofmann.

Grupe, O. (1997). Olympismus und olympische Erziehung. Abschied von einer großen Idee? In O. Grupe (Ed.), *Olympischer Sport – Rückblick und Perspektiven* (pp. 223–243). Schorndorf: Hofmann.

GutsMuths, J. C. F. (1793). *Gymnastik für die Jugend*. Dresden: Limpert (Faksimile-reprint 1929).

GutsMuths, J. C. F. (1804). *Gymnastik für die Jugend*. Rudolfstadt: Hain. (2nd revised edtion; Faksimile-reprint 1999.)

Haan, N., Aerts, E., & Cooper, B. (1985). *On moral grounds: The search for a practical morality*. New York: New York University Press.

International Olympic Committee (IOC) (2015). *Olympic Charter*. Lausanne: IOC.

Kohlberg, L. (1981). *The philosophy of moral development*. San Francisco, CA: Harper & Row.

Krüger, A. (2009). Die Olympische Erziehung im Spätwerk Coubertins. In R. Naul, A. Krüger, & W. Schmidt (Eds.), *Kulturen des Jugendsports. Bildung, Erziehung und Gesundheit* (pp. 15–38). Aachen: Meyer & Meyer.

Müller, N. (1975). Olympische Erziehung. In F. Thaller, & H. Recla (Eds.), *Signale der Zeit* (pp. 133–140). Schorndorf: Hofmann.

Müller, N. (1998). Olympische Erziehung. In O. Grupe, & D. Mieth (Eds.), *Lexikon der Ethik im Sport* (pp. 385–395). Schorndorf: Hofmann.

Müller, N. (1995). *Olympia zwischen Idealität und Realität. Die Internationale Olympische Akademie im Spiegel der Vorträge 1961–1994*. Niedernhausen: Schors.

Müller, N. (2004). *Olympic Education*. Online available under http://olympicstudies.uab.es/eng/lec/pdf/muller.pdf (accessed June 25, 2017).

Müller, N. (2006). The idea of peace as Coubertin's vision for the modern Olympic movement: development and pedagogic consequences. *The Sport Journal, 9*(1). Online available under https://www.thesportjournal.org/2006/Journal/vol.9-No/Mueller.asp (accessed June 25, 2017).

Naul, R. (2007). *Olympische Erziehung*. Aachen: Meyer & Meyer Verlag.

Naul, R. (2010). *Olympic Education*. Oxford: Meyer & Meyer Publ. (2nd corr. editon.)

Naul, R. (2016). Die Spiele und ihre Idee. Aufgaben und Ziele der Olympischen Erziehung. In DOA (Ed.), *Olympia ruft: mach' mit! Basiswissen Olympische Spiele* (pp. 54–58). Frankfurt/M.: DOA.

Naul, R., Krüger, M., Geßmann, R., & Wick, U. (2017). Germany – Formal Olympic Education at schools and informal Olympic learning in sport clubs. In R. Naul, D. Binder, A. Rychtecky, & I. Culpan (Eds.), *Olympic Education. An international review* (pp. 177–191). London/New York: Routledge.

Nikolaus, I. (2014). *Die Olympische Idee Pierre de Coubertins als erzieherische Herausforderung für die weltweite Olympische Bewegung*. Kassel: Agon.

Piaget, J. (1975). *The child's conception of the world*. New York, NY: Littlefield.

Rosenbaum, S., & Schulze, A. (1928). Die Auswirkungen einer täglichen Schulturnstunde. In DAL 2 (128); 3 (118–120); 5 (268–271); 6 (208–211); 7 (237–241), 8 (271–273).

Stolyarov, V., & Rodichenko, V. (2017). Russia: our model and system of Olympic Education. In R. Naul, D. Binder, A. Rychtecky, & I. Culpan (Eds.), *Olympic Education. An international review* (pp. 238–252). London/New York: Routledge.

Whitehead, M. (2001). The concept of physical literacy. *European Journal of Physical Education, 6*(2), 127–138.

Handball – From a Women's Game to a Men's Sport

Gertrud Pfister
University of Copenhagen

Introduction

I have known Gudrun since 1980, when she was my colleague, an excellent administrator, teacher and scholar at the *Freie Universität* in Berlin, where I worked from 1980 to 2000. We became good friends, conducted several skiing courses together, cooperated in several research projects and have stayed in connection ever since. One of our major joint adventures was the project *Frauen an die Spitze*, a large study about women, sport and leadership which provided topics for several publications and also had a political impact on sport. In 2007, the group led by Gudrun and myself was honoured with the prestigious *Margherita-von-Brentano-Award* for research at the *Freie Universität Berlin* (https://www.frauenrat.de/fileadmin/Website_Archiv/files/Doll-Tepper.pdf).[1]

Gudrun has authored and co-authored over 350 publications in sport sciences with a focus on adapted physical activity and sport for persons with a disability as well as on sport politics and policies. However, she did not stay in the ivory tower of intellectual pursuits, she also acts as a sport pedagogue and – in particular – as a politician who aims to have an impact to improve the situation of various marginalised groups in sport and in other areas of their lives. She also was and is engaged in a large number of national and international sport organisations, e. g. until 2008 as President of the International Council of Sport Science and Physical Education (ICSSPE), the world's largest network of organisations and institutions concerned with sport, sport science and physical education (http://www.icsspe.org/about/history-intent). Currently, she is also Vice-President of the German Olympic Sports Confederation (DOSB) and a member of the Women in Sport Commission of the IOC. Her activities and merits are reflected in numerous awards, for example, two honorary doctorates and an honorary professorship. She also received several prestigious international and national honours, including the FIEP Gold Cross of Honor of Physical

---

[1] Gudrun Doll-Tepper is member of the scientific council of the German Handball Federation which was founded in 2014.

Education and the Paralympic Order of the International Paralympic Committee (IPC).

Gudrun's long and impressive CV shows, that she is multi-talented – a good athlete, an excellent scholar, a popular educator, and a successful sport politician. Therefore it was easy to find numerous suitable topics for a contribution to her *Festschrift*, but it was difficult to find an issue which shows Gudrun from a new perspective. I decided to focus in this article on Gudrun as a sports woman. In 2007, she described her involvement in numerous sports as follows: »My whole life I was active in various sports. As many girls in this time period, I was a member of a *Turnverein* (gymnastic club), engaged in athletics and began later to play handball. For many years I played handball and basketball, also in major leagues.« Asked why she did not become a professional athlete, Gudrun answered that she did not want to focus on one discipline and that she loved to learn new sports, e. g. skiing. Although she started late – when she was 21 years of age – she became an enthusiastic ski instructor and conducted skiing classes for physical education students at the *Freie Universität*. I have precious memories about the weeks in the mountains with Gudrun and a group of young people who were eager to master the art of skiing. Whereas I focused in a contribution to Gudrun's *Festschrift* in 2006 on one of her scientific interests, I selected for this publication a topic with a focus on one of her favourite sports: Team handball – not the least because she was and is a team player on and off the pitch.

For sport scholars, handball is of particular interest because the development of the game and its characteristics are in several ways exceptional: handball is one of the few games of the *Turners* (adherents of German gymnastics) which became a modern sport and one of the few sports (maybe even the only one) which underwent a *gender transformation* as it was invented for and played by girls and women before it turned to a fast, sometimes even aggressive sport for boys and men.

Worldwide, team handball is played in relatively few countries and regions, but it has gained a relatively large role in the Nordic countries and in Germany. In Germany, handball is quite popular taking the fifth place with regard to the number of memberships in sport federations. In 2016, the most popular sport, with over

7 million members, was football. The next places are taken by shooting, and tennis with around 1.4 million members each. Then comes team handball with nearly 757,000 memberships (statistics provided by the DSOB)[2], of which 37% are girls and women – the gender difference occurs in all age groups. Thus handball mirrors the situation in other sports which are also dominated by boys and men – the few exceptions are sport acrobatics, dancing, figure skating, and volleyball.

Excursion: *Turnen* and its Influence on Sport and Games

The origins of handball are closely intertwined with the development of *German gymnastics*, *Turnen*, a concept and a *movement* which is rooted in the German history and connected with the political events and the pedagogical movements of the 18th and 19th centuries (e.g. Pfister, 2003a).

One of the *founding fathers* of modern *body cultures* in Germany (and beyond) was the Philanthropist Johann Christoph GutsMuths (1759–1839) whose system of *gymnastics* included numerous games and exercises, influencing and changing traditional physical activities and *sports* not only in Germany, but also in many other countries. Inspired by the ideas of the Enlightenment, the Philanthropists, adherents of a pedagogical reform movement, developed a revolutionary form of education whose purpose was to teach (male) pupils to become useful citizens guided by reason. Since these reformers assumed that knowledge and reason could only develop through human action, i.e. through physical activities and sensory perception, they considered bodily exercise as an indispensable part of education of boys and men. GutsMuths emphasised in particular the importance of playing and published a book with a collection of games which included *handball*, a game, where individuals hit a ball with the palm of their hand against a wall (GutsMuths, 1796, p. 96).

One of the German followers of GutsMuths, Friedrich Ludwig Jahn (1778–1852), regarded as the *father* of *Turnen*, developed a form of gymnastics for boys and men, which aimed at a *national education* and a preparation for war. The

---

2 See the membership statistics of the German Olympic Confederation. https://www.dosb. de/fileadmin/sharepoint/Materialien%20%7B82A97D74-2687-4A29-9C16-4232BAC7D C73%7D/Bestandserhebung_2016.pdf

overarching aims of the *Turners* were the liberation of Prussia from French occupation, the eradication of the feudal order, and the foundation of a German nation state. Since 1811, Jahn and a rapidly growing group of followers met outside of Berlin and engaged in various games and exercises. *Turnen* quickly spread, and by 1818 around 6,000 Turner practiced e. g. in Prussia on roughly 100 sites (see Jahn & Eiselen, 1816; e. g. Ohmann, 2009).

Turnen (the term was coined by Jahn) is an all-embracing concept of physical education which included various sorts of physical activities. Among them were not only numerous exercises on apparatus, but also running, jumping, lifting, climbing, fencing, and wrestling, as well as swimming, and playing games. The facilities installed at the Turner grounds reflected the needs and *philosophy* of the *Turner*. For jumping exercises, for instance, there were high jump *facilities* and ditches for the long jump as well as a little hill from which the young men could jump down. A tree was used for various balancing exercises (today the balance beam is used exclusively in women's gymnastics). Most conspicuous were the climbing trees and wooden *towers* with ladders, poles and ropes which could be climbed in various ways. The nearby woods were used for games such as hide and seek or playing war with attacks and raids on the *enemy* (Jahn & Eiselen, 1816).

The programme of the *Turners* shows that the exercises distinguished *Turnen* fundamentally from sport but its norms, values, intentions and principles. *Modern sport* is based on the quantification of performance, its assessment through competitions, and the comparison of results independent of time and place, which makes the setting and breaking records possible (Guttmann, 2012; see also Maguire, 2006). The exercises of the *Turners*, e. g. the forms of running, reflect the different principles: Jahn lists, for example, numerous kinds of running, including *zigzag* running, running backwards or *running up a hill*. Running could either focus on speed or on endurance and can be conducted either with or without baggage. Endurance running is characterized as follows: »The prize goes to the person who covers the largest distance in the shortest time … and arrives at the finish neither exhausted nor depleted of strength.« This means that endurance races could not be operationalised – for how could one measure the depletion of strength? »Therefore it was impossible to compare performances beyond an actual race and to set and to break records (see Guttmann,

2012). Jahn also advocated the principle of *relative performance*, meaning that performances were evaluated according to the athlete's bodily capacities e.g. with regard to weight and height. Games played a considerable role in Jahn's programme; most of them were imitations of war with ambushes and mock attacks. However, *Die Deutsche Turnkunst*, recommends also the *German ball game* which is similar to dodge ball (Jahn & Eiselen, 1816, p. 252).

Since *Turnen* promised to make young men fit and able to fight for their country, it was – at least for a while – given the support of the Prussian authorities. However, after the wars of liberation (1813–1815), the *Turners'* dreams of a German nation state did not come true as the newly founded Confederation of German States attempted to restore the old order and banned the reform movements. Therefore, the *Turnplätze* (gymnastic grounds) were closed down and Jahn was imprisoned for several years. Only in the 1840s, *Turnen* was readmitted and some of the gymnastic exercises were used in physical education in secondary schools.

Although the *Turnplatz* was meant to be used by *everybody*, it was in practice accessible to only one half of the population: to boys and men. In Jahn's book *Die Deutsche Turnkunst* (A Treaties of Gymnastics) the *bible* of the *Turners*, girls and women are not even mentioned. It was only during the prohibition of the *Turner* movement in the 1930s, that the benefit of bodily exercise for public health was given greater recognition and that the first physical education courses were provided for girls. However, females had to wear long skirts and should avoid strenuous and *improper* exercises. Therefore it is striking that an *aggressive* sport such as team handball had been originally a girls' game (Pfister & Langenfeld, 1980; Pfister, 2006b).

Team Handball – Origins and First Developments

In the wake of the *modernisation* of Western societies in the 19th century sports of English origin became popular in Germany and many traditional games and exercises adopted its principles. This was also the case for handball which was played in several European countries, e.g. Bohemia, Denmark, Sweden or the Ukraine. In Germany handball had been invented and propagated by adherents of the so-called *Spielbewegung* (games movement) which initiated reforms of traditional physical education and advocated for the adoption of sports and games, e.g. football and handball, in the schools. Among the most influential leaders of this movement were Konrad Koch (1846–1911) and August Hermann (1835–1906) who both worked at a *Gymnasium* (high school) in Braunschweig. Koch translated the football rules into German and founded a football club at his school. He also invented *Raffball*, a predecessor of modern handball (Hoffmeister, 1986; Eggers, 2014, p. 19). In 1915, Hermann created a similar team game, named *Torball*, where the ball had to be passed among all team members until one of the players could score a goal. *Torball* was considered as suitable to the physical training of the *weaker sex* and was played mainly by girls and women.[3]

However, as many other sports and games, handball was affected by *sportification processes* which also influenced the *gender of the game*. Carl Schelenz, a successful track athlete and a teacher of the Berlin Physical Education College, modified the rules of *Torball* in 1919 (Eggers, 2014, 32 et seq). The new game was played with 11 players on a larger field and with a larger goal. These and other changes made the game more aggressive and as such more attractive for men.[4] In 1936, men's team handball was played in the Olympic Games. However, the game was dropped and returned to the Olympics only in 1976. Since then men's and women's tournaments have been integrated into the Olympic programme (see e.g. http://www.sports-reference.com/olympics/).

The development of team handball differs in several ways from the histories of other sports, in particular with regard to the participation of both genders. In contrast to many other sports, handball changed its gender from a women's to men's sport. However, it also demands skills and practices which are commonly associated with masculinity.

---

3 http://www.bchandball.ca/index.php/about/whatisteamhandball/history-of-handball
http://www.echo-online.de/sport/lokalsport/handball/wissenschaftlichen-beirat-ist-weg weisender-schritt-in-die-zukunft_15536395.htm
http:/www.sports-reference.com/olympics/

4 welt-des-sports.com: Geschichte; Memento vom 12. August 2011, *Internet Archive*.

Handball – Gender Changes
Women's roles in handball

Although *Turner* clubs had already started to offer courses for schoolgirls from mid-century onwards, adult women were not allowed to take part in gymnastics and games until the 1890s. This changed partly due to the influence of the games movement, which advocated physical fitness for girls and women, for *the strong are born of the strong*. Whereas, however, the majority of doctors and educators recommended games of moderate physical strain suited to the female disposition, the doctor Alice Profé and a number of other progressive gymnastics teachers wished to make (almost) all games permissible for girls (Pfister & Langenfeld, 1982; Pfister, 1991). Georg Thiele, for example, editor of GutsMuths' book about games, was of the opinion that »as far as girls are concerned, it is a proven fact today that the build of the organs of locomotion and the need to train them are the same for both sexes. Thus, generally speaking, the same games can be played by both boys and girls [...] only in the case of football, Reiterball, and a few others might there be reservations about letting girls play them« (Thiele, 1914, p. 44).

Tambourine ball in particular emerged as a suitable girls' game while most throwing and catching games were played by boys and men. In 1909 the gymnastics instructor Marie Meyer developed *Königsberger Ball* as a team game for women, where the ball is not thrown but hit with the fist or arm into the opponents' goal (Bernett, 1995, p. 23). Aiming and throwing a ball with force was looked upon as a man's affair, requiring abilities and skills that women were not credited with.

In search of interesting exercises and »in order to give our lady gymnasts the opportunity of playing outdoor games in the cold part of the year« (Riekhoff 1943, p. 62), the Women's Committee of the Berlin Gymnastics Society (*Berliner Turnrath*) along with its chairman, Max Heiser, experimented with a number of throwing and catching games – also those which were played in other German cities and in other countries (Eggers, 2014, p. 11 et seq). From these games Heiser developed, together with female gymnasts, a ball game for women where the ball was thrown and caught and the players aimed at scoring goals. Sport historian Bernett (1995, p. 23) considers this game named *Torball* to be the »product of a complex construction« of several types of games (see also Eggers, 2014, p. 20). It is first mentioned in the announcement of a games festival held by women in the Grunewald district of Berlin on 29th August 1915: »Besides competitions of fist ball and tambourine ball there will also be competitions in *Barlauf*, *Torball* and *Ball über die Schnur*« (Riekhoff 1943, p. 58). In the following year the rules for the new game of *Torball* were made official, and Max Heiser and the Women's Committee put a great deal of effort into promoting it. Numerous training games and friendly matches soon made women's *Torball* known all over Berlin. As early as 1916 the first league games were played with five teams (see also Rieckhoff, 1943; Mielke, 2010, p. 74 ff.).

In 1917 the Berlin Gymnastics Society's Committee for Girls' and Women's Gymnastics approved the extended rules of *Torball* and its new name of *Handball*. Max Heiser is generally considered to be the founder of *Handball*, and, as the women's gymnastics instructor and chairman of the Women's Committee, he undoubtedly played a significant role in its *invention*; at the same time, however, other members of the Women's Committee – including the women gymnasts themselves – were also involved in improving the game and developing the rules (Eggers, 2014, p. 20). Writing in 1941, for example, Else Schelenz, the wife of Carl Schelenz, emphasised: »At the start *Torball* was only played by women gymnasts belonging to the Berlin Gymnastics Society. They introduced it and drew up the rules. Heiser's rules came about in collaboration with us since, of course, he wasn't a player« (quoted in Riekhoff, 1943, p. 64). Riekhoff characterised the new Handball rules as follows: »The rules of play in Handball are partly taken from those of *Raffball*, *Korbball* and football, although adapted as far as possible to suit women players« (Riekhoff, 1943, p. 5). The game was played on a small field (50m x 20m) in teams of eleven players. Running with the ball was not allowed, it could be held by the players for only five seconds and it belonged to the player who touched it last; »Grappling with others for the ball is not permitted« (Riekhoff, 1943, p. 8). A game consisted of two halves of 20 minutes each. The ball used was either a fist ball or a football. Similar games were played in other German cities and in other countries (Eggers, 2014, p. 11 ff.).

Played with these rules, handball was scarcely a strenuous or aggressive game. The »nature of women's play« was supposed to be defensive rather than offensive (Braungardt, 1922, p. 28). It was generally agreed that »for women, any kind of physicality in games is absolutely preposterous« (Amberger 1921, p. 16). What mattered was first and foremost cooperation between players. Throwing and catching were the crucial elements. While kicking the ball with the foot was considered masculine, catching at least was connoted with femininity. Whether, here, the phenomenological notion that catching, i.e. receiving, had to do with conceiving and was thus a women's activity is a moot point. The influential philosopher, anthropologist and psychologist F.J.J. Buytendijk, at any rate, commented: »Kicking differs essentially from throwing. For one thing, kicking is by nature more aggressive than throwing; for another, throwing is linked to catching, i.e. receiving, whereas kicking is linked to kicking back. […] One can certainly throw like a girl, but one can only kick like a man. […] No one has ever succeeded in getting women to play football« (Buytendijk, 1953, p. 20). The question whether girls and women really did not want to throw or maybe also kick a ball and the reasons for the assertion of the inadequacy of females in handling a ball cannot be discussed here. Lack of training may have been the most important reason. As we know today, girls and women do not have any problems to throw or to kick balls.

Team handball becomes a men's sport

Carl Schelenz is considered to be the *inventor* of men's team handball. In 1917, together with fellow club members of the Berlin Gymnastics Club of 1850 (BTV 1850), Schelenz played a throwing and catching game similar to *Raffball* both in the gym and on the field. He was also a women's sports instructor at the club and, in this capacity, he was involved in the development of *Torball* and, later, Handball for women (Riekhoff, 1943, p. 64). However, the success and spread of handball did not really come about until 1919, when Schelenz, in his capacity as instructor of the umbrella organisation of the *bourgeois* sport movement (*Deutscher Reichsausschuss für Leibesübungen*), was commissioned to develop a game for soldiers returning from the front. The traditional *Turner* games demanded neither strength nor endurance and thus no longer appeared suitable for the »earnest fight between men's teams« (Riekhoff 1943, p. 99). Football was seemingly too difficult and liable to cause injuries. Since women's handball did not appeal to men, Schelenz set about *sportifying* this game. The new rules presented early in 1920 were similar to the rules of *Torball* with two crucial changes: after three seconds or two steps the ball had to be tapped on the ground, and it could be knocked out of the opponent's hand Dribbling and grappling for the ball made handball a »fast-moving, aggressive game« (Riekhoff, 1943, p. 104; Bernett, 1995, p. 26). New was also an intentional differentiation of players' roles into goal-keeper, forwards, runners and defenders, thus introducing a specialisation of the participants.

This brief overview of the history of team handball shows that it is not a game which *automatically* developed from a traditional game, but that it was consciously constructed partly to create a counterpoint to football (Bernett, 1995). In this process the search for the *correct* rules and principles of play led to disputes over conflicting views that had to be settled. On 22nd February 1920 the first men's handball match took place in Berlin (Final score: BTV 1850 v. GutsMuths 4:1) with around one thousand spectators. This was the birth of the game of team handball, but would it be able to establish itself? Or was it, in Nikolaus Bernett's words in the *Deutsche Turnzeitung* (DTZ: 1920, No. 2, p. 14), a »nice game full of movement but of minor importance?«

Despite Bernett's scepticism team handball enjoyed a rapid rise in popularity in the years that followed. By 1927 around 1,000 women's and 1,200 men's teams had been formed (see, for example, Bernett, 1995). The proportion of women among the players amounted to roughly 20%.

Team handball's rise in popularity is due to various factors. Fühler (1925) attributed the appeal of the game partly to the natural movements of throwing and catching, which made the game easy to learn. Apart from this, football fields could be used as facilities, balls and outfits were cheap and the rules were straightforward. A further factor that undoubtedly played a role, however, was that team handball was propagated as a German alternative to football. Handball, remarked Fühler, is a »truly German game, invented by Germans, taught and propagated by Germans; and this notion of play has been taken out into the world by Germans« (Fühler, 1925, p. 10; translation GP). It was this attempt to define handball as a national sport, however, that contributed later to the exclusion of women, who were unsuitable as subjects of national identification. Women took away from the game its aura of struggle and toughness; if women could play real handball, it couldn't be a game for real German men.

In the *Weimar Republic* team handball was catered for by both the umbrella organisation for *Turnen*, the *Deutsche Turnerschaft* (DT), and the German athletics association, the *Deutsche Sportbehörde für Leichtathletik* (DSB). The *DT* laid claim to team handball since it followed the tradition of *Turnen* games while the *DSB* used the game as an alternative sport for athletes in the winter months. Moreover, team handball was played in the workers' sports association, the

Arbeiter-Turn- und Sportbund (ATSB), in which *Raffball* continued to be popular alongside handball, and in the Catholic sports organisation *Deutsche Jugendkraft*. Largely due to the ideological disputes over sports politics between the *Turnen* and sports movements, the bourgeois *Turner* and sports associations only came to an agreement on a common book of rules in 1928. Even so, the *DT* and *DSB* still had their own leagues and held separate championships until 1932. As in all other sports, however, there was no cooperation with the workers' sports movement on team handball (Bernett, 1995; Eggers, 2014, p. 24 ff.).

The process of *sportification* resulted in team handball, too, becoming international. In 1925 the first international game in the history of team handball was played in Halle (Saale), in which the German (men's) team lost to Austria 3:6. In 1928 an international handball federation was founded, and in 1928 and 1932 demonstration handball matches were played at the Olympic Games. In 1936 field handball became an Olympic discipline for men (Eggers, 2014, p. 75). Women's handball internationals did not take place until 1930, the first of them, against Austria, being held at the Women's World Games organised by the International Women's Sport Federation in Prague (Pfister, 2000).

Handball and the myth of the weaker sex

The *sportification* of handball described above gave rise to doubts about its suitability for the weaker sex. The key factors were, firstly, the rule that the ball could be knocked out of the opponent's hand and, secondly, throwing at the goal. With the *DT's* rules from 1921 women's handball was by large adapted to the men's game, although the field and the goals for women were smaller than in men's handball. Women were permitted to seize and play the opponent's ball (*Sport und Spiel*, 1921, 38, p. 157) which met with severe criticism from opponents of such »outrages«, who not only envisaged »ears being boxed«, »hair flying around« and »noses bleeding« (»because of the great sensitivity of women's nasal mucous membranes«) but also feared much worse effects such as »internal injuries ... below the belt« with the resultant risks for child-bearing. Thus, they called for »respect for female beings« (*Märkische Turnzeitung*, 1921, 11, p. 738). Because of the numerous protests the *DT* undertook a further change of the rules, with the result that women were again prohibited from grappling with other players for possession of the ball (DTZ, 05.08.1922, p. 329). But this was not the end of the affair: in spite of the *special rules* for women the game was still regarded by many sports and officials of the *Turner* as being not only rough and offensive to watch but also strenuous and a risk to the women's health. And, after all, should women really be spending their Sundays travelling around town and hanging around at sports grounds, when their real place, ordained by nature, was the kitchen and home?

The more team handball became an aggressive sport, the fiercer were the attacks against women playing the game. In 1925 the *DT's* Games Committee attempted to abolish the league games for women with the following justification: »The rough way in which the players fight for the ball, the great demands placed on the body by strenuous association games and throwing the ball at the goal, which is best done with as much force as possible – all this is not suited to the particular nature of the female body. After strenuous games most women players have shown signs of complete exhaustion and players have repeatedly appeared in a condition unworthy of womanhood« (Dehmlow, 1926, p. 283). Instead of handball, it was added, women should play *Korbball* since an action like throwing the ball into a basket »demands skill rather than strength and suits the female disposition better since it is gentler and more agreeable than throwing a ball at a goal« (*Handball* 05.01.1925, 1, p. 1). Here, it must be remembered that women in the *DT* played the game on a smaller field and with a smaller goal than the men.

The *DT* officials' proposal to abolish women's team handball provoked an outcry of indignation. In a statement issued on 30th January 1925 instructors and female players declared that the game was indeed compatible with the strength and capabilities of the female body, and none of the women players had suffered exhaustion or harm to their health. Furthermore, they wrote, there was nothing *un-ladylike* about throwing a ball at a goal. On no account did the women want to give up playing handball and threatened to leave the *DT* and join the *DSB*. A handball committee member demanded that the women should be allowed to decide for themselves: »Why should we men tell the women what to do?«, he remarked. A specialist doctor, finally, stated that from a medical point of view there was no reason for »depriving our lady gymnasts of their beloved game of handball«. Thereupon, the relevant bodies of the *DT* had no other choice but to pass a resolution in the summer of 1925 retaining women's team handball as a sport (*Handball* 29, 21.07.1925).

Women in the *DSB*, just like the men, played handball on football pitches with football goals. The attempt in 1925 to allow women to fight for the ball met with fierce criticism in the *DSB* as well and had to be abandoned (Sparbier, 1926, p. 26). Here, too, the view that women were not suited to the exertions and aggressive play required by the game was widespread (cf. e.g. Kierblewski, 1987, p. 65). Therefore, it was suggested, among other things, that the area of the playing field should be reduced. Although there was no call in the *DSB* for team handball to be abolished generally, the regional associations were given a free hand in deciding. Thus, the women in the West German Games Association were only allowed to play handball as a *sociable game*.

Opposition to women's team handball also arose in the workers' gymnastics and sports movement (ATSB). This happened in spite of the fact that the *proletarian sports movement*, committed as it was to socialism, in many respects presented a progressive image of womanhood and, very early on, granted women in its own association, the ATSB, membership rights and the opportunity of a say in the association's affairs. Women in the ATSB also played handball according to the same rules and on the same playing field as the men. Despite the workers' sports movement's claim to uphold sexual equality, the conviction was firmly anchored that the attributes and roles of men and women were different, unalterable and ordained by nature. Thus, according to the women's gymnastics instructor Georg Benedix, the most important aspect of women's sport ought to be the »value of the physical exercises for health and beauty«. Contests should be adapted to women's capabilities. In 1929 the women's gymnastics instructors at county level stated categorically: »League games, knock-out competitions and championships are not suitable for women.« However, this radical view was not able to assert itself. Women's league games continued to be played, as can be gathered from sports reports, for example in the Social Democratic newspaper *Vorwärts* (see also Pfister, 1991; Pfister, 2003b).

In the 1930s handball spread to Norway, where it immediately took on a female appearance. Since the Norwegian national sports were skiing and ski jumping, handball was a sport that was scarcely taken up by men, with the result that it developed into a women's game – but that is another story (cf. von der Lippe, 1988).

Theoretical considerations

The discussions about women's participation in handball and in gymnastics and sports in general as well as the arguments for and against females playing this game are based on and supported by the gender ideologies and gender roles, in particular by the norms and ideals of femininity of the time.

From a constructivist perspective, handball is *gender play*, an issue of gendered discourses, embedded in the gender order and doing gender. The realisation that gender is a social construct, is currently taking root in popular wisdom. Judith Butler's provocative claim (e. g. 1990) that the duality of gender is created in discourse and is continuously reproduced in line with the social ideas about femininity and masculinity has not only become common in feminist literature but has also spread to newspapers, magazines and popular literature.

According to Lorber (e. g. 1994), Connell (2008) and numerous other scholars, gender is a social construct, firmly anchored in all social structures and institutions from the family to language; it is *embodied* in all interaction, and internalised and enacted by all individuals. Thus, gender always has an individual, an interactional and an institutional side to it. It is, on the one hand, a key category, used by societies to constitute their social order. On the other hand, individuals adopt the existing roles and rules, the images and scripts of gender duality in lifelong processes (*projects*, according to Connell) of socialisation. Interacting with their social and natural surroundings, girls and boys and men and women develop identities in and through *cultural practices*; in doing so, they assimilate a *gendered* social reality and at the same time represent – and thus reinforce – the symbolic order of gender duality (Lorber, 1994; Connell, 2008). »Gender is both something we do and something we think with, both a set of social practices and a system of cultural meaning« (Rakow, 1986, p. 19).

Sport is one of the few areas of our *high-tech* society in which one still finds a segregation of the sexes. In sport the body plays a key role, for sport always involves the presentation of the body, be it a demonstration of physical strength, endurance and aggressiveness or of beauty and elegance. And, here, the differences in performance seem to provide conclusive proof of the *natural* hierarchy of the sexes. Doing sport, too, is always *doing gender*, i. e. presenting oneself as an athlete, but as a female athlete or as a male athlete – although it must be added that some sports *dramatise* gender more than others. Whether consciously or subconsciously – gender has a constant influence on everybody's life.

In sport too people's characteristics and their actions, their body shapes and their movements are perceived through the prism of gender duality and interpreted along gender lines. The *sport culture* specific to each gender is influenced and dominated not only by the images and practices of the different sports but also by the roles enacted by sportsmen and sportswomen, by their *doing gender*. According to Lorber, sport and media sport »construct men's bodies to be powerful, women's bodies to be sexual« (Lorber, 1994, p. 43).

Sport, however, is also a social field in which gender can not only be produced but also deconstructed and modified as the way the body is used, the sporting practices and performances provide an opportunity to decode gender arrangements, to negotiate and – to a certain degree – to change them (Heywood, 1998; Pfister, 2010).

Doing handball is *doing gender*
The debates around the gender of handball must be interpreted against the backdrop of the gender order and the ideals and discourses connected with it. Although, as a result of Germany's defeat in the First World War, numerous traditional institutions, rules and norms disintegrated, although women were granted political rights under the Weimar constitution and although fashions and ideals of beauty changed, women continued to be the *other sex* which was discriminated against due to numerous written and unwritten laws and rules. It must be added, however, that differing notions about men and women and their roles existed in the various political, social and cultural environments of the Weimar Republic.

Women's sports, also handball, were constructed along the lines of the prevailing myths of womanhood, in order to avoid contradictions between being a woman and playing handball. Taking part in this cooperative and not very strenuous game could even be interpreted as demonstrative femininity.

The growing concern about girls and women playing handball had first and foremost to do with handball's gradual change from a recreational *Turner* game to a combative and aggressive sport. Schelenz and people who shared his views endeavoured to make the game competitive, strenuous, physical and potentially dangerous in order to suit male tastes which were oriented towards games like football, the national sport in Germany since the 1920s. Even today team handball connotes roughness and toughness. Consequently, it is a common prejudice that women who play *real* handball are not particularly feminine.

The labelling of sports as masculine or feminine is by no means based on individual interpretations, however. Rather, the body, along with physical activities and various forms of performances, including sport, play an important role in the re-production of the gender order and in *doing gender*. Sports, or at least certain types of sports, have served, and still serve today to construct and perform masculinity. As Dunning (1986) demonstrated using the example of rugby, sport is an important resource for the preservation of men's identity and domination in times when the balance of power between the sexes shifts, as was the case in the 1920s, but also in the 1960s or after the turn of the millennium. Women who played *men's sport* such as handball refuted myths of the weaker sex and challenged the widely held belief in men's superiority and in the traditional gender hierarchy. Thus, the attempts to keep women away from the handball fields (and other sports such as e.g. football) involved much more than just sport; they had to do with the gender order of the society as a whole. It must also be taken into account, that handball was considered as a *German game*. Because national sports produce, present and preserve myths of masculinity specific to the society, they have been and still are considered to be male domains (Pfister, 2006a).

The extent to which handball and other sport games, e.g. football or basketball, differ and why in other countries, for example Denmark and Norway, handball is a women's sport, should provide sufficient material for discussion. But this would go beyond the scope of this essay.

Not only sports but also leadership in sport organisations underwent crucial changes with regard to women's involvement, although the top positions in sport organisations are still dominated by men. Gudrun Doll-Tepper, however, managed to break the *glass ceiling* to reach the top – she is an exception, but also a pioneer and a role model.

References

Amberger, G. W. (1921). *Das Handballspiel*. Leipzig, Zürich: Grethlein.

Bernett, H. (1995). Geschichte des Handballspiels. Vom lokalen Experiment zum Weltsport. In J. Meynert (Hrsg.), *Und auch der Handball ist rund* (pp. 19–49). Bielefeld: Westfalen Verlag.

Braungardt, W. (1922). *Handball und Faustball*. Braunschweig, Hamburg: Westermann.

Butler, J. (1990). *Gender Trouble: Feminism and the Subversion of Identity*. New York, London: Routledge.

Buytendijk, F.J.J. (1953). *Das Fußballspiel. Eine psychologische Studie*. Würzburg: Werkbund.

Connell, R. (2008). *Gender*. Cambridge: Polity.

Dehmlow, F. (1926). *Turnspiele für Deutschlands Jugend* (9th edition). Langensalza: Beltz.

Dunning, E. (1986). Sport as a Male Preserve. *Theory, Culture, and Society, 3* (1), 79–90.

Eggers, E. (2014). *Handball. Geschichte eines deutschen Sports* (3rd edition). Göttingen: Verlag Die Werkstatt.

Fühler, B. (1925). *Das Handballspiel*. Berlin: Weidmann.

GutsMuths, J. C. F. (1796). *Spiele zur Übung und Erholung des Körpers und des Geistes*. Schnepfenthal: Buchhandlung der Erziehungsanstalt.

Guttmann, A. (2012). *From ritual to record. The nature of modern sports* (Updated edition). New York: Columbia University Press.

Heywood, L. (1998). *Bodymakers*. Rutgers, NJ: Rutgers University Press.

Hoffmeister, K. (1986). Ein Braunschweiger Lehrer als Begründer der Schulspiele in Deutschland. Professor Dr. phil. Konrad Koch (1846–1911). In A. Krüger (Hrsg.), *Beiträge zur niedersächsischen Sportgeschichte* (pp. 14–68). Duderstadt: Mecke.

Jahn, F. L., & Eiselen, E. (1816). *Die Deutsche Turnkunst*. Berlin.

Kierblewski, R. (1987). *Die Entwicklung des Handballspiels in Berliner Turn- und Sportvereinen*. Examensarbeit, Berlin.

Lippe von der, G. (1988). *Gla handball*. Oslo: Pax.

Lorber, J. (1994). *Paradoxes of Gender*. New Haven, CT: Yale University Press.

Maguire, J. (2006). *Power and global sport: zones of prestige, emulation and resistance*. London: Routledge.

Mielke, G. (2010). *Vermarktung des Spitzenhandballs: eine ökonomische Analyse der Handball-Bundesliga Frauen.* Wiesbaden: Gabler.

Ohmann, O. (2009). *Friedrich Ludwig Jahn.* Erfurt: Sutton.

Pfister, G. (1991). Mädchenspiele – zum Zusammenhang von Raumaneignung, Körperlichkeit und Bewegungskultur. *Sportunterricht, 40,* 165–176.

Pfister, G. (2000). Die Frauenweltspiele und die Beteiligung von Frauen an Olympischen Spielen. In M. Behrendt, & G. Steins (Eds.), Sportgeschichte. Berichte und Materialien. *Sporthistorische Blätter, 7/8,* 157–171.

Pfister, G. (2003a). Cultural confrontations: German Turnen, Swedish gymnastics and English sport. European diversity in physical activities from a historical perspective. *Sport in Society, 6* (1), 61–91.

Pfister, G. (2003b). »Doing gender« im Handballspiel – Geschlechterdiskurse und -inszenierungen in den 20er Jahren des 20. Jahrhunderts. In J. Schutová, & M. Waic (Eds.), *Turnen und Sport der Frauen in den böhmischen und anderen mitteleuropäischen Ländern* (pp. 282–292). Prag: Nationalmuseum.

Pfister, G. (2006a). Auf den Leib geschrieben – Körper, Sport und Geschlecht. In I. Hartmann-Tews, & B. Rulofs (Eds.), *Handbuch Sport und Geschlecht* (pp. 26–40). Hofmann: Schorndorf.

Pfister, G. (2006b). The future of football is female!?: On the past and present of women's football in Germany. In A. Tomlinson & C. Young (Eds.), *German football: history, culture, society* (pp. 93–126). London: Routledge.

Pfister, G. (2010). Women in sport – gender relations and future perspectives. *Sport in Society, 13* (2), 234–248.

Pfister, G., & Langenfeld, H. (1980). Die Leibesübungen für das weibliche Geschlecht – ein Mittel zur Emanzipation der Frau? In H. Ueberhorst (Ed.), *Geschichte der Leibesübungen, Vol. 3/1* (pp. 485–521). Berlin, München, Frankfurt: Bartels & Wernitz.

Pfister, G., & Langenfeld, H. (1982). Vom Frauenturnen zum modernen Sport. In H. Ueberhorst (Ed.), *Geschichte der Leibesübungen. Vol. 3/2* (pp. 1007–1077). Berlin: Bartels & Wernitz.

Rakow, L. (1986). Rethinking Gender Research in Communication. *Journal of Communication, 36,* 11–26.

Riekhoff, W. (1943). *Historische Untersuchungen über die Vorläufer und Anfänge des Deutschen Handballspiels* (Doctoral dissertation, Universität Hamburg).

Sparbier, J. (1926). *Wettspielregeln für Schlagball, Faustball, Handball.* Berlin: Weidmannsche Buchhandlung.

Thiele, G. (1914). *Johann Christoph Friedrich Gutsmuths. Spiele zur Übung und Erholung des Körpers und Geistes für die Jugend, ihre Erzieher und alle Freunde unschuldiger Jugendfreuden* (9th edition). Hof: Lion.

Institutes of Higher Education and the Olympic Games[1]

Uri Schaefer
President ICSSPE

The Olympic Games are recognised as the world's foremost sports competition, with over 200 nations represented and more than 10,000 athletes participating in the Summer Games. Whilst the Olympic Games last for 16 days, the preparation for an event like the Olympic Games lasts for about 7 years. In fact, preparatory work begins before the International Olympic Committee announces the next host city of the Games, in conjunction with a bid which has the potential in itself to help promote and develop the bidding city. This is also the case in regard to the next decision of the International Olympic Committee relating to the host city of the 2024 and the 2028 Olympic Summer Games. The two cities that have reached the final stage of the bidding process are Los Angeles and Paris.

It is well documented that the magnitude of the impact of the Olympic Games in post-modern societies can be felt in many countries around the world. The Games have influenced ordinary people and athletes alike, as we will demonstrate in this paper.

The Olympic Games and other mega-sporting events inspire us, either as educators in academic and non-academic institutions, or within the public sector, or school setting, to learn and implement the spirit and ideas of the Games on a daily basis.

»The goal of the Olympic Movement is to contribute to building a peaceful and better world by educating youth through sport practice without discrimination of any kind and in the Olympic Spirit, which requires mutual understanding with a spirit of friendship, solidarity and fair play« (International Olympic Committee, 2015).

In light of this aim and the spirit of the Olympic Games, I see it as an important task to assist educators in institutions of higher education, physical education

---

1 This paper is based on a presentation given at the International Olympic Academy, Greece, on May 27, 2017.

teachers and sport coaches with educational material which allow them to reflect upon the above mentioned goals. Ideally, this will be done in a way that will inspire children and adolescents to engage in physical activity and sport, and thus recognise the long lasting benefits of being physically active no matter where – in a school setting, sport club, a community centre or elsewhere.

Besides the global recognition of sporting performance and competition, sport participation at the grassroots level and informal physical activity, especially among adolescents, is facing challenges partly evoked by modern city construction, traffic, new technologies, increasing costs of sporting activities etc. This again has led to an increase of non-communicable diseases in all age groups worldwide. We face absurd conditions where parents have to convince their children to go outside, while in the past they had to urge them to come home for dinner.

Jacques Rogge, Past President of the International Olympic Committee, recognised these negative phenomena. In order to ensure on-going participation in the Olympic Games in the years to come, and in order to support leading agencies like United Nations, especially UNESCO and WHO, in the fight against child and youth inactivity, he initiated the Youth Olympic Games in 2007 (Youth Olympic Games, 2009). The Youth Olympic Games are targeted specifically at teenagers. The first Summer Youth Olympics Games were held in August 2010 in Singapore, while the first Winter Youth Olympics took place in January 2012, in Innsbruck, Austria. The Games included, apart from the actual sporting events, a cultural and educational programme that every participant was obliged to participate in.

Jacques Rogge's idea and hope was that the young participants also take part in the Olympic Youth Academy during the Games and would become *sport ambassadors* in their respected cities and home countries, thus leading to a growing awareness for the positive benefits inherit in organised sports (Youth Olympic Games, 2009). He was convinced that »The Youth Olympic Games can provide a magnet to attract back youth who turn their back on sports when they reach adolescence« (Johnston, 2010). But he was also aware that it would take years before the Youth Olympic Games would have a significant impact on children's health and physical activity habits, citing the example of the 116 years needed for the IOC to reach its present status (Youth Olympic Games, 2009).

However, we should not just see the promotion of physical activity in the context of the above; we need to think how Olympism could contribute to a physically active and sportive lifestyle of all members of society. Knowing that one of the most important reasons for dropping out from sport participation is the lack of fun (Harel et al., 2015), it is evident that the way physical education and sport are provided need to be analysed and, where needed, improved. Here I see an important role for policy makers as well as for educators at institutes of higher education.

The Olympic Games have the potential to deliver lasting benefits that can considerably impact and improve a community and its image and can also promote further development and future planning towards a community which encourages various forms of physical activity. The International Olympic Committee's policy is that the Games must provide far more than just good memories from the sporting events.

Through the analysis of the Olympic legacies, the spirit and idea of Olympism can be better understood and its possible implementation in the microcosms of institutes of higher education and school settings, by leveraging their potential on various societal and individual levels.

Among the main Olympic legacies are sporting, social, environmental, urban and economic development which in turn may contribute to more satisfaction and self-esteem (International Olympic Committee, 2013).

The mission and role of the IOC is »to promote a positive legacy from the Olympic Games to the host cities and host country« (Olympic Charter, 2015). These legacies might be perceived differently in different host cities, yet possessing at the same time common basic characteristics.

It is therefore expected that educators in higher education will critically use findings for their research and teaching. Hopefully, we will be able to observe a growing level of physical activity and sport participation among all age groups – all leading to improvement in health, and at the same time of performance at the elite level.

Sporting Legacies

Despite different sporting traditions across the world, the International Olympic Committee, host city and country and the general public are expecting that, as a result of the bidding process and the implementation of the Games, performance and participation numbers grow. However, from several Games we know that athletes of the host country win more medals than during other Games whereas a growing number in sporting participation and physical activity cannot be observed in all the host Olympic cities. To ensure that this legacy happens, a close co-operation between the policy level, the sporting and education systems is needed.

This is the expected direct impact of the bidding cities and countries on their citizens. In Great Britain, for instance, prior and following the London Olympics 2012, *Places People Play* invested GBP 20 million to benefit 377 community sports projects across England. This impact inevitably led to an increase in the population's awareness of the importance of being physically active. This can also be found – albeit not with the same financial investments – among students in institutions of higher education specialising in physical education.

Social Legacies

Fundamental principles of Olympism embrace education, respect for ethical principles including the opponent, human dignity, mutual understanding, the spirit of friendship, solidarity, and fair play, while rejecting all forms of racial, religious, political and gender discrimination.

Accordingly, culture and education have always been an integral part of the Olympic Games and the Opening and Closing ceremonies of the Games provide unique opportunities for the host country to introduce and expose its culture to the world and thus motivate foreign visitors to come and explore the country. The Seoul Games served as an example of this idea. South Korea was, at the beginning of the 1980s, relatively unknown in many parts of the Western world. Throughout the Games many people around the world could watch South Korea's cultural programmes which resulted in an increased integration of South Korea into the rest of the world. Likewise, the Sydney 2000 Olympic Games, and its Arts Festival, named the *Harbour of Life*, enabled the people across the world to be educated and introduced to the multicultural nature of Australian society, among others, the country's rich indigenous heritage and contemporary Aboriginal art.

Educators at institutions of higher education are expected to motivate and educate their students – future teachers and coaches – how to turn social inclusion, loyalty, respect and equality into learning objectives.

Environmental Legacies

Over the last decades, sustainability has become a growing policy area in many parts of the world which is strongly connected to research and educational institutions, the corporate sector and various other areas of the global human society. Inevitably, it has affected the sports movement and the Olympic Games as well. In 1994, the late IOC President, Juan Antonio Samaranch stated: »The International Olympic Committee is resolved to ensure that the environment becomes the third dimension of the organisation of the Olympic Games, the first and second being sport and culture« (Chappelet, 2008). Acting on this statement, in 1996 the IOC added *environment* as a third pillar to its vision for Olympic Games (Chappelet, 2008). It requires bidding cities to provide a comprehensive strategy to protect the environment in all planning and implementation phases as well as after the Games (Chappelet, 2008). This initiative was most notably acted upon in 2000, at the 27th Sydney Olympics which were considered as the first Games to be environmentally minded. The eco-friendly Olympic Village housing ended the myth, that green technology is too expensive and laid the foundation for future planning of *Green Games*. Thus the Beijing 2008 Olympic efforts to host environmentally friendly games resulted in over 160 projects aiming to meet the goal of *Green* Games through improved water quality, implementation of sustainable energy sources, and education in environmental topics.

During the Games, the athletes benefit most from these initiatives, but in the long term, the citizens will also feel the improvement of the environmental conditions supported by the idea that »The IOC's role and part of the Olympic Agenda 2020 is… to encourage and support a responsible concern for environmental issues, to promote sustainable development in sport and require that the Olympic Games are held accordingly« (Olympic Agenda 2020). This has resulted in the implementation of friendlier public transport, new sustainable energy resources across Olympic

Parks, new green parks, improved water and air quality, including major non-material environmental legacies related to Summer and Winter Olympic Games which have a strong impact on the nature (International Olympic Committee, 2013). It is therefore important that institutions of higher education address environmental aspects in the programmes they provide for students on various levels.

Urban Legacies

For all bidding cities it is a great opportunity to address urban changes. By making the candidate city an attractive place to live in or to visit, a bid and the conduct of the Games can help cities to achieve long-term goals and create a higher quality of life for their residents and increase the city's appeal.

These changes apply to almost every department in the city, among these transportation, sanitation, energy, water supply, waste management, sport, education, health, and culture. In London as part of the preparation for the Games, one of the largest regeneration projects in Europe took place »with the Olympic Park being constructed in what was previously one of the most deprived areas of the city« (International Olympic Committee, 2013). In Vancouver, among others, public transport has been expanded, wasteland has been decontaminated, abandoned industrial sites have been redesigned and made available for the public; other host cities have developed accessible neighbourhoods and invested in bike and walking lanes.

As for the institutions of higher education it is of importance to include urban planning into respective sport management programmes and create an understanding for the needs of the local population.

Economic Legacies

One of the most significant economic impacts of staging the Olympic Games is the increased level of economic activity and the increase in the Gross Domestic Product (GDP) that host cities have experienced. Another way to evaluate and look at the economic legacies is to source out the enormous investment by the host city and country during the 6 to 7 years during the preparations. *Transport to London* invested GBP 6.5 billion in transport infrastructure. Ten new railway lines and thirty new bridges are connecting London communities nowadays because of the Games.

It was also reported that at least sixty Games related projects promoted greener travel, including a GBP 10 million investment to upgrade pedestrian and cycling routes across London. Furthermore, independent analysts reported that the Games preparations were a major factor in the 1.2 per cent reduction in the unemployment rate in early 2012 (International Olympic Committee, 2013).

There is much more to write concerning the economic contribution to most Olympic host cities, but it should be understood that failures were also reported following the London Games and other Olympic host cities, some of which have faced some great financial debts as a result of organising and hosting the Games.

As we have outlined, the Olympic Games created many Olympic legacies which have impressive positive impacts on the host cities, on the countries and on the inhabitants. But there are also many other additional positive outcomes to the Games which this paper did not explore, such as: promotion of healthy living across the life span, learning to train and to compete, making new friends, international collaboration, and others.

Olympic Legacies and Their Impact on Teaching at Institutions of Higher Education

Dispite all the positive impact, we must realise that the aspiration for better performances and success, the Games also have a relatively long list of negative outcomes, among them we can point out doping, corruption, match fixing, bribery, fraud, athlete and child abuse, sexual harassment, sport injuries due to overtraining, and exploitation to name the significant ones only. The International Olympic Committee and other stakeholders have taken measures and are cooperating to meet the challenges related to the above. In this regard, it should be emphasised that the protection of clean athletes and the fight against doping are high on the agenda of the IOC.

All these challenges as well as the previously addressed positive legacies must be addressed in academic programmes at institutions of higher education.

In what has been presented so far my intention has been to create awareness among future physical educators and coaches of the huge impact they have on future participation of children and adolescents in physical activity and their view on sport especially. This said, I am convinced that sport provides a unique opportunity, a *laboratory*, to learn for the future. I encourage young visitors of the International Olympic Academy to accept the opportunities that lie in their professional life. I am not only thinking of those students who study sport management, architecture, sports law or sports medicine; on the contrary, I would like everybody to understand that all professionals, volunteers, athletes, officers and other groups are part of a structure that can have a positive impact on personal and societal development. And in order to better understand this I encourage educators and institutes of higher education to create scenarios that allow for a personal entry point to the respective theme or topic and thus lead to a better understanding for the needs of everybody participating in physical activity and sport or for those indirectly affected by both. It is not about *us* and *them*; instead, through personal experiences we learn about our roles that either support developments that have very little in common with Olympic values or contribute to sustainable change for the benefit of all parts of society. In this sense I very much support the idea of experimental learning which should be applied wherever possible and which has its roots in concepts that have been further developed by well-known pedagogues over the past centuries.

Building on this, I ask the visitors of the International Olympic Academy to consider to also act as an entrepreneur and to initiate new ideas and activities based on the Olympic Spirit.

In Israel, for example, six years ago, the sport administration in the Ministry of Culture and Sport initiated a project named *The Children's Olympics*. Since then, the project is organised by the sport administration in collaboration with the communities in Israel and is held at the Wingate Institute, Israel's National Sport Centre every year on the first Friday of the month of May when children are out of school. The National Olympic Committee of Israel, the National Paralympic Committee, the lottery and Special Olympics of Israel, support the event. Some 5,000 young athletes aged between seven to sixteen years old, are transported with their coaches from over 80 communities across the country to take part in a one-day competition in over 20 different sport disciplines.

Following the opening ceremony, when all the participants are marching into the stadium and thus imitate the start of the Olympic Games, the competitions begin. They are all opened by Israeli top athletes following a short address when they share their personal thoughts about Olympic legacies with the young athletes. This is a unique opportunity for all the participants to experience on a small and very limited, but meaningful manner the Olympic spirit hoping that it will lead to long-lasting sport participation. Every participant is a winner and everyone gets a medal for participation.

This paper indicates that educators at institutes of higher education use the Olympic Games as a catalyst for a better understanding of human movement, advocate for the benefits associated with an active lifestyle, and educate for human and Olympic values.

Summarising the message of this paper, it is inevitable that major sporting events such as the Olympic Games can and should be used by educators in institutes of higher education. The Games are, in this sense, a unique platform from which to draw ideas and learn for the future.

References

Chappelet, J.L. (2008). Olympic Environmental Concerns as a Legacy of the Winter Olympics. *The International Journal of the History of Sport, 25* (14), 1884–1902.

Harel, Y. et al. (2015). *Patterns of physical activity among children and adolescent in Israel 2014.* School of Education; Bar-Ilan University.

International Olympic Committee (2013). *Olympic Legacy* (pp. 5–65). Lausanne: International Olympic Committee.

International Olympic Committee (2015). *The Olympic Charter.* http://stillmed. olympic.org; September 2015.

Johnston, P. (2010). *Youth Olympic Games Can Stop Kids Leaving Sport: Rogge.* http://www.reuters.com/article/us-olympics-rogge-idUSTRE62M0XH20100 323; March 2017.

Olympic Agenda 2020. http://www.org.olympic>documents; 18. November 2014.

Olympic Charter (2015). https://stillmed.olympic.org/Documents/olympic_ charter_en.pdf; 14. August 2017.

Youth Olympic Games (2009). *(YOG) Fact Sheet, 2009*; http://multimedia.olympic.org/pdf/en_report_1423.pdf; March 2017.

Frauen im Sport: Totales Eigenleben
Ein Gespräch mit Shokouh Navabinejad[1]

Guido Schilling
Chair ICSSPE Editorial Board 1997–2003

Shokouh Navabinejad (links im Bild)

Guido: Du hast in den USA studiert und kennst so auch den amerikanischen Sport gut. Wo liegen aus deiner Sicht die Hauptunterschiede zwischen der Organisation des Sports in den USA und im Iran bzw. anderen islamischen Ländern?

Shokouh: Unser Frauensport ist total getrennt vom Sport der Männer. Frauen sind so auch Trainerinnen, Kampfrichterinnen und Managerinnen geworden. Sie mussten in den nationalen Verbänden Spitzenpositionen übernehmen. Es gibt wohl kaum ein anderes Land wie den Iran, wo im Sport so viele gut ausgebildete und spezialisierte Frauen mitarbeiten.

Guido: Das ist fast ein Gegensatz zu unseren Strukturen, wo sich die früher getrennten Organisationen der Frauen und der Männer zusammengeschlossen

---

1 Zum Zeitpunkt des Interviews war Dr. Shokouh Navabinejad Professorin an der Teachers Training University und Direktorin des Women's Network of non-governmental organisations in Iran.

haben. Ist diese strikte Trennung nicht auch hinderlich, weil so viele Parallelstrukturen nötig sind?

Shokouh: Es gibt für uns keine anderen Möglichkeiten, weil die islamische Staatsform das so vorschreibt. Aber das ist ja eigentlich gut für die Frauen, sie müssen so ihre Identität suchen.

Der Sport hilft den Frauen sich zu emanzipieren. Sie müssen in den eigenen Organisationen ja auch Führungseigenschaften entwickeln, damit sie ihre Teams betreuen und führen können. Natürlich arbeiten wir aber auch mit den Organisationen der Männer zusammen.

Guido: Ist die Emanzipation der Frauen im Sport auch auf andere Bereiche übertragbar?

Shokouh: Ja sicher. So haben wir seit 2001 an der Universität Teheran ein *Center for Women's Studies (CWS)*, das ein Netzwerk zur Förderung der Frauen in Ländern gründete, wo Persisch gesprochen wird. Das Netzwerk will Frauen anhalten und ermutigen sich national und international aktiv an der Entwicklung der Gesellschaft zu beteiligen. Das Netzwerk will Kontakte und auch Wissen zur Verfügung stellen und so Frauen befähigen sich für ihre Anliegen erfolgreich einzusetzen.

Guido: Zurück zum internationalen Sport. Wie können junge Frauen mit dieser Geschlechtertrennung im Sport umgehen? Möchten sie nicht auch im internationalen Sport mitmachen? Sie stehen ja sehr im Abseits und dürfen nicht einmal als Zuschauerinnen bei einem Fußballspiel mit Männermannschaften dabei sein.

Shokouh: In der Tat sind wir mit der strikten Geschlechtertrennung im Sport sehr gefordert. Das Eigenleben des Frauensports in den islamischen Ländern hatte und hat zwar sicher Vorteile, aber auch große Nachteile: Der Sport findet kaum Platz in den Familien.

Außerdem verlieren unsere Athletinnen die Motivation, wenn sie nicht im Weltsport mitmachen können. Auch das Fernsehen in unserem Land bietet ihnen keine Plattform, denn Fernsehübertragungen von Sportveranstaltungen mit Frauen sind nicht erlaubt. Wir müssen da unbedingt eine Lösung finden. Vielleicht kann die Bekleidung der Frauen in den diversen Sportarten so sein, dass sie den islamischen Kleidervorschriften entspricht. Wir müssen vermehrt in Erscheinung treten, sichtbar werden.

Inklusion im schulischen und außerschulischen Sport – im Fokus der Heterogenitätsdimension Behinderung

Heike Tiemann und Sabine Radtke
Universität Leipzig und Universität Paderborn

Der Inklusionsbegriff wird aktuell in geradezu inflationärer Weise gebraucht. Häufig geschieht dies in Abgrenzung zum Integrationsbegriff, nicht selten werden die beiden Begriffe allerdings auch synonym verwendet. Die unterschiedliche Bedeutung der Termini ruft immer noch Irritationen hervor und die Frage nach »terminologische[m] Spiel oder konzeptionelle[r] Weiterentwicklung« (vgl. Hinz, 2002, S. 354) steht offenkundig im Raum.

Im Rahmen dieses Beitrags soll ein Verständnis von Inklusion zugrunde gelegt werden, welches im Kontext der Verabschiedung und Ratifizierung der UN-Behindertenrechtskonvention steht und eine spezifische Heterogenitätsdimension, nämlich die Kategorie Behinderung, fokussiert. Ziel des Aufsatzes ist die Auseinandersetzung mit der Frage des Umgangs mit Behinderung in unserer Gesellschaft unter Berücksichtigung des schulischen und außerschulischen Sports. Dabei können aus historischer Perspektive verschiedene aufeinander aufbauende Phasen identifiziert werden: von der Phase der Segregation/Separation über die der Integration zur Inklusion (vgl. Radtke, 2011). In diesem Kontext wird verdeutlicht, dass es sich bei einer Begrenzung auf die Kategorie Behinderung um eine eindimensionale Sichtweise handelt, die mit Blick auf den Ansatz der Pädagogik der Vielfalt und dem *Diversity*-Ansatz seine Vervollständigung erfährt. Darauf aufbauend werden ausgewählte Themenstellungen des aktuellen wissenschaftlichen Inklusionsdiskurses diskutiert. Den Beitrag beschließen persönliche Worte der Autorinnen an Gudrun Doll-Tepper.

1 Der Weg von der Segregation zur Integration

Das Jahr 1888 kann mit der Gründung der *Taubstummen-Turnvereinigung Berlin* als der Beginn des (separierten) organisierten Behindertensports in Deutschland betrachtet werden (vgl. ebd.). Infolge des Ersten Weltkriegs und der aus ihm hervorgegangenen vielen Menschen mit *Kriegsbeschädigungen* kam es zu einer zumindest zeitweilig schnell voranschreitenden Entwicklung des sogenannten

Versehrtensports. Zur Verbesserung des Gesamtbefindens erhielten viele Kriegsverwundete in Lazaretten die Möglichkeit an ärztlich überwachten sportlichen Übungen teilzunehmen (vgl. Tiemann, 2006). Ihr Enthusiasmus überdauerte den Weltkrieg jedoch nicht und nur wenige setzten ihre sportlichen Aktivitäten weiter fort (vgl. Guttmann, 1979). Der Zweite Weltkrieg führte zu einer neuen Belebung des Sports von Menschen mit Behinderung. Haep (1988, S. 21) spricht von etwa 1,5 Millionen *Kriegsversehrten* als *Keimzelle des Behindertensports*. In einer Reihe von Lazaretten des Zweiten Weltkrieges wurden Übungsstätten für sportliche Aktivitäten eingerichtet (vgl. Lorenzen 1961). Nach dem Krieg kam es auch außerhalb dieser Institutionen in der gesamten Bundesrepublik zur Gründung von Sportgruppen, initiiert von den Betroffenen selbst. Um eine einheitliche Entwicklung des Sports zu sichern, bildete sich 1951 als Zusammenschluss von fünf Vereinen mit etwa 5500 Mitgliedern die *Arbeitsgemeinschaft Deutscher Versehrtensport*, die 1952 umbenannt wurde in *Deutscher Versehrtensportverband* (DVS) (vgl. Haep 1988). Während in den 1950er Jahren männliche Kriegsversehrte in den Vereinen dominierten, differenzierte sich die Mitgliederstruktur mit der Zeit zusehends im Hinblick auf Geschlecht, Lebensalter und Art der Behinderung. Fortan nahmen weniger Kriegsinvaliden als vielmehr Menschen mit angeborener oder durch Unfall bzw. Krankheit erworbener Behinderung an Sportaktivitäten teil. Mit der Umbenennung des Dachverbands für den Sport von Menschen mit Behinderung 1975 in *Deutscher Behindertensportverband (DBS)* verschoben sich die Inhalte des ursprünglichen Versehrtensports in Richtung Rehabilitations-, Breiten- und Leistungssport. Zusammenfassend bleibt festzuhalten, dass in den 1950er und 1960er Jahren eine klare Trennung der Sportaktivitäten von Menschen mit und ohne Behinderung bestand.

Parallel zu der Entwicklung im Bildungssystem[1] wurden Mitte der 1970er Jahre erstmals integrative Ansätze im Sport in Bezug auf Menschen mit Behinderung diskutiert. So war es Ziel dieser Integrationsbewegung, Freizeitsportangebote für das gemeinsame Sporttreiben von Menschen mit und ohne Behinderung zu

---

1 Die Diskussion über *Integration* wurde in der Sonderpädagogik um 1970 eröffnet. 1973 entstand nach dreijähriger Beratungszeit des Fachausschusses *Sonderpädagogik* der Bildungskommission des Deutschen Bildungsrates das erste bildungspolitische Dokument, das die gemeinsame Beschulung von Kindern mit und ohne Behinderung empfiehlt (Titel: *Zur pädagogischen Förderung behinderter und von Behinderung bedrohter Kinder und Jugendlicher*).

schaffen, um Berührungsängste abzubauen und gemeinsame Aktivitäten voranzutreiben (vgl. Doll-Tepper, 2012). Parallele Entwicklungen waren im Bildungsbereich zu verzeichnen, als neben den bestehenden Schulen mit unterschiedlichen sonderpädagogischen Förderschwerpunkten auf Initiative engagierter Eltern vereinzelt Pilotprojekte zur integrativen Beschulung entstanden (vgl. z. B. Ziebarth, 2010).

Auf dem Gebiet der Integration in den organisierten Sport leisteten Eltern eines Sohnes mit Down-Syndrom Mitte der 1970er Jahre Pionierarbeit. Sie setzten sich im *ASC Göttingen von 1846 e. V.* für das gemeinsame Sporttreiben von Kindern und Jugendlichen mit und ohne Behinderung ein. Das Projekt wurde als *Göttinger Modell* bekannt und führte zur Gründung des bis heute bestehenden Fachbereichs *Integration durch Sport* im ASC Göttingen. In Anlehnung an das Göttinger Modell gingen in verschiedenen Städten weitere integrative Modellprojekte an den Start, die sich im Laufe der Zeit entweder als Abteilungen in allgemeinen Sportvereinen oder als eigene Integrationssportvereine weiterentwickelten. Bis heute gibt es zahlreiche Beispiele der Organisation integrativer Spiel- und Sportfeste, wobei die umfassende Einbindung von Menschen mit Behinderung (zumal von Menschen mit schwerer Mehrfachbehinderung) in das soziale Gesamtgeschehen oft noch als Herausforderung empfunden wird (vgl. Fediuk, 2008). Festzuhalten bleibt, dass Segregation und Integration keine klar gegeneinander abzugrenzenden Phasen sind, sondern dass bis heute beide parallel nebeneinander bestehen.

Im Gegensatz zum Begriffsverständnis aus (sport-)soziologischer Perspektive wird aus Sicht der aktuellen Inklusionspädagogik die Phase der Integration als eine Vorstufe zur Phase der Inklusion betrachtet, wobei *Integration* im Verständnis der 1970er Jahre im weitesten Sinne mit Assimilation gleichzusetzen war.

2 Von der Integration zur Inklusion

Während der Inklusionsbegriff im deutschsprachigen Raum lange Zeit kaum bekannt war und Begriffsgebrauch und Diskussion seit Anfang der 2000er Jahre zunächst vor allem auf die akademischen Fachkreise der Sonder- und Heilpädagogik beschränkt blieben, hat der Diskurs um Inklusion im internationalen Raum eine wesentlich längere Tradition. Fälschlicherweise wird zuweilen behauptet, dass der Diskurs um Inklusion erst mit der 1994 in Salamanca stattfindenden UNESCO-Weltkonferenz *Pädagogik für besondere Bedürfnisse: Zugang und Qua-*

lität begann. Der Ursprung des Diskurses um die Begrifflichkeit in Abgrenzung zu *Mainstreaming* und *Integration* setzte jedoch bereits früher im angloamerikanischen und angelsächsischen Raum ein (vgl. Radtke, 2016).

Die sogenannte Salamanca-Konferenz von 1994 stellte jedoch insofern einen Meilenstein dar, als hier die *Deklaration von Salamanca* verabschiedet wurde, die die inklusive Erziehung hervorhebt, indem sie als Leitprinzip feststellt, dass Schulen »alle Kinder, unabhängig von ihren physischen, intellektuellen, sozialen, emotionalen, sprachlichen oder anderen Fähigkeiten aufnehmen sollen« (Schnell, 2006, S. 10). Im Kontext der Deklaration ist darauf hinzuweisen, dass in den ins Deutsche übersetzten Dokumenten häufig nicht der Begriff Inklusion, sondern fälschlicherweise der Begriff Integration verwendet wird.

Inklusionspädagoginnen und -pädagogen heben hervor, dass es zwischen den Begriffen Integration und Inklusion allerdings durchaus eine klare Abgrenzung bzw. Weiterentwicklung im Hinblick auf die Teilhabe von Menschen mit Behinderung an gesellschaftlichen Lebensbereichen gibt: »Inklusion beansprucht in der Tat [...] einen Paradigmenwechsel« (Hinz, 2002, S. 3). Gemäß diesem Ansatz wird ein Individuum (einer sozialen Randgruppe) im Zuge eines Integrationsprozesses in ein bestehendes System aufgenommen, welches ursprünglich nicht analog seiner Bedürfnisse konzipiert worden ist. Infolgedessen muss dieses Individuum aus eigener Kraft versuchen sich an das bestehende System mit seinen kulturellen Standards anzupassen (vgl. Radtke, 2011). So lautet in Bezug auf den Integrationsprozess im Handlungsfeld Sport die Frage: Was muss eine sportinteressierte Person mit Behinderung tun, um an einem bestehenden Sportangebot teilnehmen zu können? Dieses Begriffsverständnis entspricht einem assimilatorischen Integrationsverständnis.

Im Gegensatz dazu erfordert der inklusive Ansatz weniger einen Anpassungsprozess auf individueller Ebene als vielmehr einen Veränderungsprozess auf institutioneller Ebene. Insofern muss im Rahmen des Inklusionsprozesses der Frage nachgegangen werden, wie Sportangebote auf allen Ebenen (Breiten-, Schul- und Spitzensport) gestaltet sein müssen, um die Teilhabe aller Mitglieder einer heterogenen Gesellschaft mit all ihren vielfältigen sozialen Merkmalen zu ermöglichen. An dieser Stelle ist zu betonen, dass aus Sicht der Inklusionspädagogik das Begriffsverständnis von Inklusion keinesfalls ausschließlich auf die Kategorie Behinderung zu beziehen ist, sondern viel weiter zu fassen ist und weitere Vielfaltsdimensionen wie z.B. Geschlecht, Alter, Ethnie, Religion und sexuelle Orientierung mit einbezieht (vgl. Fediuk, 2008; Tiemann, Schulz & Schmidt-Gotz, 2007). Die Pädagogik der Vielfalt[2] findet sich wiederum im *Diversity*-Ansatz wieder, dessen Ziel es ist, Menschen mit all ihren Unterschieden im gesellschaftlichen Kontext zu berücksichtigen, einzubeziehen und daraus folgend als Ganzes von dieser Vielfalt zu profitieren (vgl. Stuber, 2009). Es bleibt demzufolge festzuhalten, dass es zwischen dem politischen und pädagogischen Inklusionskonzept und dem aus Wirtschaft und Organisationsmanagement stammenden *Diversity*-Ansatz Parallelen gibt. Im Sinne des auf dem Potenzialprinzip beruhenden *Diversity*-Ansatzes wird eine Behinderung nicht mehr als ein Defizit der betroffenen Person betrachtet, das – mit dem Ziel der Anpassung an die gesellschaftliche Norm bedarf.

Einen besonderen Impuls in der Inklusionsdebatte ging von dem durch die Generalversammlung der Vereinten Nationen im Jahr 2006 verabschiedeten und in Deutschland durch Bundestag und Bundesrat im Jahr 2009 ratifizierten Übereinkommen über die Rechte der Menschen mit Behinderungen zur gleichberechtigten gesellschaftlichen Teilhabe, aus. Die sogenannte Behindertenrechtskonvention (BRK) ist die erste verbindliche Völkerrechtsquelle, die die Menschenrechte von Personen mit Behinderung zum Thema hat, und in der Literatur als *Inklusionsmotor* beschrieben wird (Degener, 2009, S. 200). Entscheidend für das gesamte Bildungssystem ist Artikel 24 der Konvention, der die Vertragsstaaten verpflichtet, ein *inclusive education system at all levels* (Bundesgesetzblatt Jahrgang 2008, S. 1436) zu gewährleisten. Während in der völkerrechtlich bindenden englischen Fassung der Begriff der Inklusion (*inclusion*) verwendet wird, wurde in der deutschsprachigen Übersetzung der BRK von einem *integrativen Bildungssystem auf allen Ebenen* gesprochen. Dieser Übersetzungsfehler wurde von vielen Fach- und Behindertenverbänden kritisiert und als bewusste und gewollte Entstellung und Entschärfung des emanzipatorischen Gehalts der Konvention angeprangert (vgl. Frühauf, 2008).

---

2 Das hier formulierte Verständnis von einer Pädagogik der Vielfalt geht über das von Prengel (1993) hinaus, die diesen Terminus geprägt hat und in ihren Ausführungen drei Vielfaltsdimensionen in den Mittelpunkt stellt: Ethnische Zugehörigkeit, Geschlecht und Behinderung.

Artikel 30 (5) der Konvention beinhaltet unter dem Titel *Teilhabe am kulturellen Leben sowie Erholung, Freizeit und Sport* die Forderung nach der gleichberechtigten Teilnahme an Sportaktivitäten auf allen Ebenen, was sowohl das inklusive Sporttreiben gemeinsam mit Menschen ohne Behinderung als auch behinderungsspezifische Settings beinhaltet. Mit der rechtsverbindlichen Verankerung der Konvention sind alle gesellschaftlichen Kräfte und so auch der Sport gefordert, sowohl auf institutioneller als auch auf personeller Ebene entsprechende Grundvoraussetzungen für den Inklusionsprozess zu schaffen. Der Deutsche Olympische Sportbund (DOSB) hat mit den drei Behindertensportverbänden[3] bereits 2013 ein Positionspapier zum Thema veröffentlicht. Auch in diesem wird auf die *Wahlmöglichkeiten zwischen behinderungsspezifischen und gemeinsamen Angeboten in Sportvereinen* hingewiesen (DOSB, 2013, S. 3).

3 Der wissenschaftliche Inklusionsdiskurs in ausgewählten Handlungsfeldern des Sports

3.1 Inklusion im Schulsport

Die Geschichte des deutschen Schulwesens ist seit jeher von Separierung und Spezialisierung geprägt. Noch heute gehört Deutschland zu den wenigen Ländern weltweit, in denen lediglich rund 31 Prozent der Schülerinnen und Schüler mit sonderpädagogischem Förderbedarf an Regelschulen unterrichtet werden (vgl. Klemm, 2015). Die Ratifizierung der Behindertenrechtskonvention zieht nach sich, dass die im Schulwesen Verantwortlichen nicht mehr umhin kommen sich mit dem Phänomen der Heterogenität im Klassenzimmer auseinanderzusetzen. In Bezug auf den wissenschaftlichen Diskurs im Rahmen der deutschen Sportpädagogik/-didaktik ist festzustellen, dass man hier lange gegenüber Inklusionsbestrebungen – im Gegensatz zur kritischen Auseinandersetzung auf internationaler Ebene – die Augen verschlossen hat (vgl. Hölter, 2011). Die in Deutschland in den letzten Jahren formulierten Ansätze und Modelle zum Umgang mit Diversität im Sportunterricht (vgl. z. B. Fediuk, 2008; Weichert, 2008; Tiemann, 2013; Tiemann, 2016) haben in der Sportlehrerinnen- und Sportlehrerausbildung erst in den letzten Jahren Berücksichtigung gefunden. Während

---

3 Hierbei handelt es sich um den Deutschen Behindertensportverband (DBS), Special Olympics Deutschland (SOD) und den Deutschen Gehörlosen-Sportverband (DGS).

in anderen Ländern die Auseinandersetzung zum Beispiel mit dem Thema *Adapted Physical Activity* (APA) schon lange selbstverständlich ist (vgl. Doll-Tepper, 2003), wird in Deutschland erst in den letzten Jahren verstärkt über verpflichtende Lehrmodule mit Inhalten zum inklusiven Unterricht nachgedacht.

Neben den notwendigen Kenntnissen und Kompetenzen von Sportlehrerinnen und -lehrern in Bezug auf einen inklusiven Sportunterricht und neben der Barrierefreiheit von Sportstätten ist es jedoch die Haltung der Lehrkräfte, der bei der Umsetzung schulischer Inklusion eine Schlüsselposition zukommt: Ihre positive Einstellung ist entscheidend für eine gelungene Gestaltung von inklusivem Unterricht (vgl. De Boer, Pijb & Minnaert, 2011, S. 331). Die Beantwortung der Frage, wie eine Lehrerin oder ein Lehrer zur Inklusion steht, ob sie oder er in der Vielfalt der Schülerinnen und Schüler eine Bereicherung, Chance und positive Herausforderung sieht oder diese eher negativ beurteilt, ist ausschlaggebend für den Inklusionsprozess (vgl. Tiemann, 2013).

3.2 Inklusion im außerschulischen Sport – das Beispiel des Leistungssports

Während in Deutschland die Sportstrukturen fast ausschließlich von Segregation geprägt sind, setzt man sich in anderen Ländern, wie beispielsweise Kanada und Großbritannien, schon seit rund 20 Jahren auf der Organisationsebene mit dem Thema Inklusion auseinander (im Folgenden vgl. Radtke, 2011; 2013; Radtke & Doll-Tepper, 2010; 2014). So wurde in Kanada Anfang der 1990er Jahre von der Dachsportorganisation *Sport Canada* als Top-Down-Strategie die Devise ausgegeben, dass der Zuständigkeitsbereich der für die einzelnen Sportarten zuständigen Sportfachverbände auf der nationalen Ebene von nun an den Behindertensport einschließe. Bei Nichteinhaltung drohten den Verbänden finanzielle Sanktionen. Die Folgen der gleichberechtigten Einordnung von Sportlerinnen und Sportlern mit und ohne Behinderung in ein und denselben Sportverband sind gleichwertige finanzielle Fördermaßnahmen sowie – dies zumindest im Falle von Mitgliedern der britischen Paralympics-Mannschaften – gleichwertige Prämien nach Medaillengewinnen.

Das Ausmaß des Kontaktes zwischen Nationalmannschaftsmitgliedern mit und ohne Behinderung, begünstigt durch die Durchführung von gemeinsamen Trainingslagern sowie Meisterschaften, differiert international zwischen den einzelnen Sportarten mitunter erheblich. In Deutschland bestehen beispielsweise in den Bereichen Reiten und Rudern auf der Leistungssportebene Kooperationen mit dem jeweiligen Nichtbehindertensportverband. Der Deutsche Schützenbund, der neben weiteren Verbänden eine Kooperation von Behinderten- und Nichtbehindertensport eingegangen ist, wartete im Januar 2011 mit einem Novum im deutschen Sport auf: Gemäß einem Beschluss des Gesamtvorstandes des Schützenbundes darf die Paralympics-Siegerin Manuela Schmermund, die im Rollstuhl sitzt, in der Bundesliga gemeinsam mit *Fußgängern* starten.

Es bleibt aber festzuhalten, dass es im internationalen Vergleich in Deutschland im Hinblick auf eine generelle sportartspezifische Zusammenführung von Behinderten- und Nichtbehindertenbereich in den Spitzenverbänden derzeit noch Handlungsbedarf gibt (vgl. Radtke, 2013).

4 Aktuelle Entwicklung im außerschulischen Sport

Im Kontext der Umsetzung von Inklusion lassen sich eine Reihe von Entwicklungslinien identifizieren: Beispielsweise wurde zur Beurteilung, aber auch zur Planung und Umsetzung von inklusiven Settings von den britischen Pädagogen Mel Ainscow und Tony Booth der sogenannte Index für Inklusion entwickelt, der inzwischen international vielfach u. a. zur Initiierung von Schulentwicklungsprozessen eingesetzt wird. Der Index für Inklusion ist ein Fragenkatalog, der ursprünglich für Schulen und Kindertagesstätten entwickelt wurde und der aus einer Art *Checkliste* mit über 500 Fragen besteht, die dabei helfen sollen, eine Einrichtung auf Aspekte wie Teilhabe und Vielfalt bzw. Ausgrenzung und Diskriminierung zu überprüfen (vgl. Montag Stiftung Jugend und Gesellschaft, o. J., S. 4). Die Idee des Index für Inklusion wurde in unterschiedlichen Zusammenhängen aufgegriffen und ausdifferenziert, z.B. in Form des Kommunalen Index für Inklusion der Montag Stiftung (2011), des Index für Inklusion in Kindertageseinrichtungen der GEW (2017) oder auch des Index für Inklusion im und durch Sport, herausgegeben vom Deutschen Behindertensportverband (DBS) mit dem Ziel einen Beitrag zu leisten, »dass in Deutschland das Entstehen inklusiver Sportlandschaften weiter vorangebracht wird« (Deutscher Behindertensportverband, 2014, S. 6).

Auch der DOSB hat mit seinem bereits oben erwähnten Positionspapier ein für den organisierten Sport richtungsweisendes Dokument vorgelegt (zur Inklusionsdebatte im DOSB vgl. Doll-Tepper, 2016). In diesem Papier werden die Leistungen des organisierten Sports dargestellt, das Verständnis von Inklusion verdeutlicht und Orientierung für die Sportverbände gegeben. Es wird unter anderem hervorgehoben, dass der DOSB und seine Mitgliedsorganisationen Informationen zum Thema Inklusion allgemein, aber auch zu Aktionen und übergreifenden Maßnahmen sowie zu guten Beispielen sammeln und verbreiten (vgl. DOSB, 2013, S. 5). 2015 folgte das Strategiekonzept des DOSB, in dem unter anderem Chancen und Risiken, Stärken und Schwächen sowie wichtige Handlungsfelder der Inklusion differenziert dargelegt werden (vgl. DOSB, 2015). In einer Stellungnahme von 2016 hat sich der DOSB gemeinsam mit dem Deutschen Behindertensportverband, dem Deutschen Gehörlosenverband und Special Olympics Deutschland zum Gesetzentwurf der Bundesregierung zur Stärkung der Teilhabe und Selbstbestimmung von Menschen mit Behinderungen geäußert und eine eigene Forderungen formuliert.

Von der Beauftragten der Bundesregierung für die Belange behinderter Menschen geht eine weitere wichtige Maßnahme aus: *Die Landkarte der inklusiven Beispiele*, welche online einsehbar ist. Nicht nur in Bezug, aber auch auf den Sport gerichtet, lassen sich in diesem Kontext bundesweit inklusive Projekte identifizieren.

5 Persönliche Worte anstelle eines Fazits

Die beiden Autorinnen sind Gudrun Doll-Tepper seit langer Zeit durch die gemeinsame Wirkungszeit an der Freien Universität Berlin verbunden. Heike Tiemann wurde in ihrem Studium schon sehr früh von Gudrun Doll-Tepper inspiriert von der Idee der Integration und letztlich auch der Inklusion. Als Mitwirkende der deutschsprachigen APA-Pionierbewegung gehörte sie dem Helferteam des legendären, in der politischen Aufbruchsstimmung des Jahres 1989 in Berlin (West) stattfindenden *ISAPA (International Symposium on Adapted Physical Activity)* an, bei dem unter der Leitung von Gudrun Doll-Tepper das Kunststück gelang im Internationalen Congress Centrum (ICC) der Stadt einen Kongress mit über 1.000 Teilnehmenden in einem Fachgebiet zu organisieren, das der deutschsprachigen Wissenschaftscommunity bis dahin quasi gänzlich unbekannt war: *Adapted Physical Activity (APA)*. Gudrun Doll-Tepper war es, die Heike Tiemann anregte in der ersten Kohorte von Studierenden am mit anderen von Gudrun entwickelten und ins Leben gerufenen Studiengang *Adapted Physical Activity* teilzunehmen. Der *European Master in Adapted Physical Activity* stellte letztlich einen bedeutenden Grundstein der wissenschaftlichen Karriere Heike Tiemanns dar.

Sabine Radtke arbeitete von 2001 bis 2013 als Wissenschaftliche Mitarbeiterin im Arbeitsbereich *Integrationspädagogik, Bewegung und Sport*, den Gudrun Doll-Tepper nach Schließung eines der ehemals größten deutschen sportwissenschaftlichen Institute begründet hatte und so der Sportwissenschaft an der FU Berlin zumindest noch zu einem Standbein verhalf. Als *Mitbewohnerin* in der sogenannten *Fabeck-WG* arbeitete Sabine Radtke gemeinsam mit Gudrun Doll-Tepper und der damals in Kopenhagen ansässigen Gertrud Pfister im Wissenschaftsprojekt *Frauen an die Spitze*, in dessen Rahmen die Unterrepräsentanz von Frauen in Führungspositionen des Sports untersucht wurde. Anschließend führten Gudrun Doll-Tepper und Sabine Radtke gemeinsam mehrere erfolgreiche Forschungsprojekte zum Thema *Paralympischer Sport* durch, was der thematische Ausgangspunkt für die heutige Expertise von Sabine Radtke in ebendiesem Themenfeld darstellt.

Wir wissen die lange Zusammenarbeit mit Gudrun Doll-Tepper sehr wertzuschätzen! Gudrun ist eine äußerst charismatische Person, von der wir in unserer Zeit als Nachwuchswissenschaftlerinnen vorgelebt bekommen haben, wie man mit großer Leidenschaft und Authentizität sowohl in der Fachcommunity als auch vor den Studierenden für die eigenen Themen eintreten, sie mitreißen und sie auf diese Art und Weise sensibilisieren kann. Nicht zuletzt ist die Zusammenarbeit mit Gudrun Doll-Tepper neben aller Leistungsbezogenheit stets mit viel Humor, Spaß und familiärer Vertrautheit verbunden; etliche gemeinsame Aktivitäten, vor allem auch Reisen zu internationalen Tagungen und Kongressen sind uns so in Erinnerung geblieben. Die Begeisterung und Leidenschaft für unser großes gemeinsames Thema *Heterogenität im Sport*, die uns von Gudrun Doll-Tepper stets vorgelebt wurde und durch die wir in unserer Wissenschaftssozialisation stark geprägt sind, versuchen wir, die wir nun mittlerweile selbst Professorinnen sind, genauso an unseren eigenen wissenschaftlichen Nachwuchs weiterzugeben.

Literatur

Bundesgesetzblatt (Jahrgang 2008 Teil II Nr. 35, ausgegeben zu Bonn am 31. Dezember 2008). *Gesetz zu dem Übereinkommen der Vereinten Nationen vom 13. Dezember 2006 über die Rechte von Menschen mit Behinderungen sowie zu dem Fakultativprotokoll vom 13. Dezember 2006 zum Übereinkommen der Vereinten Nationen über die Rechte von Menschen mit Behinderungen.*

DBS (Hrsg.) (2014). *Index für Inklusion im und durch Sport.* Frechen: Deutscher Behindertensportverband.

De Boer, A., Pijb, S.J. & Minnaert, A. (2011). Regular primary schoolteachers' attitudes towards inclusive education: a review of the literature. *International Journal of Inclusive Education, 15*(3), 331–353.

Degener, T. (2009). Die UN-Behindertenrechtskonvention als Inklusionsmotor. *RdJB, 2*, 200–219.

Doll-Tepper, G. (2003). Adapted Physical Activity. In P. Röthig & R. Prohl (Hrsg.), *Sportwissenschaftliches Lexikon* (S. 16–18). Schorndorf: Hofmann.

Doll-Tepper, G. (2012). Inklusiver Sport – Wege zu einer langfristigen Sicherung von Teilhabechancen. In F. Kiuppis & S. Kurzke-Maasmeier (Hrsg.), *Sport im Spiegel der UN-Behindertenrechtskonvention* (S. 80–90). Stuttgart: Kohlhammer.

Doll-Tepper, G. (2016). Inklusion im und durch Sport – Entwicklungen und Perspektiven aus der Sicht des DOSB. In I. Hunger, S. Radtke & H. Tiemann (Hrsg.), *Dabei sein ist (nicht) alles. Inklusion im Fokus der Sportwissenschaft* (S. 103–109). Hamburg: Feldhaus.

DOSB (2013). *Inklusion Leben. Gemeinsam und gleichberechtigt Sport treiben.* Frankfurt am Main: Deutscher Olympischer Sportbund.

DOSB (2015). *Strategiekonzept. Inklusion im und durch Sport.* Frankfurt am Main: Deutscher Olympischer Sportbund.

Fediuk, F. (2008). *Sport in heterogenen Gruppen. Integrative Prozesse in Sportgruppen mit behinderten und benachteiligten Menschen.* Aachen: Meyer & Meyer.

Frühauf, T. (2008). Von der Integration zur Inklusion – ein Überblick. In A. Hinz, I. Körner & U. Niehoff (Hrsg.), *Von der Integration zur Inklusion. Grundlagen – Perspektiven – Praxis* (S. 11–32). Marburg: Lebenshilfe.

GEW (2017). *Index für Inklusion für Kindertageseinrichtungen. Gemeinsam leben, spielen und lernen.* Frankfurt am Main: Gewerkschaft Erziehung und Wissenschaft.

Guttmann, L. (1979). *Sport für Körperbehinderte*. München: Urban und Schwarzenberg.

Haep, H. (1988). Spiegelbild gesellschaftlicher Entwicklung. Geschichte des organisierten Behindertensports in Deutschland. In U. Genzler (Hrsg.), *Comeback. Sport für Behinderte* (S. 21–28). München: Mosaik.

Hinz, A. (2002). Von der Integration zur Inklusion – terminologisches Spiel oder konzeptionelle Weiterentwicklung? *Zeitschrift für Heilpädagogik, 53*, 354–361.

Hölter, G. (2011). Schulsport in der Förderschule – Bestandsaufnahme und Perspektiven. *sportunterricht, 60*(1), 14–21.

Klemm, K. (2015). *Inklusion in Deutschland. Daten und Fakten*. Gütersloh: Bertelsmann Stiftung.

Lorenzen, H. (1961). *Lehrbuch des Versehrtensports*. Stuttgart: Ferdinand Enke Verlag.

Montag Stiftung Jugend und Gesellschaft (2011). *Kommunaler Index für Inklusion, ein Arbeitsbuch*. Bonn: Montag Stiftung Jugend und Gesellschaft.

Prengel, A. (1993). *Pädagogik der Vielfalt: Verschiedenheit und Gleichberechtigung in interkultureller, feministischer und integrativer Pädagogik*. Opladen: Leske + Budrich.

Radtke, S. (2011). Inklusion von Menschen mit Behinderung im Sport. *Aus Politik und Zeitgeschichte, 16–19*, 33–38.

Radtke, S. (2013). Zwischen Inklusion und Exklusion: Internationaler Vergleich von Systembedingungen für einen erfolgreichen Leistungssport: erste Ergebnisse eines Forschungsprojekts. In V. Anneken (Hrsg.), *Inklusion durch Sport – Forschung für Menschen mit Behinderungen* (S. 43–63). Köln: Sportverlag Strauß.

Radtke, S. (2016). Zum pädagogischen Inklusionsdiskurs im nationalen und internationalen Raum. Grundlegende Entwicklungsschritte im Bildungswesen sowie im Bereich des Sports. In I. Hunger, H. Tiemann & S. Radtke (Hrsg.), *Dabei sein ist (nicht) alles. Inklusion im Fokus der Sportwissenschaft* (S. 11–39). Hamburg: Feldhaus.

Radtke, S. & Doll-Tepper, G. (2010). *Ist-Analyse von Talentsichtung und -förderung im Behindertensport in den deutschen Landesverbänden und im Ausland (Pilotstudie)*. Bonn: BISp.

Radtke, S. & Doll-Tepper, G. (2014). *Nachwuchsgewinnung und -förderung im paralympischen Sport. Ein internationaler Systemvergleich unter Berücksichtigung der Athleten-, Trainer- und Funktionärsperspektive*. Köln: Sportverlag Strauß.

Schnell, I. (2006). Wir haben damals übermorgen angefangen – sind wir schon im Heute gelandet? *Zeitschrift für Inklusion.* Februar 2006. Abgerufen am 01. Juli 2017 von http://www.inklusion-online.net/index.php/inklusion-online/article/view/188.

Stuber, M. (2009). *Diversity – Das Potenzial-Prinzip.* München: Luchterhand.

Tiemann, H. (2006). *Erfahrungen von Frauen mit Körperbehinderung im Hochleistungssport – eine empirische Untersuchung.* Hamburg: Dr. Kovac.

Tiemann, H. (2013). Inklusiver Sportunterricht: Ansätze und Modelle. *Sportpädagogik, 37(6),* 47–50.

Tiemann, H. (2016). Konzepte, Modelle und Strategien für den inklusiven Sportunterricht – internationale und nationale Entwicklungen und Zusammenhänge. *Zeitschrift für Inklusion, 0(3),* abgerufen am 05. Juli 2017 von http://www.inklusion-online.net/index.php/inklusion-online/article/view/382/303.

Tiemann, H., Schulz, S. & Schmidt-Gotz, E. (Hrsg.) (2007). *International, inklusiv und interdisziplinär – Perspektiven einer zeitgemäßen Sportwissenschaft.* Schorndorf: Hofmann.

Weichert, W. (2008). Integration durch Bewegungsbeziehungen. In F. Fediuk (Hrsg.), *Inklusion als bewegungspädagogische Aufgabe* (S. 55–95). Baltmannsweiler: Schneider Verlag.

Ziebarth, F. (2010). Gelingensbedingungen für eine inklusive Pädagogik. *Sonderpädagogik in Berlin, 2,* 5–10.

Frauen an die Spitze – Förderung von Frauen im gemeinnützig organisierten Sport in Deutschland

Petra Tzschoppe
Universität Leipzig und Vizepräsidentin Deutscher Olympischer Sportbund

Für den Deutschen Olympischen Sportbund (DOSB) ist die gleichberechtigte Teilhabe von Frauen und Männern am Sport ein Ziel, zu dem er sich in der Präambel seiner Satzung bekennt: »Der DOSB fördert die tatsächliche Durchsetzung der Gleichstellung von Frauen und Männern und wirkt mit gezielter Frauenförderung auf die Beseitigung bestehender Nachteile hin. Er begreift die Förderung von Vielfalt als Gewinn für Sport und Gesellschaft ...«[1] Diese Formulierung verweist zugleich auf noch immer bestehende Barrieren für eine in allen Feldern des Sports gleichrangige Partizipation von Frauen. Um die Defizite hinsichtlich der Beteiligung von Frauen an Führungspositionen im Sport abzubauen, wurde von der Mitgliederversammlung im Dezember 2014 mit der neuen Satzung auch eine Geschlechterquote beschlossen. In allen Gremien des DOSB müssen nun Frauen und Männer zu jeweils mindestens 30 Prozent vertreten sein. Bei Einzelwahlen und bei den Mitgliedern des DOSB-Präsidiums gilt dies als Soll-Quote – ein grundlegender Beschluss, der ohne Gegenstimme gefasst wurde.

Die Einführung dieser Geschlechterquote resultiert freilich auch daraus, dass vorhergegangene Appelle und Absichtserklärungen in puncto gleichberechtigter Beteiligung von Frauen an Führungspositionen nur unzureichend gefruchtet hatten. Auch wenn das Thema *Sport für Mädchen und Frauen* als Motiv die gesamte Geschichte von der Gründung des Deutschen Sportbundes (DSB) bis zum aktuellen Wirken des DOSB durchzieht, sind die Auswirkungen auf verschiedene Handlungsfelder recht unterschiedlich. Markante Veränderungen werden vor allem in der Beteiligung von Mädchen und Frauen am aktiven Sporttreiben sichtbar. Hier sind in den vergangenen Jahrzehnten deutliche Zuwächse erreicht worden. Als der DSB 1950 gegründet wurde, waren es vor allem junge Männer, die unter seinem Dach in knapp 20.000 Vereinen ihrer Begeisterung für den Wettkampfsport

---

1 Deutscher Olympischer Sportbund (DOSB) (2015). *Satzung des DOSB*. Unter: https://www.dosb.de/fileadmin/sharepoint/DOSB-Dokumente%20%7B96E58B18-5B8A-4AA1-98BB-199E8E1DC07C%7D/Satzung.pdf

nachgingen. Der Anteil an Mädchen und Frauen unter den 3,2 Millionen Einzelmitgliedern betrug lediglich 10 Prozent. Seither ist die Zahl weiblicher Mitglieder stetig gewachsen, unter den mittlerweile mehr als 27 Millionen Mitgliedschaften in den mehr als 90.000 Sportvereinen weisen sie einen Anteil von 40 Prozent auf.

Vertraten anfangs noch viele Männer, aber auch Frauen, die Position, dass körperliche Konstitution, biologische Bestimmung des weiblichen Körpers und gesellschaftliche Rolle mit der Ausübung der meisten Sportarten nicht vereinbar seien, verloren in den Folgejahren solche Sichtweisen an Einfluss. Einhergehend mit gesellschaftlichen Modernisierungsprozessen veränderte sich Ende der 1960er Jahre auch das Frauenbild im Sport erkennbar. DSB-Präsident Willi Daume war überzeugt, dass der Deutsche Sportbund die angepeilte Schwelle von 10 Millionen Mitgliedern zu den Spielen 1972 in München nur überspringen würde, wenn es gelänge »die Frau für den Sport zu gewinnen«. So betonte er 1967 die Bedeutung des Frauensports und kritisierte, »...so lässt das Verständnis für ihn und seine gebotene Repräsentation in den eigenen Reihen entschieden zu wünschen übrig«. (Deutscher Sportbund, 2001, S. 22). Der Bundestag des DSB verabschiedete 1968 in Stuttgart die Resolution *Zum großen Schritt des Frauensports in die Gesellschaft von morgen* und beschloss ein Bündel von Maßnahmen, mit denen eine deutlich stärkere Beteiligung von Frauen in Sport und Sportpolitik eingefordert wurde. Bis 1970 stieg die Zahl weiblicher Mitglieder auf mehr als 2,8 Millionen an, dies entsprach einem Anteil von etwas mehr als einem Viertel an den Gesamtmitgliedern. Es gab jedoch längst noch nicht im hinreichenden Maß entsprechende breitensportliche Angebote. So argumentierte der damalige DSB-Präsident Willi Weyer ähnlich wie sein Amtsvorgänger: »Immer noch ist die Hälfte unserer Vereine ohne Angebot für Frauen. Sie haben noch immer nicht begriffen, dass ein ausgewogenes Programm für beide Geschlechter eine existenzielle Frage der Turn- und Sportvereine ist.« Er hielt 1976 eine Entwicklung für möglich, in der das Verhältnis von Frauen und Männern im Sport ebenso wie in der Bevölkerungsstatistik 1:1 betragen würde, und äußerte dafür konkrete Wünsche. Dazu gehörten »Chancengleichheit für alle Frauen im Sport«, keine reinen Männerclubs mehr, die er als Geschlechter-*Apartheid* des Sports bezeichnete, sowie »nicht nur einige wenige Sportarten«, sondern Öffnen der Fülle des Sports für den breiten Kreis am Sport interessierter Frauen (vgl. Deutscher Sportbund, 2001, S. 23). Mit eben diesem Anspruch diskutierte die Vollversammlung des Bundesausschusses Frauensport 1983 das Thema *Sport für alle – aller Sport für Frauen?* aus philosophischer und soziologischer Sicht. Die Frage, in welcher Weise Vereinsangebote und Vereinskulturen zu verändern sind, um für Mädchen und Frauen attraktiv zu werden und weibliche Mitglieder gewinnen zu können, war auch in den Folgejahren prägend für die Aktivitäten, etwa 1988 als Gegenstand einer gemeinsamen Fachtagung mit dem Bundesausschuss Breitensport und der Deutschen Sportjugend (dsj) unter dem Thema *Im Verein ist Sport am schönsten – auch für Mädchen und Frauen?*. Eine weitere Aufwertung erfuhr das Anliegen, als 1996 erstmals ein Bundestag des DSB unter einem *Frauenthema* tagte: *Mädchen und Frauen im Sport: Mit uns in die Zukunft!* (Deutscher Sportbund, 2001, S. 47). Vereine und Verbände griffen diese Impulse für eine Sportentwicklung, mit der Mädchen und Frauen stärker einbezogen werden, auf. Dies spiegelte sich auch in wachsenden Mitgliederzahlen wider, im Jahr 2000 war die Zahl weiblicher Sportvereinsmitglieder auf mehr als 10 Millionen angewachsen, ihr Anteil an der Gesamtmitgliedschaft auf 39 Prozent.

Weit weniger zählbare Erfolge waren beim Bemühen mehr Frauen in Führungspositionen zu bringen, zu verzeichnen. Auf allen Ebenen – ob in Vereinen, Fachverbänden oder Landessportbünden – stellten sie auch im Jahr 2000 in den Führungsgremien noch immer lediglich eine Minderheit. Auch im Präsidium des DSB selbst waren Frauen noch längst nicht gemäß ihrem Anteil in der Mitgliedschaft beteiligt, obwohl es über die Jahre eine Reihe von Anläufen gegeben hatte.

1950, bei Gründung des DSB, bestand das Präsidium ausschließlich aus Männern, zumindest der Platz einer Beisitzerin wurde für eine Frau freigehalten, um eine spätere Benennung durch eine Frauenvollversammlung zu ermöglichen. Auf diese Weise gelangte 1951 die erste Vorsitzende des *Frauenausschusses im DSB*, Grete Nordhoff, mit Sitz und Stimme ins Präsidium. Sie übte diese Funktion bis 1968 aus, über den gesamten Zeitraum blieb sie die einzige Frau im Präsidium. Zu Beginn der Amtszeit ihrer Nachfolgerin Inge Bausenwein änderte sich dies. Mit der Wahl von Wally Schuster, der Vorsitzenden des Fachausschusses *Mädchenarbeit*, und Grete Busch als zusätzlicher Beisitzerin ins Präsidium verfügten 1968 drei Frauen über Sitz und Stimme im Präsidium (vgl. Deutscher Sportbund, 2001, S. 71). Dies fand eine Entsprechung auch in der Resolution *Zum großen Schritt des Frauensports in die Gesellschaft von morgen*, die vom DSB-Bundestag im Jahr 1968 verabschiedet wurde. Diese Resolution forderte u. a. Maßnahmen, um eine »größere Beteiligung der Frauen an der Führung des

Sports auf Vereins-, Landes- und Bundesebene, auch in den herkömmlich von Männern ausgeübten Ämtern« zu erreichen. Die Forderung verdeutlichte nicht nur, dass der Anteil von Frauen in Führungspositionen bis dato ausgesprochen gering war. An ihr ist auch das vorherrschende Rollenverständnis abzulesen, nach dem Frauen allenfalls die Position einer Frauen- bzw. Mädchenwartin vertraten, ihnen in den anderen Handlungsfeldern die Kompetenz zumeist abgesprochen wurde (vgl. Tzschoppe, 2017, S. 258).

Um Frauen an sportpolitischen Entscheidungsfindungen zumindest etwas stärker zu beteiligen, verabschiedete die Frauenvollversammlung 1970 einen Antrag, mit dem gefordert wurde: »Bei Mitgliedsorganisationen mit mehr als 50.000 Mitgliedern sollen die weiblichen Mitglieder durch mindestens eine Delegierte vertreten sein.« Damit formulierten sie den ersten frauenpolitischen Quotierungsantrag im DSB, er scheiterte jedoch bereits im Präsidium des DSB (vgl. Deutscher Sportbund, 2001, S. 71). Weitere Anträge zur Quotierung bei der Ausübung des Stimmrechtes folgten 1976, 1994 und 1998, sie blieben jeweils ohne Erfolg. Die Festlegung von verbindlichen Quoten war in all der Zeit konträr diskutiert worden, auch unter den Frauen selbst gab es erhebliche Vorbehalte. Als schließlich der Bundestag 1989 das Thema *Frauenförderpläne im DSB – Bilanz und Perspektiven der Frauenarbeit* erörterte, wurde in der Folge vom Hauptausschuss des DSB ein Frauenförderplan für den Geltungsbereich des Präsidiums verabschiedet. Mit diesem wurde ein Frauenanteil von 25 Prozent in Präsidium und Gremien des DSB bis 1994 anvisiert, allerdings nicht als verbindlicher Richtwert, sondern lediglich als Orientierung (vgl. Deutscher Sportbund, 2001, S. 75). Verschiedene Sportverbände verabschiedeten gleichfalls Frauenförderpläne, um Unterstützungsmaßnahmen und Zielperspektiven für Frauen festzulegen. Deren geringes Maß an Verbindlichkeit war ganz offensichtlich nicht geeignet die angestrebten Veränderungen herbeizuführen, eine nennenswerte Steigerung des Frauenanteils in den Führungsgremien war nicht zu verzeichnen. So lag auch zu Beginn des neuen Jahrtausends, 50 Jahre nach der Gründung des DSB, der Frauenanteil im DSB-Präsidium unter 20 Prozent. Noch gravierender hielt sich die Unterrepräsentanz von Frauen in den Präsidien der Mitgliedsorganisationen: bei den Landessportbünden mit einem Frauenanteil von 14 Prozent, bei den Spitzenverbänden mit nicht einmal 10 Prozent. 25 Spitzenverbände hatten zu diesem Zeitpunkt ihre Präsidien gar komplett mit Männern besetzt (vgl. Deutscher Sportbund, 2002).

Wie ist die Diskrepanz zwischen der stetig wachsenden Zahl sportaktiver Frauen einerseits und der andererseits kaum gegebenen Teilhabe an wichtigen Ämtern in den Sportorganisationen zu erklären? Welche Barrieren bestehen im Sport für Frauen auf dem Weg in Spitzenfunktionen? Werden sie gehindert oder sind sie nicht interessiert? Je offensichtlicher wurde, dass weder Frauenförderpläne noch diverse Willensbekundungen relevante Veränderungen bewirkten, desto mehr wuchs der Bedarf auf diese Fragen über Alltagsvermutungen hinausgehende, wissenschaftlich fundierte Antworten geben zu können.

Das Projekt *Frauen an die Spitze*

Aus diesem Erfordernis und dem Fehlen von systematischen und verallgemeinerungsfähigen Studien zur Problematik der Marginalisierung von Frauen in Führungsgremien des Sports (vgl. Pfister, 2004a, S. 7) erwuchs die Initiative für ein Projekt. 2001 startete das vom Bundesministerium für Familie, Senioren, Frauen und Jugend finanziell geförderte Vorhaben. Geleitet wurde es von Gudrun Doll-Tepper gemeinsam mit Gertrud Pfister. Unter dem programmatischen Titel *Frauen an die Spitze – Aktionsbündnis zur Steigerung des Frauenanteils in den Führungspositionen des Sports* wurde in Zusammenarbeit mit den Sportorganisationen nach den Gründen für diese Unterrepräsentanz geforscht. Ziel des Projekts war es, ausgehend von einer systematischen Analyse der Teilhabe an Führungspositionen, Ursachen zu identifizieren und Erklärungsansätze für die Minderbeteiligung von Frauen zu diskutieren. Die im wissenschaftlichen Teil des Projekts gewonnenen Erkenntnisse bildeten die Grundlage für Konzepte und Maßnahmen, die gemeinsam mit Sportverbänden im Praxisteil des Projekts durchgeführt und evaluiert wurden. Publiziert wurden die Ergebnisse in mehreren von Gudrun Doll-Tepper zusammen mit Gertrud Pfister sowie weiteren Autorinnen herausgegebenen Veröffentlichungen.

Das Projekt war nicht nur durch eine enge Partnerschaft zwischen Wissenschaft und Sportpraxis geprägt. Das wissenschaftliche Teilprojekt zeichnete sich dadurch aus, dass sowohl bei den theoretischen Überlegungen als auch bei den empirischen Untersuchungen vielfältige Zugänge und Betrachtungsweisen berücksichtigt wurden. Sowohl Organisationsstrukturen als auch die individuelle Akteursperspektive fanden in den Analysen Beachtung. All dies macht die Auseinandersetzung mit den Erkenntnissen auch aus heutiger Perspektive

lohnenswert. Daher werden im Folgenden Herangehen und Hauptergebnisse noch einmal skizziert.
- Für die theoretischen Überlegungen zu Ursachen und Hintergründen der Geschlechterhierarchien im Sport wurden diverse Theorieansätze aus anderen gesellschaftlichen Bereichen herangezogen und nach der Übertragbarkeit von Theorien und Befunden aus anderen gesellschaftlichen Bereichen wie Politik und insbesondere Wirtschaft auf Sportorganisationen gefragt (vgl. Pfister, 2004a). So wurden etwa Thesen und Ansätze aus der Arbeitsmarktforschung und Organisationssoziologie zum Handeln in Sportorganisationen in Bezug gesetzt.

- Die Darstellung internationaler Tendenzen hinsichtlich der Beteiligung von Frauen in Entscheidungsgremien erweiterte den Blickwinkel und ermöglichte es die Situation in Deutschland im Vergleich zu internationalen und nationalen Sportorganisationen verschiedener Länder einzuordnen (vgl. Pfister, 2004b).

- Für das deutsche Sportsystem wurde mit einer Organisationsanalyse Einblick in die Strukturen der Verbände und die Zusammensetzung der Entscheidungsgremien angestrebt. Mehr als 11.000 Daten über Führungskräfte wurden aus den Jahrbüchern ausgewählter Sportorganisationen[2] erfasst und ausgewertet und so zunächst ein Überblick zur Geschlechterverteilung in Führungspositionen hergestellt (vgl. Meck, 2004).

Weiterhin wurden im empirischen Teil mittels qualitativer und quantitativer Befragungen die Ebene der Individuen in den Forschungsfokus gerückt und in mehreren Teilstudien Motive, Einstellungen, Zielsetzungen und Wünsche, Lebenszusammenhänge und Biografien von aktiven, potenziellen und bereits wieder ausgeschiedenen Führungskräften erkundet.
- In der Teilstudie zu Biografien von Frauen in ehrenamtlichen Führungspositionen im deutschen Sport wurde mittels leitfadengestützter Interviews gefragt, wie weibliche Führungskräfte das Ehrenamt in ihren Lebenszusammenhang integrieren, welche Motive Frauen in Führungspositionen haben, ob es Barrieren beim Aufstieg gab und gibt und inwieweit weitere Aufstiegsambitionen

---

2 Neben dem Jahrbuch des Sports (DSB) 2002-2003 mit Daten zur Dachorganisation sowie allen Mitgliedsorganisationen wurden im Speziellen die Jahrbücher des Deutschen Eissport-Verbandes, des Deutschen Tischtennis-Bundes und des Deutschen Ruderverbandes analysiert.

bestehen. Befragt wurden insgesamt 23 Frauen, die auf Landes- und Bundesebene des Sportsystems ehrenamtliche Führungspositionen ausübten (vgl. Radtke, 2004).

- Auf der Basis einer quantitativen Befragung wurden Ehrenamtskarrieren vor dem Hintergrund der jeweiligen beruflichen und sportlichen Laufbahn, der familiären Situation und in Bezug auf soziodemografische Daten von weiblichen und männlichen Führungskräften im deutschen Sport analysiert. Mit dem Anliegen geschlechtsspezifische Unterschiede aufzudecken, erfolgte hierzu eine Vollerhebung bei allen Präsidiumsmitgliedern von DSB und NOK, Landessportbünden und Spitzenverbänden, dabei war mit 413 verwertbaren Fragebögen ein Rücklauf von immerhin 59,3 Prozent zu verzeichnen (vgl. Radtke & Pfister, 2004).

- Eine weitere Teilstudie ging der Überlegung nach, inwiefern bei Übungsleiterinnen und Übungsleitern ein Potenzial für die Übernahme von Führungspositionen auf verschiedenen Ebenen des Sportsystems liegen könnte. Inwieweit Ehrenamtliche in Vereinen eine Ressource zum Ausgleich des Defizits an weiblichen Führungskräften darstellen, wurde am Beispiel des Deutschen Turnerbundes (DTB) mit einer quantitativen Befragung untersucht. Der DTB schien auf Grund des Kontrastes zwischen seiner hohen Zahl weiblicher Mitglieder und Übungsleiterinnen und den mehrheitlich männlichen Spitzenfunktionären besonders geeignet, allerdings blieb hier der Fragebogenrücklauf mit lediglich 5 Prozent unter den Erwartungen (vgl. Sliep, 2004).

Ableitend aus den Erkenntnissen dieser Untersuchungen wurde mittels qualitativer Befragungen vertiefend weiteren Fragestellungen nachgegangen:
- Zum einen wurde der mögliche *Einstieg in die Führung* von aktiven und ehemaligen Hochleistungssportlerinnen und -sportlern in den Blick genommen. Mit dem Ziel deren Potenzial als künftige Führungskräfte auf der Basis ihrer Persönlichkeitseigenschaften sowie ihrer Kenntnisse und Erfahrungen im Sportsystem zu analysieren, wurden neun (ehemalige) Spitzensportlerinnen und acht Spitzensportler befragt (vgl. Radtke, 2005b).

- Zum anderen wurde der Aspekt *Ausstieg aus der Führung* vertieft. Mit der Drop-out-Studie wurden geschlechtsspezifische Ursachen für den vorzeitigen

Karriereabbruch von weiblichen und männlichen Führungskräften analysiert. Mittels qualitativer Biografieforschung ging es darum Einflussfaktoren zu identifizieren, die zur Aufgabe des bis dato höchsten Ehrenamtes geführt haben, neun Frauen und sieben Männer wurden hierzu befragt (vgl. Radtke, 2005a).

Aus der Vielschichtigkeit dieser Teilstudien resultierte eine Fülle von Ergebnissen, die entsprechend dokumentiert wurden. Einige grundlegende Aussagen werden im Folgenden noch einmal herausgehoben:
Funktionen im Sport werden nicht über Einstellungs- oder Berufungsverfahren, sondern über Wahlen besetzt. Hier besteht ein deutlicher Unterschied zwischen profitorientierten Unternehmen und Sportorganisationen mit ehrenamtlicher Führung, die Selektionsprozesse im Sport gestalten sich daher oft noch schwieriger und intransparenter. Häufig steht nur ein Kandidat zur Wahl, weil bereits im Vorfeld ohne festgelegte Rekrutierungsverfahren die Weichen gestellt werden. Im Sinne des Prinzips der *homosozialen Reproduktion* tendieren die im Sport überwiegend aus Männern bestehenden Gremien dazu wiederum das eigene Geschlecht zu bevorzugen. Wie Ergebnisse der Arbeitsmarktforschung eindeutig belegen, fühlen Frauen sich durch wenig transparente Rekrutierungs- und Wahlverfahren benachteiligt und sind es auch tatsächlich, dies trifft für den Sport ebenso zu (vgl. Pfister, 2004a, S. 38).

Darüber hinaus kommt es im Sport in zahlreichen anderen Situationen zur Einflussnahme über persönliche Beziehungen. Männer verfügen deutlich mehr über die Netzwerke, die in Sportorganisationen enorm bedeutsam sind – sei es um Zugang zu finden, Einblicke zu gewinnen oder Entscheidungen vorzubereiten.

In Sportorganisationen existieren zumeist relativ wenige Zielvorgaben und auch wenige auf konkrete Ziele ausgerichtete Strukturen und Regeln, mit Ausnahme der sportlichen Erfolge und der Mitgliederzahlen verfügen sie über wenig Maßstäbe und keine Evaluierungsinstrumente. Diese wenig formalisierten Strukturen leisten der Geschlechtersegregation ebenfalls Vorschub, wie aus der Organisationsforschung belegt ist (vgl. Pfister, 2004a, S. 39).

Typisch für ehrenamtlich geführte Organisationen ist zudem die große Bedeutung von *Austauschbeziehungen*. Gute Beziehungen zu anderen Verbänden, zur Wirtschaft und zur Politik zu haben, wirkt sich für einen Verband in vielerlei Hinsicht positiv aus. Daher werden häufig Seiteneinsteigerinnen bzw. Seiteneinsteiger aus anderen Bereichen in Führungsgremien von Sportverbänden gewählt, die sich davon einen Zuwachs von Ressourcen erhoffen. Dass zumeist Männer auch in anderen gesellschaftlichen Bereichen die Machtpositionen innehaben, verbessert ihre Chancen hochrangige Positionen im Sport zu erhalten (vgl. ebd.).

Ein weiterer Aspekt ist, dass gerade in Führungspositionen des Sports eine Verbindung von Macht und Männlichkeit inszeniert wird, die *großen alten Männer des Sports* dienen Nachwuchsfunktionären als Modelle. Frauen haben dagegen nur wenige Vorbilder in den Führungsgremien, an denen sie sich orientieren können.

Es werden zwei vorrangige Motive herausgestellt, die Frauen veranlassen sich auf der Führungsebene ehrenamtlich zu engagieren. Es handelt sich erstens um den Anreiz etwas aktiv mitzugestalten und dabei Einfluss zu nehmen, und zweitens um den Anreiz, soziale Beziehungen aufzubauen und daraus folgend Anerkennung und Wertschätzung von außen zu erfahren (vgl. Radtke, 2005b, S. 122).

So wird zusammenfassend festgestellt, dass das Fehlen von Frauen *an der Spitze* zum einen mit den Lebenszusammenhängen, Motiven und Ressourcen potenzieller weiblicher Führungskräfte zusammenhängt. Zum anderen sind es aber auch die Strukturen von Sportverbänden, Aufgaben und Erwartungen, Beziehungen, Normen, Regeln und Interaktionen, die als Barrieren wirken und Frauen den Aufstieg in Führungspositionen erschweren (vgl. Pfister, 2004a, S. 40).

Im Ergebnis der Analysen des Wissenschaftsteils sowie aus den Erfahrungen der ersten Projektphase wurden schließlich fünf praxisrelevante Arbeitsfelder abgesteckt, aus denen heraus Handlungsempfehlungen abzuleiten sind:

1. Veränderungen der Strukturen
Der Frauenanteil in Führungspositionen ist um so geringer, je höher der mit dem Amt verbundene Zeitaufwand ist und je länger die Amtsperioden sind, daher sollten Regelungen und Satzungen so gestaltet werden, dass die satzungs- und strukturbedingten Barrieren beim Zugang ins Ehrenamt und in ehrenamtliche Führungspositionen für Frauen abgebaut werden.

2. Organisationsentwicklung

Die Organisation der Verbandsarbeit erscheint oft nicht mehr zeitgemäß, da sie Mehrfachbelastung der Frauen mit Beruf, Familie und Ehrenamt ebenso wenig berücksichtigt wie die allmähliche Neuorientierung junger Väter. In Zusammenarbeit mit interessierten Verbänden sollten neue, flexible Rahmenbedingungen für das Ehrenamt erarbeitet werden, die es Frauen (und auch Männern) erleichtern ehrenamtliche Tätigkeiten und Teilhabe an Führungspositionen mit beruflichen und familiären Anforderungen zu vereinbaren.

3. Gezielte Ansprache von Frauen

Frauen, die bereits Führungspositionen innehaben, sind zu diesen größtenteils von außen angeregt worden. Mit dem Wissen um die Bedeutung von gezielter Ansprache und Motivation sollten Mentoring- und Coaching-Programme in den Mitgliedsorganisationen weiter vorangetrieben werden.

4. Umsetzung von Gender Mainstreaming in den Verbänden

Frauenvertreterinnen betonten den Bedarf an Unterstützung bei der praktischen Umsetzung von Gender Mainstreaming in ihren Verbänden. Dazu sollten entsprechende Fortbildungsmaßnahmen oder Fachtagungen angeboten sowie Arbeitshilfen für die Verbände erarbeitet werden. In enger Kooperation mit dem DSB sollen gemeinsam Umsetzungsstrategien entwickelt und Aktivitäten gebündelt werden.

5. Weiterentwicklung des Profils der Frauenvertreterinnen bzw. Frauenbeauftragten

Die Strukturen der Verbandsarbeit entsprechen vielfach nicht mehr der Lebensrealität junger Frauen, aber auch nicht der der Männer. Daher sollte das Profil der Frauenvertreterin bzw. der Frauenbeauftragten grundlegend geprüft werden, mit der Orientierung das Amt im Sinne des Diversity Managements auf den Bereich Personalentwicklung auszudehnen.

Diese Arbeitsfelder kamen in der zweiten Projektphase im Verbund mit der Sportorganisation auf den Prüfstand. Unter Leitung von Gudrun Doll-Tepper wurden diese Maßnahmen in enger Zusammenarbeit mit dem DSB, insbesondere mit der Vizepräsidentin Ilse Ridder-Melchers, in einer Reihe von Mitgliedsorganisationen[3] praktisch umgesetzt und evaluiert. Hierbei zeigte sich die grundsätzlich große Bereitschaft zum ehrenamtlichen Engagement im Sport. Hoch geschätzt wurde dabei wiederum die soziale Komponente, also etwas gemeinsam mit anderen im Team zu tun. Als ebenso wichtiges Motiv bestätigte sich das Bestreben Verbandsleben aktiv mitzugestalten, wobei starre Verbandsstrukturen kritisch thematisiert wurden. Bemängelt wurde neben dem hohen Zeit- und Arbeitsaufwand zudem die mangelnde Anerkennung des ehrenamtlichen Engagements. Hier liegen Ansatzpunkte für Veränderungen (vgl. Biskup, 2005).

Erklärtes Ziel aller im Projekt Mitwirkenden war es also *Frauen an die Spitze* zu bringen.[4] Wie dieses Anliegen realisiert werden konnte, war unmittelbar nach Projektende schwerlich zu beantworten. Daher scheint es durchaus angemessen, zwölf Jahre nach Abschluss des Projektes einige Aspekte noch einmal in den Blick zu nehmen.

Aktuelle Situation zur gleichberechtigten Teilhabe von Frauen in Führungspositionen

Im Jahr 2016 zeichneten die Ergebnisse der Befragung der Mitgliedsorganisationen im DOSB zur Umsetzung von Gleichstellung in Führungspositionen folgendes Bild:

Ehrenamtliche Organe und Gremien des DOSB und der Mitgliedsorganisationen

Der Anteil von Frauen im gewählten Präsidium des DOSB liegt bei 30 Prozent. Die beschlossene Geschlechterquote wurde auch für die vom DOSB berufenen Kommissionen realisiert. Dies gilt ebenso für die von der Vollversammlung der Athletinnen und Athleten gewählte Athletenkommission. In den ehrenamtlichen Führungsgremien der Mitgliedsorganisationen werden diese Werte dagegen nicht erreicht, nur wenige von ihnen haben bislang analog zur Satzung des DOSB

---

3 Beteiligte Mitgliedsorganisationen: Bund Deutscher Radfahrer, Deutscher Fechter-Bund, Deutscher Handballbund, Deutscher Ruderverband, Deutscher Tennis Bund, Deutscher Turnerbund, Landessportbund Hessen, Landessportbund Nordrhein-Westfalen, Allgemeiner Deutscher Hochschulsportverband

4 Für die wertvollen Ergebnisse des Projektes *Frauen an die Spitze* erhielten Gudrun Doll-Tepper und ihr Team von Sportwissenschaftlerinnen der FU Berlin 2005 den am höchsten dotierten deutschen Frauenförderpreis, den Margherita-von-Brentano-Preis.

verbindliche Regelungen festgeschrieben. Dennoch lässt sich auch hier ein kontinuierlicher, wenn auch langsamer Zuwachs an Frauen in Führungspositionen erkennen. Mittlerweile beträgt ihr Anteil in den Präsidien der Landesportbünde fast 25 Prozent, vier Bünde haben einen Frauenanteil von mehr als 30 Prozent in ihren Präsidien. Dem stehen 10 Landessportbünde mit einem Frauenanteil von weniger als 30 Prozent gegenüber. In den Spitzenverbänden ist der Wert auf knapp 18 Prozent gestiegen. Allerdings realisieren lediglich acht Spitzenverbände in ihren Präsidien eine Frauenbeteiligung von mindestens 30 Prozent. Hingegen wird von 32 Verbänden die mit der DOSB-Satzung empfohlene 30-Prozent-Schwelle nicht erreicht, darunter sind sechs Verbände, deren Präsidien komplett ohne weibliche Mitglieder agieren. Auf Grundlage einer Quotierung ragt im Bereich der Verbände mit besonderen Aufgaben der DJK-Sportverband mit 55,6 Prozent Frauenanteil im Präsidium heraus.

In den Diskussionen um gleichberechtigte Teilhabe an Führungspositionen ist im Sport in der Vergangenheit zumeist der Bereich ehrenamtlichen Engagements in den Blick genommen worden. Mittlerweile wird zunehmend auch der Bereich hauptberuflicher Führungspositionen betrachtet.

Geschlechterverteilung im Hauptberuf[5] in den Geschäftsstellen von DOSB und Mitgliedsorganisationen
Während mehr als die Hälfte der Mitarbeitenden im DOSB weiblich sind, liegt der Frauenanteil bei den hauptberuflichen Führungspositionen nur bei etwa einem Viertel. Im Vorstand des DOSB beträgt der Anteil lediglich 20 Prozent. Auf der Ebene der Mitgliedsorganisationen verschärft sich diese Diskrepanz noch. Alle Landessportbünde verfügen über hauptberufliches Personal, in fast allen ist mehr als die Hälfte der Mitarbeitenden weiblich. In den hauptberuflichen Führungsgremien hingegen liegt der durchschnittliche Anteil von Frauen bei lediglich 13,5 Prozent. In mehr als der Hälfte der Landessportbünde arbeitet die hauptberufliche Verbandsführung sogar gänzlich ohne Frauen. Bei den Spitzenverbänden ist die Ausstattung mit hauptberuflichem Personal sehr unterschiedlich ausgeprägt, die Zahlen liegen in einer Spanne von 272 bis einem bzw. einer Mitarbeitenden. Im Durchschnitt ist auch hier mehr als die Hälfte der Mitarbeitenden

---

5 Als hauptberuflich werden Personen bezeichnet, die in einem sozialversicherungspflichtigen Arbeitsverhältnis (inkl. 400-Euro-Jobs) angestellt sind.

in den Geschäftsstellen weiblich. Hingegen beträgt der Anteil von Frauen in den, teilweise auch kollegial geführten, hauptberuflichen Führungsgremien lediglich 28,6 Prozent, wobei hier ebenfalls mehr als die Hälfte der Verbände keine Frau in der hauptberuflichen Führung haben (vgl. DOSB, 2016b).

Delegierte zu Mitgliederversammlungen
Wenngleich auch beim Anteil weiblicher Delegierter zu DOSB-Mitgliederversammlungen ein moderater Zuwachs zu verzeichnen ist, spiegelt sich die gewachsene Zahl weiblicher Mitglieder bis heute nicht angemessen wider. Laut Satzung des DOSB (DOSB, 2015) sollen die Mitgliedsorganisationen »mindestens 30 Prozent weibliche und mindestens 30 Prozent männliche Delegierte zur Mitgliederversammlung entsenden« (§ 12, Abs. 2). Bei der 11. Mitgliederversammlung des DOSB 2015 waren weniger als 20 Prozent der Delegierten Frauen, sie sind also nicht angemessen vertreten, wenn es darum geht, weitreichende sportpolitische Entscheidungen zu treffen. Dies gilt analog auch für Mitgliederversammlungen und Hauptausschüsse der Mitgliedsorganisationen: Auch bei diesen stellen Frauen durchschnittlich nur 19,7 der Delegierten (vgl. DOSB, 2016b).

Aktivitäten
Um eine stärkere Repräsentanz von Frauen in Führungspositionen zu erreichen, engagiert sich der DOSB in der Weiterentwicklung des Projektes *Frauen an die Spitze* im Rahmen seiner Strategie *Gemeinsam an die Spitze!* Diverse Projektergebnisse sind in entsprechenden konkreten Maßnahmen umgesetzt und verstetigt worden. Dazu gehören diverse Mentoring-Programme in den Sportorganisationen. 2012 startete der DOSB unter dem Motto *Mit dem gemischten Doppel an die Spitze!* ein einjähriges Mentoring-Programm. Ziel dieses Projektes ist es, weibliche Nachwuchskräfte zu motivieren Führungspositionen zu übernehmen und sie auf diesem Weg durch erfahrene Führungskräfte zu unterstützen. Im besonderen Fokus des DOSB-Mentoring-Programms stehen ehemalige Spitzensportlerinnen, die im Anschluss an ihre sportliche Laufbahn auch eine ehrenamtliche oder berufliche Karriere – ob als Funktionärin oder Trainerin – im gemeinnützig organisierten Sport anstreben. Mittlerweile ist der dritte Durchlauf des Mentoring-Programms abgeschlossen und positiv evaluiert worden. Weitere erfolgreiche Maßnahmen sind die Führungstalente-Camps mit den Effekten von Motivation, Qualifikation und Netzwerk-Bildung. Zudem werden Mitgliedsorganisationen mit Organisationsberatungen unterstützt (vgl. DOSB, 2016c).

Das Thema wird auch weiterhin im Zentrum der gleichstellungspolitischen Aktivitäten des DOSB stehen. Die Delegierten der 11. DOSB-Frauen-Vollversammlung haben 2016 einstimmig die *Strategischen Eckpunkte zum Themenfeld Gleichstellung im Sport des DOSB bis 2020* beschlossen und dabei diese vier Handlungsfelder herausgestellt:
1. Gleichstellung in Führungspositionen,
2. Förderung von Trainerinnen und Kampfrichterinnen,
3. Kampf gegen sexualisierte Gewalt,
4. Geschlechtergerechte Darstellung in den (Sport-)Medien.

Für die Weiterentwicklung und Umsetzung dieser *Strategischen Eckpunkte* wurden Arbeitsgruppen eingerichtet, mit denen Expertisen über den Bereich der Sportorganisation hinaus aus anderen gesellschaftlichen Bereichen wie Wirtschaft, Politik, Wissenschaft und Medien zusammengeführt und genutzt werden, um das Ziel der gleichberechtigten Teilhabe von Frauen und Männern auf allen Ebenen zu erreichen – gemäß dem Anspruch *Gemeinsam gewinnen*.

Frau an der Spitze – ein persönlicher Nachtrag

Mehr Frauen an die Spitze von Sportorganisationen zu bringen, das ist ganz offensichtlich ein langer Weg, für den es viele Schritte braucht. Sehr bedeutsam für die Bereitschaft eine Führungsposition anzustreben, sind auch entsprechende Vorbilder. Für Frauen ist es wichtig, dass es Vorbilder gibt, um sich an ihnen zu orientieren und ihnen nachzustreben. Davon finden sich im Sport noch immer zu wenige. Aber es gibt sie zweifellos. Gudrun Doll-Tepper ist eine Frau *an der Spitze*, sie hat über ihr wichtiges Projekt für mehr Frauen in Führungspositionen hinaus ungezählte starke Impulse gesetzt. Sie hatte und hat selbst seit Jahrzehnten zahlreiche unterschiedliche Ämter auf verschiedenen Feldern des Sports, national wie international, ausgefüllt. All diese Spitzenämter prägt sie nicht nur mit ihrer fachlichen Kompetenz, Akribie, Ausdauer und diplomatischem Geschick. Mit ihrer gesamten Persönlichkeit, nicht zuletzt ihrem Humor, ist Gudrun Doll-Tepper einfach herausragend. Sie inspiriert und ist ein so wichtiges Vorbild, indem sie das Thema *Frauen an die Spitze* lebt.

Literatur

Biskup, C. (2005). Evaluation der Praxismaßnahmen. In G. Doll-Tepper, G. Pfister & S. Radtke (Hrsg.), *Karrieren in Führungspositionen des Sports – Ein- und Ausstiege* (S. 151–211). Köln: Sport & Buch Strauß.

Deutscher Olympischer Sportbund (DOSB) (2015). *Satzung*. Zugriff unter https://www.dosb.de/fileadmin/sharepoint/DOSB-Dokumente%20%7B96E58B18-5B8A-4AA1-98BB-199E8E1DC07C%7D/Satzung.pdf

Deutscher Olympischer Sportbund (DOSB) (2016a). *Bestandserhebungen*. Zugriff unter http://www.dosb.de/de/service/download-center/statistiken/

Deutscher Olympischer Sportbund (DOSB) (2016b). *Bestandserhebungen*. Zugriff unter http://www.dosb.de/fileadmin/fm-frauen-im-sport/DOSB-Gleichstellungsbericht_2016.pdf

Deutscher Olympischer Sportbund (DOSB) (2016c). *Gleichstellung im Sport*. Zugriff unter www.dosb.de/gleichstellung

Deutscher Olympischer Sportbund (DOSB) (2016d). Zugriff unter http://www.dosb.de/de/gleichstellung-im-sport/service/news/detail/news/mehr_vorbilder_fuer_frauen_in_fuehrungspositionen_im_sport/

Deutscher Sportbund (2001). *Mitmachen. Mitdenken. Mitlenken! 50 Jahre Frauen im Deutschen Sportbund*. Frankfurt am Main: DSB.

Deutscher Sportbund (2002). *Jahrbuch des Sports 2002/2003*. Niedernhausen: Schors.

Doll-Tepper, G. & Pfister, G. (Hrsg.) (2004). *Hat Führung ein Geschlecht? Genderarrangements in Entscheidungsgremien des deutschen Sports*. Köln: Sport und Buch Strauß.

Doll-Tepper, G., Pfister, G. & Radtke, S. (Hrsg.) (2005). *Karrieren in Führungspositionen des Sports – Ein- und Ausstiege*. Köln: Sport und Buch Strauß.

Doll-Tepper, G., Pfister, G. & Radtke, S. (Hrsg.) (2006). *Progress Towards Leadership – Biographies and Career Paths of Male and Female Leaders in German Sports Organisations*. Köln: Sport und Buch Strauß.

Doll-Tepper, G., Pfister, G., Scoretz, D. & Bilan, C. (Hrsg.) (2005). *Sport, Women and Leadership, Congress Proceedings*. Köln: Sport und Buch Strauß.

Meck, S. (2004). Organisationsanalyse ausgewählter Sportverbände. In G. Doll-Tepper & G. Pfister (Hrsg.), *Hat Führung ein Geschlecht? Genderarrangements in Entscheidungsgremien des deutschen Sports* (S. 213–238). Köln: Sport und Buch Strauß.

Mevert, F. (2002). *50 Jahre Deutscher Sportbund. Geschichte, Entwicklung, Persönlichkeiten* (2., erw. u. überarb. Auflage). Niedernhausen: Schors.

Pfister, G. (2004a). Frauen in Führungspositionen – theoretische Überlegungen im deutschen und internationalen Diskurs. In G. Doll-Tepper & G. Pfister (Hrsg.), *Hat Führung ein Geschlecht? Genderarrangements in Entscheidungsgremien des deutschen Sports* (S. 10–48). Köln: Sport und Buch Strauß.

Pfister, G. (2004b). Frauen in Führungspositionen des Sports – internationale Tendenzen. In G. Doll-Tepper & G. Pfister (Hrsg.), *Hat Führung ein Geschlecht? Genderarrangements in Entscheidungsgremien des deutschen Sports* (S. 49–64). Köln: Sport und Buch Strauß.

Radtke, S. (2004). Interviewstudie: Biographien von Frauen in ehrenamtlichen Führungspositionen im deutschen Sport. In G. Doll-Tepper & G. Pfister (Hrsg.), *Hat Führung ein Geschlecht? Genderarrangements in Entscheidungsgremien des deutschen Sports* (S. 65–142). Köln: Sport und Buch Strauß.

Radtke, S. (2005a). Ausstieg aus der Führung: geschlechtsspezifische Ursachenanalyse für den vorzeitigen Karriereabbruch von männlichen und weiblichen Führungskräften in Sportverbänden (Drop-Out-Studie). In G. Doll-Tepper, G. Pfister & S. Radtke (Hrsg.), *Karrieren in Führungspositionen des Sports – Ein- und Ausstiege* (S. 67–150). Köln: Sport & Buch Strauß.

Radtke, S. (2005b). Einstieg in die Führung? Das Führungskräftepotenzial von ehemaligen Hochleistungssportlerinnen und Hochleistungssportlern für das deutsche Sportsystem. In G. Doll-Tepper, G. Pfister & S. Radtke (Hrsg.), *Karrieren in Führungspositionen des Sports – Ein- und Ausstiege* (S. 5–66). Köln: Sport & Buch Strauß.

Radtke, S. & Pfister, G. (2004). Quantitative Befragung: Biographien von weiblichen und männlichen Führungskräften im deutschen Sport. In G. Doll-Tepper & G. Pfister (Hrsg.), *Hat Führung ein Geschlecht? Genderarrangements in Entscheidungsgremien des deutschen Sports* (S. 143–212). Köln: Sport und Buch Strauß.

Sliep, K. (2004). Quantitative Befragung: Übungsleiterinnen – ein Führungskräftepotenzial? In G. Doll-Tepper & G. Pfister (Hrsg.), *Hat Führung ein Geschlecht? Genderarrangements in Entscheidungsgremien des deutschen Sports* (S. 239–260). Köln: Sport und Buch Strauß.

Tzschoppe, P. (2017). Sport für alle – Sport und Sportpolitik von und für Frauen und Mädchen in Deutschland. In D. Jütting & M. Krüger (Hrsg.), *Sport für alle – Idee und Wirklichkeit* (S. 248–265). Münster: Waxmann.